PURSUING HUMAN STRENGTHS

A POSITIVE PSYCHOLOGY GUIDE

PURSUING HUMAN STRENGTHS

A POSITIVE PSYCHOLOGY GUIDE   SECOND EDITION

Martin Bolt

Late of Calvin College

Dana S. Dunn

Moravian College

WORTH
PUBLISHERS

A Macmillan Education Imprint
New York

Publisher: Rachel Losh
Associate Publisher: Jessica Bayne
Senior Acquisitions Editor: Christine Cardone
Executive Marketing Manager: Katherine Nurre
Assistant Editor: Catherine Michaelsen
Managing Editor: Lisa Kinne
Senior Project Editor: Jane O'Neill
Associate Media Editor: Anthony Casciano
Director of Design, Content Management: Diana Blume
Cover Designer: Blake Logan
Text Designers: Lissi Sigillo & Blake Logan
Art Manager: Matthew McAdams
Photo Editor: Sheena Goldstein
Senior Production Supervisor: Susan Wein
Composition: codeMantra
Printing and Binding: RR Donnelley
Cover Illustration: Marie Bertrand/Illustration Source

Library of Congress Preassigned Control Number: 2015948999

ISBN-13: 978-1-319-00448-4
ISBN-10: 1-319-00448-2

Worth Publishers
One New York Plaza
Suite 4500
New York, NY 10004-1562
www.worthpublishers.com

To the memory of three exceptional positive psychologists
who had many strengths and shared them with others:
Martin Bolt, Christopher Peterson, C. R. Snyder

About the Authors

Martin Bolt, late professor of psychology at Calvin College, received his PhD from Michigan State University. For 38 years, he was professor of psychology at Calvin College, where he taught classes in general and social psychology. He wrote and regularly revised instructional resources to accompany the many editions of David Myers' *Psychology* and *Social Psychology* textbooks. He was the first recipient of Calvin's Presidential Award for Exemplary Teaching (1997) and published the first edition of *Pursuing Human Strengths* in 2004. Martin is remembered for his passion for teaching psychology, his innovative teaching methods, and his mentoring of students and faculty.

Dana S. Dunn is professor of psychology and assistant dean for special projects at Moravian College in Bethlehem, PA. He earned his PhD in experimental social psychology from the University of Virginia and his BA in psychology from Carnegie Mellon University.

A fellow of the American Psychological Association (APA) and the Association for Psychological Science (APS), Dunn is active in the Society for the Teaching of Psychology (STP-APA Division 2) where he served as president in 2010. In 2013, Dunn received the Charles L. Brewer Distinguished Teaching of Psychology Award from the American Psychological Foundation and in 2015 he was the APA's Harry Kirke Wolfe lecturer. He is a member of the editorial boards of several journals and is a frequent speaker at national and regional psychology conferences. Dunn is a past board member of the Eastern Psychological Association (EPA) and formerly served on the program committee for the National Institute for the Teaching of Psychology (NIToP).

The author of over 150 articles, chapters, and book reviews, Dunn writes about the teaching of psychology, the social psychology of disability, and liberal education. He is the author or editor of more than 20 books and writes a blog on the teaching of psychology called "Head of the Class" for *Psychology Today.* He is currently editor-in-chief of the *Oxford Bibliographies (OB): Psychology.*

At Moravian, Dunn has held various leadership positions, including serving as chair of the department of psychology for six years and acting chair of the department of philosophy for three-and-a-half years. As past director of the Learning in Common (LinC) curriculum, Dunn oversaw Moravian's general education program.

Contents

Preface to the Second Edition

As George Harrison noted, "All things must pass." All things do pass and, most poignantly, of course, the people in our lives do, as well. Martin Bolt, late professor of psychology at Calvin College, conceived, wrote and published the first edition of *Pursuing Human Strengths*. He was renowned as an exemplary teacher, and his passion for psychology and its positive possibilities to improve and serve the lives of others was apparent on every page he wrote. In my view, as the new author, the appeal of the first edition was Bolt's writing voice—friendly, concerned, ever interested, and excited to share scientific and pedagogical insights about positive psychology with his readers. But his goal was to share psychology and its helpful applications with each reader, not in a formal way but in one that created a bond. In this second edition, I have worked to preserve that wonderful voice and to add to it in ways that I hope will forge connections between readers, the text, and the pursuit of human strengths.

The basic structure of *Pursuing Human Strengths* is retained here. The chapters and their original order, as well as most topics, self-assessments, and critical thinking exercises, remain. Naturally, I have added to the text by inserting new or updated material, including a closing chapter as well as new or revised exercises; some scales have been revised and updated since the first edition was published, and I have usually elected to include the most recent versions herein. The scientific literature in positive psychology has expanded considerably over the last decade. As a result, this edition boasts more than 210 new references. I have also added my own views on various topics, issues, and questions. By doing so, I am not replacing Bolt's perspective; rather, I am complementing it by encouraging readers to think about the ways that positive psychology can enhance their daily lives and promote well-being across their life spans. That sounds like a tall order, but it's one that is implicit in Bolt's vision, which is both intact and expanded here in the new edition.

Like Dr. Bolt, I welcome comments and suggestions for ways to improve subsequent editions of *Pursuing Human Strengths*. I encourage motivated readers to share their ideas with me and with the editorial team.

A Flexible Overview of Positive Psychology

Any instructor or student interested in a brief but comprehensive overview of the still young field of positive psychology will be interested in reading and using this book. Although the book was designed as a supplementary work for use in introductory or general psychology courses (where it has been quite popular), it also lends itself to stand-alone courses or seminars on positive psychology. As you will see in the next section, the book's chapters complement the standard chapter topics in virtually all introductory psychology books. At the same time, the book can stand on its own, allowing instructors to use each chapter's discussions as a way to enter more deeply into major topics in positive psychology. Some instructors, for example, might assign the book as a reading in a capstone course wherein students explore how positive psychological themes can inform their relationships with others as well as their own thoughts on the nature of happiness and how to live a good life. Students not only find the writing style to be both accessible and engaging, they enjoy the various exercises and self-assessments that bring the concepts and theories of well-being alive—and applicable to their daily experiences.

Where Does This Book Fit into the Introductory Psychology Course?

In utilizing the discipline's scientific methodology and diverse theoretical perspectives to study all dimensions of optimal human functioning, one could argue that positive psychology is simply psychology (Sheldon & King, 2001). Indeed, the 11 human strengths covered in this brief book map well onto the organization of general psychology texts. For both teachers and students, the topic of human flourishing provides an integrating theme for what sometimes seems to be a loosely connected collection of topics in the psychology course.

Here's an overview of how this book's specific chapters connect to psychology's key concepts, along with a short summary of each chapter. You will see, for example, that Chapter 2, which deals with love, reinforces many key themes covered in developmental psychology, while Chapter 5, "Wisdom," extends traditional coverage of thought and intelligence. Note that there are many other possible ways to connect this material to introductory psychology (and other courses, as well), but this outline provides one valid way to begin. The introduction presents positive psychology's central themes and provides a basis for working through the entire book, so you will want to read it first. Otherwise, the chapters are self-contained units (with occasional cross-references to other chapters) that may be read in any order and do not depend on one another for comprehension.

Chapter 1   Introduction

This first chapter provides an overview of the themes of positive psychology and is a prelude to the rest of the book. This is the place to start regardless of how or where the rest of this book is being used. In this chapter we are reminded that psychology's major theoretical perspectives suggest that we are both creatures and creators of our world. Chapter 1 focuses on the many different factors that affect our thinking and behavior, but it emphasizes that those who think they can influence and control their world are more likely to initiate intentional actions, persist in pursuing goals, and attain more in virtually every area of life. This chapter introduces the core strength of responsibility, which is central to developing other strengths.

Chapter 2   Love

Both nature and nurture contribute to **human development**. This chapter specifically recognizes the interaction of heredity and environment in the formation of social bonds. Infant attachment styles carry over to adult relationships. Secure attachment in early life predicts social competence in adulthood. People not fortunate enough to have developed secure attachment styles can still change, and there are many ways to foster the closeness, care, communication, and commitment common to all intimate bonds.

Chapter 3   Empathy

The organization and interpretation inherent in **perception** are evident in our social judgments. We tend to see people's behavior as reflecting their traits, and thus we often overlook their life situations and influences from the environment. By assuming the perspective of others, we come to see what they see and to feel what they feel. This chapter reminds us that empathy enables us to live with greater purpose, and research suggests that empathy may promote genuine altruism. Positive psychologists recognize that assuming the perspective of those who have injured us represents a special challenge. Nonetheless, forgiveness is linked to well-being and health.

Chapter 4   Self-Control

The study of **learning** highlights the power of immediate rewards and helps us to understand the difficulties of self-control. Psychologists have examined the evolutionary, developmental, and cultural factors that are involved in resisting small, immediate rewards in favor of choosing more rewarding delayed outcomes. Contemporary cognitive theory emphasizes the importance of setting goals. Once a goal has been set, self-regulation reflects a process of feedback control. Recent research contributes to both the understanding of and possible solutions for a wide range of self-control problems, including exercising willpower and developing grit in order to satisfy long-term goals.

Chapter 5   Wisdom

Research on **intelligence** shows that productive living requires more than academic aptitude. Recent studies of emotional and successful intelligence have expanded to take wisdom into consideration. People with wisdom have good judgment and offer sound advice in important but uncertain life situations. Wisdom researchers therefore ask people to reason about difficult life dilemmas. We see how wise people carefully balance their short- and long-term interests with those of others, are committed to values of truth and justice, and are keenly aware of the human capacity for self-deception. With little effort, we can learn to exercise some everyday wisdom and creativity.

Chapter 6   Commitment

Psychologists make an important distinction between intrinsic and extrinsic **motivation**. When important human strivings bring little immediate joy or satisfaction, commitment enables us to persevere in meeting our need for competence, relatedness, and autonomy. We see how obligation merges with enthusiasm when our goals have lasting meaning or value. For example, when our work is a vocation, life is purposeful and satisfying. Being committed to causes or a direction can also enable us to develop and display resilience in the face of unexpected turmoil.

Chapter 7   Happiness

After decades of focusing on negative **emotions**, psychologists are now also examining the positive emotions of joy, life satisfaction, and happiness. In considering important predictors of happiness, we learn how people's perceptions of their life situations often prove more important to their sense of well-being than objective circumstances. For example, how we spend money can lead to more happiness than does the money itself, just as the desire to maximize all of life's outcomes may foster feelings of regret. Savoring life's best moments facilitates a sense of well-being, and those who live gratefully are happier as well.

Chapter 8   Self-Respect and Humility

Personality theorists show how our self-understandings organize our thoughts and feelings. They debate the merits of high self-esteem; too much is too much. We see that examining where people find their self-worth helps us to understand the paradoxical links between self-esteem and behavior. Unlike narcissists, humble people have an awareness of their inherent value and are able to "forget themselves." They view their weaknesses and strengths realistically. By admitting pride, by seeking accurate feedback, and by taking a cosmic perspective, we cultivate healthy self-respect.

Chapter 9   Hope

Psychological disorders such as depression are often marked by a sense of hopelessness. **Therapy** works, in part, by restoring optimism and hope to demoralized people. Optimists seem to cope better—and more constructively—with stressful life events and actually live longer than pessimists. Hopeful people have the motivation to keep moving toward their goals and the ability to generate routes to achieve them. This chapter reminds us that hope survives best in community. Hopeful people have a strong support network and join with others in the pursuit of collective well-being.

Chapter 10   Friendship and Social Support

The study of friendship is central to **social psychology**. By providing social support, friends foster both our psychological and physical well-being. We see how people regard trust, honesty, and understanding as important features of their closest relationships. Social support is integral to our individual adjustment to life's ups and downs, and one careful analysis of friendship regards intimacy and caring as its core ingredients. Friends share a communal relationship in which they are mutually responsive to one another's needs.

Chapter 11   Epilogue: Meaning and Flourishing

We complete our review by reflecting on how to **flourish** by continuing to use principles and concepts from positive psychology in daily life, including finding **meaning**.

What's New in this Edition
Chapter 1   Introduction

New section defining positive psychology and reviewing its brief history

New self-assessment of flourishing (having many psychological resources and strengths to call upon) that is paired with a reassessment in the final chapter

Discussion of key factors of happiness (the "happiness pie") highlighting which personal factors we can change and which ones are fixed

New activity: Thinking of your best possible self

Chapter 2   Love

New activity: Reflecting on happiest and most painful memories

Discussion of John Gottman's research on marital communication patterns that predict divorce

Chapter 3   Empathy

New discussion of the power of forgiveness

New self-assessment of how people react to personal transgressions

Review of why helping others allows us to help and benefit ourselves

Chapter 4   Self-Control

New discussion of the place of "guilty pleasures" in our lives

New material on willpower and whether this self-regulation acts like a muscle

New self-assessment: Internet Addiction

New discussion of the GRIT scale, a measure of passion and perseverance for achieving long-term goals

Chapter 5   Wisdom

New discussion of our limited ability to predict accurately how we will feel in the future (affective forecasting)

New critical thinking exercise on Attention Restoration Theory (ART)

Chapter 6   Commitment

New discussion of intrinsic versus extrinsic motivations

New discussion of positive institutions and their importance to positive psychology

New section on psychological resilience and ways to foster it

Chapter 7   Happiness

New discussion of subjective well-being and happiness

New discussion of the Mills College Yearbook Study, which deals with genuine smiles and long-term happiness and well-being

New critical thinking exercise on opportunities for prosocial spending of money

Updated self-assessment: the Maximization Scale

New discussion of savoring and ways to extend pleasurable experiences

New material on the benefits of expressing gratitude

New discussion of capitalization (responding positively to others' good news) and recognizing and addressing unhappiness

Chapter 8   Self-Respect and Humility

New discussion distinguishing high self-esteem from narcissism

New discussion of demonstrating balance in order to benefit from humility

Chapter 9   Hope

Updated self-assessment: the Revised Life Orientation Test (LOT-R)

New discussion of the benefits of optimism

New material on the behavioral impact of hope and hopeful connections to other people

Chapter 10   Friendship and Social Support

New material on the consequences of ostracism and ostracizing others

Chapter 11   Epilogue: Meaning and Flourishing

This is a new chapter that explores meaning and flourishing—all the material is new

Acknowledgments

Books are never solo affairs and, in this particular case, I am building on the solid foundation created by the original author. As Professor Bolt was in the first edition, I too am very grateful to the scholar-researchers whose assessment tools and inventories provide a significant portion of the content of *Pursuing Human Strengths*. By graciously allowing their work to be reproduced, these colleagues provide readers with the opportunity to reflect on their own strengths and to engage in more active learning.

I am delighted to become a member of the Worth family of authors and am particularly grateful to my friend and Senior Acquisitions Editor Christine Cardone. We are veterans of several book projects together and I hope there will be many more. Chris's kindness and candor and her enthusiasm for publishing psychological work make writing a pleasure. In addition, my friend and fellow Worth author David G. Myers was both supportive and excited about this project from the start. Other members of the Worth staff and freelance book team who aided in the production of this edition include Senior Project Editor Jane O'Neill, Assistant Editor Catherine Michaelsen, Associate Media Editor Anthony Casciano, Copyeditor Anna Paganelli, Director of Design, Content Mangement Diana Blume, Text Designers Lissi Sigillo and Blake Logan, Senior Production Supervisor Susan Wein, Proofreader Maria Vlasak, and Indexer Alexandra Nicholson.

I am indebted to reviewers of the second edition for their helpful and thoughtful suggestions for improving the book. These colleagues include Trina Brown, Savannah College of Art and Design; Rachel Happel, Missouri State University; Mark Hopper, Loras College; Christina Jenkins, Park University; Lynn Nagle, Pennsylvania State University, Altoona; Patricia Schoenrade, William Jewell College; Jennifer Simonds, Westminster College; Christina Sinisi, Charleston Southern University; Mary Vandedorpe, Lewis University; Judy Wilson, Palomer College; Linda Waxse, Park University. A Summer 2014 Moravian College Faculty Development and Research Grant supported the writing of portions of this work. Finally, I am sincerely grateful to Martin Bolt's family, who welcomed my joining the book and building on his fine legacy.

Readers will note that this edition is dedicated to the memory of Martin Bolt, as well as to the memories of Christopher Peterson (late of the University of Michigan) and C. R. (Rick) Snyder (late of the University of Kansas). All three of these men had a decided impact on the field of psychology—positive psychology, in particular— through their scholarship, teaching, human warmth, and their particular voices as writers. They each contributed their respective spheres of influence and changed many lives for the better. All three were there when positive psychology emerged as a new subfield and each worked hard and in distinct and different ways to share its theories, research findings, practices, and practical insights with students, colleagues, scholars, and the public. The loss of Martin, Chris, and Rick was felt throughout the discipline, of course, but most acutely by their families and close friends. We can take some solace in the fact that they loved contributing to the discipline and sharing their enthusiasm with others. The words of Henry Adams ring very true for these three men: "A teacher affects eternity; he can never tell where his influence stops."

Dana S. Dunn
Moravian College
Bethlehem, PA
dunn@moravian.edu

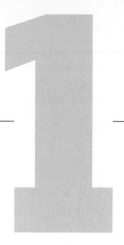

Introduction

The stream of causation from past to future runs through our present choices. —DAVID G. MYERS, 2002

We all make choices all of the time. An interesting issue for positive psychology to explore is whether our choices end up making us who we are. Perhaps making some choices rather than others allows us to develop particular strengths that represent what is best about humanity. The study of human strengths—the topic of this book— is at the core of positive psychology. *Positive psychology*, a new field within the larger discipline of psychology, aims to understand how human strengths can be used to help people flourish and be successful in life (Csikszentmihalyi & Nakamura, 2011; Lopez & Snyder, 2009). Often the worst times—and the daunting choices that accompany them—bring out the best in people. Consider a few remarkable displays of strength:

In 1940, Adolph Hitler ruled most of Europe. The Final Solution appeared on course. Sempo Sugihara, Japan's Consul General in Lithuania, seemed an unlikely roadblock. For 16 years he had provided loyal, obedient service in a variety of government posts. Sempo loved life's luxuries and was ambitious. His career goal? To become the Japanese ambassador to Russia. Nonetheless, when 200 Polish Jews gathered outside his door for help in fleeing the country, he responded. Twice he wired his home government to authorize travel visas. Rejected each time, he decided to prepare them anyway—knowingly throwing away his diplomatic career. And once started, Sempo didn't stop. Even after the consulate was shut down, he continued to write escape papers for the innocent—still frantically preparing travel visas on the train that was to take him back to Berlin. He saved thousands. For his insubordination, Sempo Sugihara lost his position. In fact, he was reduced to selling light bulbs after the war. Interviewed 45 years later about his rescue efforts, he simply said, "They were human, and they needed help." (Kenrick, Neuberg, & Cialdini, 2002, p. 304)

In spring 2003, hiker Aron Ralston found himself hopelessly pinned by a boulder that had rolled onto his arm in a remote Utah canyon. For three days he survived on some water, two burritos, and a few crumbs left in candy bar wrappers. On the fourth day he prepared his surgical table. He went through the motions of applying a tourniquet, laid out his hiking shorts to absorb blood, and in his mind worked out how to cut through his arm with a small pocket knife made dull by attempts to chip away at the rock. The next morning the operation began. "I was able to first snap the radius," he remembers, "and then within another few minutes snap the ulna at the wrist and from there, I had the knife out and applied the tourniquet and went to task. It was a process that took about an hour." Having finally freed himself, he crawled through the narrow winding canyon, rappelled down a 60-foot cliff, and walked some 6 miles before finally receiving help. Reflecting on his ordeal at a news conference a few days later, he reported, "I'm not sure how I handled it. I felt pain and I coped with it. I moved on." (Slevin, 2003, pp. A1, A11)

And in January 2009, an event that became known as the "miracle on the Hudson" occurred. Shortly after US Airways Flight 1549 took off from LaGuardia Airport, the plane flew into a flock of geese causing what is known as a "bird strike"—resulting in a rapid loss of power. The pilot, Captain Sullenberger, concluded that there was no way to land the plane at LaGuardia or any other airport in the region and quickly decided to "ditch" it in the Hudson River. A water landing was the only safe option for the passengers, crew, and people going about their business in metropolitan New York City. Sullenberger skillfully glided to the river's surface and landed it safely. There was no loss of life and all 155 people on the plane were evacuated and then rescued by local boats and ferries. The public in the United States and around the world was in awe of this rare and wonderful aviation outcome, and the manner in which the plane's well-trained crew remained calm and in control of what was a sudden and potentially catastrophic situation. Captain Sullenberger later said, "It was one of those events, in the first couple of seconds, I knew it was going to be unlike anything I had ever experienced—it was going to define my life into before and after" (Davis, 2014).

Compassion, commitment, self-control. What are the roots and fruits of human strengths such as these? And how do we foster them in ourselves and others?

After a century of studying human weakness and psychological disorders, psychologists are refocusing their attention to the brighter side of human life—on the habits and motivations that underlie human flourishing. An increasing number of psychology researchers are trying to create a more positive discipline by exploring optimal human functioning. "The main purpose of a positive psychology," says psychologist Martin Seligman (2002), "is to measure, understand, and then build the human strengths and the civic virtues." This book is not intended to be an exhaustive survey of this rapidly developing field. Rather, we will explore key directions in positive psychology research so that you may gain a broad understanding of this new approach and perhaps develop some more effective life skills in the process. This chapter introduces central themes in the scientific pursuit of human strengths, including the habits and motivations that promote vigorous growth and thriving. We begin by defining the new subfield of psychology known as positive psychology and explaining its origins.

Positive Psychology: A Definition and a Very Brief History

Positive Psychology is the scientific study of the strengths that enable individuals and communities to thrive. The field is founded on the belief that people want to lead meaningful and fulfilling lives, to cultivate what is best within themselves, and to enhance their experiences of love, work, and play. — POSITIVE PSYCHOLOGY CENTER (2015)

Where did positive psychology come from? Why did it emerge in the new millennium?

Martin Seligman (1999) is credited with initiating and coalescing interest in this new subfield. During his year as president of the American Psychological Association (APA) back in 1998, Seligman pointed out an obvious truth: Traditionally, the bulk of psychological research has emphasized people's weaknesses, such as the social, emotional, cognitive, and behavioral problems that plague them. If you are like most people, when asked what psychologists do, you might answer they help people deal with problems like depression, anxiety, and a variety of other disorders. In other words, psychologists focus on the negative rather than the positive.

Seligman wanted to change the focus—if only slightly—toward the beneficial qualities of human experience. He was in the right place at the right time, encouraging many like-minded researchers to begin to study the good in people, including how to help people build on their positive natures in order to lead happier, more fulfilling lives (e.g., Aspinwall & Staudinger, 2002; Keyes & Haidt, 2003). More than 15 years later, positive psychology has generated numerous research articles, many books (including this one), and even some journals intended to help people *flourish* or to experience high levels of well-being and low levels of mental illness (Keyes, 2009).

Which leads to a question for you, as you begin to read and respond to contents of this book: Are you flourishing? That is, are you successful in important areas of your life, including relationships, self-esteem, purpose, and optimism? Positive psychologist Ed Diener and his colleagues designed the following questionnaire to assess the degree to which people are flourishing in daily life. Take the following self-assessment, one of many you will complete in the course of reading this book, to assess your level of flourishing.

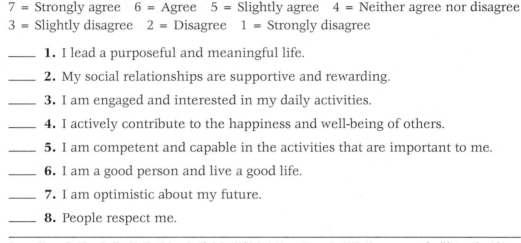

Flourishing Scale

Below are eight statements with which you may agree or disagree. Using the 1–7 scale below, indicate your agreement with each item by selecting your response for each statement.

7 = Strongly agree   6 = Agree   5 = Slightly agree   4 = Neither agree nor disagree
3 = Slightly disagree   2 = Disagree   1 = Strongly disagree

_____ **1.** I lead a purposeful and meaningful life.

_____ **2.** My social relationships are supportive and rewarding.

_____ **3.** I am engaged and interested in my daily activities.

_____ **4.** I actively contribute to the happiness and well-being of others.

_____ **5.** I am competent and capable in the activities that are important to me.

_____ **6.** I am a good person and live a good life.

_____ **7.** I am optimistic about my future.

_____ **8.** People respect me.

Source: Diener, E., Wirtz, D., Tov, W., Kim-Prieto, C., Choi, D., Oishi, S., & Biswas-Diener, R. (2009). New measures of well-being: Flourishing and positive and negative feelings. *Social Indicators Research, 39*, 247–266.

Scoring: Add the responses, varying from 1 to 7, for all eight items. The possible range of scores is from 8 (lowest possible) to 56 (highest possible). A high score represents a person with many psychological resources and strengths.

One of the goals of this book is to provide you with tools to help you flourish in your daily life. Your score on this assessment is a starting point for you. In the last chapter, you will have a chance to take this self-assessment again to see if your flourishing score has changed as a result of thinking about and developing human strengths as you work your way through the chapters in this book.

The Why of Human Behavior

Whether observing human vitality or vulnerability, virtue or vice, all of us are amateur psychologists who try to figure out other people (Heider, 1958; Malle, 2011). Everyone forms a theory of human nature. Are people basically kind and compassionate, or are they selfish and pleasure seeking? Are they rational or irrational? Is each person unique, or are people easily categorized? Different answers to these questions create different psychological worlds that affect how we think, feel, and act.

Most important, like professional psychologists, we want to know about the "why" of human behavior. We search for its underlying causes. Are the roots of human strengths such as self-control, commitment, and joy found in our genetic blueprint? In our childhood environment? Our current situation? Our personal values and choices?

Searching for the "why" leads to the most important issue of all: How much control do we have over our thoughts, feelings, and behaviors? If people were shaped solely by heredity and past experience, it would be futile to try to develop strengths. If forces beyond our control determined our motivations and behaviors, it would make little sense to pursue "virtue," strengthen our "characters," or to try to be "good" people. In fact, we regard people as acting responsibly only if they could have chosen to act differently, say, by ignoring a serious problem or failing to aid someone in distress.

Genetics and past experience are major contributors to human flourishing, but almost all of us have at least some capacity to choose, to change, and to control the direction of our lives. This book reflects the assumptions of most researchers in positive psychology—that people have the ability to build strengths such as wisdom, love, and hope in a self-directed manner.

⇒ IN REVIEW

> Positive psychology's goal is to understand and build the human strengths in an effort to help people thrive and flourish. People tend to be curious about the underlying causes of both good and bad behaviors, and to wonder about how much control we really have over our behavior. Positive psychologists argue that people can choose, change, and control their life's direction, which validates efforts to build human strengths and foster civic virtues.

Human Freedom

We are not billiard balls or rocks. We value our sense of freedom and strive to be self-determining. But what does it mean to be "free"? Consider three key components: choice (deciding life's direction), change (altering one's typical behavior patterns), and control (affecting life's outcomes).

Choice

Our experience tells us that we make choices. Indeed, decision making is life's wellspring. Consider Steven Pinker's (2002) thought experiment. Imagine for a moment not deliberating over your actions. After all, it's a waste of time; they have already all been determined anyway. Shoot from the hip, live for the moment, do what feels good. A moment's reflection on what would happen if you did try to give up decision making is illuminating: The experience of choosing is real, regardless of how the brain works or how experience shapes us. You cannot step outside of choosing or let it continue without you—because it is you.

Here's a simple example from visual perception. Different sets of arrows point across the page in opposite directions. You can choose to see the arrows pointing to the right or you can choose to see them pointing to the left. Try it. Make a choice. Does it work?

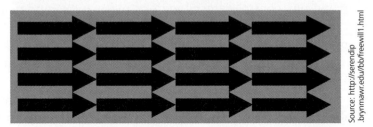

We tend to value very highly a sense of freedom and we work hard to protect our capacity to choose, even when the choice we make is a minor one (Brehm & Brehm, 1981). In fact, had we tried to dictate your choice by saying, "Now you must only see the arrows going to the left," you might well have decided, "No, I don't think so. I don't like being manipulated. I choose to see right-pointing arrows."

Imagine that someone stops you on the street and asks you to sign a petition advocating something you mildly support. As you reflect for a moment, you are told that someone else believes that "people absolutely should not be allowed to distribute or sign such petitions." How do you think you would respond? Might this blatant attempt to restrict your freedom actually increase the likelihood of your signing the petition? That is precisely what Madeline Heilman (1976) found when she staged this experiment on the streets of New York City.

Among dating couples, researchers have sometimes observed the *Romeo and Juliet effect*: The more the parents discourage the romance, the more love the partners feel for each other. Although the pattern is not inevitable, it does suggest that parents should think twice before they forbid teenagers to see each other (Brehm, Miller, Perlman, & Campbell, 2002; Driscoll, Davis, & Lipetz, 1972).

This principle works in reverse as well. Try to coerce love and it's lost. Tell a child he *must* eat his favorite dessert, and he suddenly loses his taste for it. Pressure to do what we already enjoy doing makes the activity less satisfying very quickly.

Consider Phil Zimbardo's amusing story of Nunzi, a shoemaker and an Italian immigrant (Middlebrook, 1974, p. vi).

Every day after school, a gang of young American boys came to Nunzi's shop to taunt and to tease. After attempting a variety of strategies to get the boys to stop, Nunzi came upon a solution.

When the boys arrived the next day after school, Nunzi was in front of his store waving a fistful of dollar bills. "Don't ask me why," said Nunzi, "but I'll give each of you a new dollar bill if you will shout at the top of your lungs ten times: 'Nunzi is a dirty

Italian swine. No greaseballs in our neighborhood.'" Taking the money, the boys shouted the chants in unison. The next afternoon Nunzi successfully enticed the gang to repeat their taunts for a mere half dollar. On the third day, however, he stood with a handful of dimes: "Business has not been good and I can only give you each ten cents to repeat your marvelous performance of yesterday."

"You must be crazy," said the ringleader, "to think we would knock ourselves out screaming and cursing for a lousy dime."

"Yeah," joined another, "we got better things to do with our time than to do favors for dumb guineas for only a dime." Away the boys went, never to bother Nunzi again.

Of course, when people *consistently* comply or defy—that is, conform to orders or do just the opposite—they are hardly free. *Autonomy* means acting with a sense of true choice. When autonomous, people embrace what they are doing with interest and commitment. They express their true selves (Deci, 1995). Autonomy, suggests Deci, is a fundamental human need. Is this need currently satisfied in your own life?

 **SELF-ASSESSMENT**

Autonomy

Please read each of the following statements carefully, thinking about how it relates to your life, and then indicate how true it is for you. Use the following scale to respond:

1	2	3	4	5	6	7
Not at all true			Somewhat true			Very true

_____ **1.** I feel like I am free to decide for myself how to live my life.

_____ **2.** I feel pressured in my life.

_____ **3.** I generally feel free to express my ideas and opinions.

_____ **4.** In my daily life, I frequently have to do what I am told.

_____ **5.** People I interact with on a daily basis tend to take my feelings into consideration.

_____ **6.** I feel like I can pretty much be myself in my daily situations.

_____ **7.** There is not much opportunity for me to decide for myself how to do things in my daily life.

Source: Johnston, M. M., & Finney, S. J., "Measuring basic needs satisfaction: Evaluating previous research and conducting new psychometric evaluations of the Basic needs Satisfaction in General Scale," *Contemporary Educational Psychology, 35*, 280–296. Copyright © 2010 Elsevier. Reprinted by permission.

To score your responses for this and other self-assessment activities throughout this book, you will need to learn to use a simple reversal method that may seem odd at first. For this autonomy activity, you need to reverse the numbers you gave in answer to statements 2, 4, and 7. That is, if you answered with 1, change it to 7. If you responded with 2, change it to 6. Similarly, change 3 to 5, 4 remains 4, 5 becomes 3, 6 changes to 2, and 7 becomes 1. Make these changes only for statements 2, 4, and 7. Keep the numbers in front of statements 1, 3, 5, and 6 the same. Finally, add up the numbers in front of all seven items. Scores can range from 7 to 49, with higher scores indicating that you experience a greater sense of autonomy in everyday life. Scores above the midpoint of 28 suggest that you tend to feel that you are freely making choices; scores below that midpoint indicate that you do not.

Just as restricting choice seems to undermine people's enjoyment of a task, increasing available alternatives often enhances it. Deci (1995) reports how, in one laboratory experiment, he and his colleagues varied their research participants' experience of freedom. In one group, subjects were offered a choice about which puzzles to work. In the other group, subjects were assigned puzzles. Subjects offered the simple choice spent more time playing with the puzzles and reported liking them more than participants not offered a choice.

Satisfying our need for autonomy, research suggests, is important to well-being and to personal achievement. It's a need we will come back to later in this book when we look at the factors that foster commitment.

Change

Can people change? Are they set, like plaster, or are they more pliable, like clay? Are our personal characteristics basically fixed, or are they malleable? What do you think? Can people change who they are? Can they become different or even "new" people? The following scale assesses the degree to which you believe people can change. *Entity theorists* tend to think that human characteristics are fixed. *Incremental theorists* are inclined to believe that characteristics are malleable.

 **SELF-ASSESSMENT**

Entity versus Incremental Theory

Using the scale, indicate the extent to which you agree or disagree with each statement by noting the number that corresponds to your opinion.

1 = Strongly agree   2 = Agree   3 = Mostly agree   4 = Mostly disagree
5 = Disagree   6 = Strongly disagree

_____ **1.** The kind of person someone is, is something very basic and can't be changed very much.

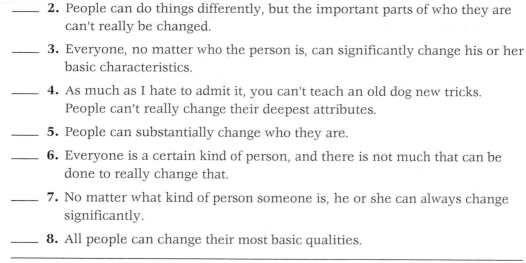

_____ **2.** People can do things differently, but the important parts of who they are can't really be changed.

_____ **3.** Everyone, no matter who the person is, can significantly change his or her basic characteristics.

_____ **4.** As much as I hate to admit it, you can't teach an old dog new tricks. People can't really change their deepest attributes.

_____ **5.** People can substantially change who they are.

_____ **6.** Everyone is a certain kind of person, and there is not much that can be done to really change that.

_____ **7.** No matter what kind of person someone is, he or she can always change significantly.

_____ **8.** All people can change their most basic qualities.

Source: From Dweck, C. S., Self-theories: Their role in motivation, personality and development. Copyright © 1999 Psychology Press (Taylor & Francis). Reprinted by permission.

To obtain a total score, first reverse the numbers you placed in front of statements 3, 5, 7, and 8. (Change 1 to 6, 2 to 5, 3 to 4, 4 to 3, 5 to 2, and 6 to 1.) Then add up the numbers in front of all eight statements. Scores can range from 8 to 48. Scores below the midpoint of 28 reflect the belief that traits are fixed (entity theory); scores above 28 indicate the belief that traits are malleable (incremental theory).

Although people at all levels of education and from all walks of life advocate each perspective, our choice of theories does make a difference—the one we choose is like a lens through which we see the social world. It affects how we think about and evaluate our own behavior, as well as how we perceive, judge, and relate to others. Most important, it affects our efforts at change.

In contrast to incremental theorists, entity theorists are more likely to think that a person's underlying character can be revealed by a single behavior or performance. This holds true for both good and bad behaviors. Entity theorists tend to believe that what they see on the outside reflects what people are like on the inside: What you see is what you get.

Taken to an extreme, this belief in a more stable social world seems to offer advantages. We could know others quickly and predict behavior more easily. If people were not mysterious, life would be simpler and more secure. Of course, in reality the world is not so simple. People are complex and don't fall neatly into the categories of those who have intelligence, self-control, and wisdom, and those who don't.

Perhaps most important, the two theories profoundly affect motivation and felt responsibility. If our traits are fixed, then there's not much we can do to change. We're stuck with who we are. The best we can do is to validate what strengths we already have and hope that they will help us win approval and avoid rejection. There is no sense in trying to promote growth in others, either. They will remain who they are in spite of our best efforts.

On the other hand, incremental beliefs that portray a dynamic self and world see the potential and even the responsibility for improvement. This mindset encourages us to look for ways to grow, to solve our problems, and to remedy our weaknesses. Small changes in the stories we tell about ourselves, for example, can change the way we see and think about ourselves and, in turn, create opportunities to act in desired ways (Wilson, 2011). The incremental beliefs perspective also encourages us to look for potential in others to help them grow.

Consider how these two belief systems play out in a specific domain—intelligence— the one most studied by Carol Dweck (2000, 2008).

CRITICAL THINKING

The Nature of Intelligence

Complete the following equation (Mueller & Dweck, 1997):

$$\text{Intelligence} = \underline{\hspace{1cm}}\% \text{ effort} + \underline{\hspace{1cm}}\% \text{ ability}$$

Now imagine that you see a puzzle labeled "Test Your IQ!" in a science magazine. You work on it for a very long time, get confused, and start over. You make very slow progress but finally solve it. How do you feel? Do you feel sort of stupid because it required so much effort? Or do you feel smart because you worked hard and mastered it?

_____

_____

Source: From Dweck, C. S., Self-theories: Their role in motivation, personality and development. Copyright © 1999 Psychology Press (Taylor & Francis). Reprinted by permission.

Finally, imagine a child who keeps getting lots and lots wrong on his or her schoolwork and asks you for help. What would you say or do?

_____

_____

_____

_____

_____

_____

Source: Dweck, 1999, p. 84.

Entity and incremental theorists respond to these questions and challenges differently. Entity theorists tend to attach greater weight to ability. They might fill out the equation this way:

Intelligence = ___35___ % effort + ___65___ % ability

For incremental theorists, things are reversed. Effort tends to be weighed more heavily than ability:

Intelligence = ___65___ % effort + ___35___ % ability

Theorists from the two camps think about effort differently. Entity theorists view making a large effort in solving the science magazine's IQ puzzle as evidence of having low intelligence. They agree with the statements "If you have to work hard on some problems, you're probably not very good at them" and "Things come easily to people who are true geniuses." Incrementalists, on the other hand, see effort as something that activates people's intelligence and allows them to use it to full advantage. They are more likely to believe "When you are good at something, working hard allows you to really understand it" and "Even geniuses have to work hard for their discoveries."

As you might imagine by now, entity and incremental theorists also respond differently to the child who is doing poorly on his or her schoolwork. Entity theorists tend to be stumped. They often have little advice because "it either comes naturally or it doesn't come." At best, they express sympathy.

However, those who believe that achievement comes only after a long, effortful process have lots of advice. One incremental theorist responded: "Do you quit a lot? Do you think for a minute and then stop? If you do, you should think for a long time—two minutes, maybe, and if you can't get it you should read the problem again. If you can't get it then, you should raise your hand and ask the teacher" (Dweck, 1999, p. 84).

People who see intelligence as fixed view their poor performance on a task as meaning that they are stupid. In fact, many indicate that whenever they fail they feel "worthless" or "like a complete loser." They also conclude, "If I didn't do as well in school as I hoped, I'd think less of myself as a person." In short, they generalize from academic performance to intelligence to personal worth. Those with a malleable view of intelligence see failure as indicating that they have to do something different in the future to succeed. Most important, they intend to do it. For these people, a specific performance may reflect something about their skill level at the moment, but it says nothing about their broader intellectual abilities. And it certainly suggests nothing about a person's worth.

Entity theorists who are afraid that they may make errors or reveal their ignorance sometimes pass up important learning opportunities. Strange, isn't it? The very notion of learning assumes that there is something you don't know. Most of life's important accomplishments require a heavy investment of effort regardless of how bright you are.

In fact, most famous geniuses worked extraordinarily hard (Dweck, 1999), and many of them had very ordinary beginnings. Charles Darwin, Leo Tolstoy, William James, John Stuart Mill, and Norbert Weiner, to name a few, were not exceptional children. As inventor Thomas Edison quipped, "Genius is 1 percent inspiration and 99 percent perspiration." Brilliant musicians, too, are more often made than born. Researchers find that, as kids, these musicians put in thousands of hours of practice. Researchers who study creativity have proposed the "10 year" rule: No truly great creative contributions come without at least 10 years of intense effort and preparation (Simon & Chase, 1973). Mozart's earliest compositions were neither original nor particularly noteworthy.

None of this means that people only pull themselves up by their own bootstraps. Social support is important. It can be foolish, cautions Dweck, to believe that a person continuing in the same environment will change without any educational or psychological help. Our personal strivings are vital, but so are external supports. Parents and teachers play a particularly important role. When students do well at something—academic work, athletics, artistic performances, difficult hobbies—adults should praise their efforts but not their abilities. When dealing with failure, however, parents and teachers should avoid making any global statements ("You lost focus on the whole game") and should instead give specific feedback on what the student did wrong ("You didn't seem focused on your swing") and what he or she might try next ("Try making your swing tighter and closer to your body next time").

Parents and teachers can also teach students to relish a challenge. Doing easy tasks is often a waste of time. The fun comes in confronting something difficult and finding strategies that work. Finally, advises Dweck, adults should help children value learning more than grades. Too often kids rely on grades to prove their worth. Sure, grades are important. But report cards and transcripts are not as significant as the skills acquired in the process of learning.

Control

Now that we've considered the importance of making our own choices and believing we can change, let's focus on how our sense of personal control affects our feelings of freedom.

Uncertainty often leads to anxiety. Hostages and prisoners of war often say that the worst part of their experience was the unpredictability of their fate. They report making every effort to maintain some sense of personal control. Among the Americans held captive by Iranians in the early 1980s, one hostage saved a bit of food from breakfast and later offered it to anyone who came to his cell. The strategy, he said, had the effect of turning his cell into a living room and he, a hostage, into a host welcoming guests.

Feelings of personal control contribute to a sense of responsibility for behavior and its consequences. We feel accountable for pursuing important objectives only if we feel competent to achieve them. Delroy Paulhus designed the following scale to measure one's sense of control in personal achievement situations.

Personal Efficacy

Indicate the extent to which you agree with each statement using the response scale.

1 = Strongly disagree   2 = Disagree   3 = Slightly disagree   4 = Neither agree nor disagree   5 = Slightly agree   6 = Agree   7 = Strongly agree

_____ **1.** When I get what I want, it's usually because I worked hard for it.

_____ **2.** When I make plans, I am almost certain I can make them work.

_____ **3.** I prefer games involving some luck over games requiring pure skill.

_____ **4.** I can learn almost anything if I set my mind to it.

_____ **5.** My major accomplishments are entirely due to my hard work and ability.

_____ **6.** I usually don't set goals because I have a hard time following through on them.

_____ **7.** Competition discourages excellence.

_____ **8.** Often people get ahead just by being lucky.

_____ **9.** On any sort of exam or competition I like to know how well I do relative to everyone else.

_____**10.** It's pointless to keep working on something that's too difficult for me.

To score your responses, reverse the numbers you wrote before statements 3, 6, 7, 8, and 10 (that is, change 1 to 7, 2 to 6, 3 to 5, 5 to 3, 6 to 2, and 7 to 1). Then add up the numbers in front of all 10 items. Scores range from 10 to 70, with higher scores reflecting a greater sense of personal control. Among one sample of college students (Burger, 2004), males and females obtained mean scores of 51.8 and 52.2, respectively.

Psychological research suggests that some people tend to have an internal locus of control—they believe that they control their own destiny. Others are inclined toward external control—they believe that their fate is determined by chance or powerful others. For example, in terms of academic achievement, students with an internal locus of control believe that their grades depend on their study habits. Those with an external locus of control believe that their grades depend on luck or perhaps their teachers' moods.

People with an internal locus of control not only do well in school, they also exercise greater control over many other aspects of their life. (Self-control is a strength we will examine more carefully in Chapter 4.) Research (Burger, 2004; Myers, 2004; Ryon & Gleason, 2014) suggests that people who see themselves as more internally controlled are more likely to do the following:

- Successfully stop smoking
- Report fewer daily hassles and anxieties
- Wear seat belts
- Display better physical health and emotional adjustment
- Practice birth control (rather than rely on fate)
- Be happy
- Have higher levels of job satisfaction
- Cope better with stress
- Delay gratification in order to achieve long-term goals

People with an internal locus of control not only show more control over their internal world, they also exercise more influence in their social worlds. They achieve more in school, are more independent, deal with marital problems more directly, and are more successful in changing other people's opinions. They are also more likely to be involved in working toward social and political change (Levenson, 1981). They take charge in many areas of life and assume more responsibility for the outcomes (Larsen & Buss, 2002).

In contrast, those who feel they have little personal control tend to avoid challenges and abandon activities when faced with setbacks, and they often suffer anxiety or depression. But if you scored low on the Personal Efficacy Self-Assessment, fear not. As we will see throughout this book, we all have the potential for change.

⇒ IN REVIEW

We value our freedom and resist others' efforts to restrict it. Choice, change, and control are three factors that powerfully affect our sense of personal freedom. Decision making is central to human experience. Autonomy seems to be a fundamental human need that is important to well-being and personal achievement. The belief that human nature can be changed affects motivation and felt responsibility. Entity theorists, who see traits as fixed, exert less effort than incremental theorists, who believe traits can be modified. People vary in their sense of personal control. People with an internal locus of control believe they shape their own destiny. People with an external locus of control believe that chance or powerful others control their outcomes. Compared with externals, internals achieve more in school, act more independently, and enjoy greater physical and psychological well-being.

Human Limits

Experiencing choice, change, and control is clearly important to human flourishing and personal development—to living both joyfully and responsibly. Yet this introduction to our study of the human strengths and virtues would be incomplete without flipping the coin over. Do we have unlimited choice? Can we change and control everything? Certainly not. Let's briefly revisit choice, change, and control to understand human responsibility more fully.

Unlimited Choice and Illusory Control

Our range of choices seems to multiply daily. People have countless choices for colleges, careers, vacation spots, and even the places they call home. Even for relatively inconsequential matters, observes Barry Schwartz (2000), decision making is challenging. Take the simple task of grocery shopping. In the breakfast food aisle, should we buy hot or cold cereal? Sugar-coated or relatively unsweetened? With or without bran? Or should we opt for the breakfast bars instead? Shopping for a car is more mindboggling. Should the car be new or used? Foreign or domestic? Automatic or manual? Coupe, sedan, or minivan? Two-door or four-door? Six-cylinder or four-cylinder? Black, white, green, blue, beige, or yellow?

It's overwhelming to have so many alternatives. With all these choices, how does one ever gather enough information to make the right decision? And when anyone finally makes a selection, how can he or she be sure that a different choice would not have produced a better outcome? "Unconstrained freedom," concludes Barry Schwartz, "leads to paralysis and becomes a kind of self-defeating tyranny" (2000, p. 81). Having too many options leaves people paralyzed, disappointed, and unfulfilled (Schwartz, 2012). Indeed, Schwartz and his colleagues find that *maximizers*—people who routinely seek to make the optimal or "best" decisions—usually report lower feelings of well-being than *satisficers*, individuals who try to make "good enough" decisions (Dar-Nimrod, Rawn, Lehman, & Schwartz, 2009; Roets, Schwartz, & Guan, 2012). Compared with satisficers, maximizers are usually on the lookout for better alternatives, tend to see even trivial decisions as challenging, and maintain high standards for themselves. What's the catch? Maximizers risk having higher levels of regret and dissatisfaction than satisficers; they also tend to be less optimistic and more depressed than their counterparts. We will explore the degree to which you are a maximizer in Chapter 7.

Manufacturers are finally learning the wisdom of limiting alternatives. Some commercial giants have streamlined the number of options they offer. Proctor & Gamble reduced the varieties of their very popular Head & Shoulders shampoo from a staggering 26 to 15. The impact? Sales climbed 10 percent (Schwartz, 2000).

So many choices may also fuel an illusion of control. When coupled with our strong desire to shape our own destiny, we may come to perceive that even chance events are under our personal control. Do you sometimes press the elevator call button even though it's already lit, thinking that somehow you will make the car arrive faster? Do you twist and turn your body after throwing the bowling ball, convinced your gyrations will make the ball knock down more pins? Most of us do these sorts of things even though we know in our heart and head that we can't speed up the elevator or put down more pins.

Gambling casinos thrive on illusory control, and people waste time and money because of it. Overactive perceptions of control can be self-defeating. Here's a vivid example (McQuaid, 1971):

> One gambler in Las Vegas blew a deep breath against the dice before every roll.
> "Do you think that brings you luck?" the man standing next to him at the crap table asked.
> "I know it does," the shooter replied with conviction. "Las Vegas has a very dry climate, right?"
> "Right," his neighbor nodded.
> "So the dice are usually very dry. I have very damp breath, and I always exhale against a six and an ace. That not only gives the six and ace a little extra weight but makes them adhere to the table when they roll across it. The opposite sides come up— the opposite sides of a six and an ace are an ace and a six."
> "Does it really work?" his neighboring partner asked.
> "Well, not all the time," the shooter admitted. "The load of condensation isn't quite heavy enough. But I've been on a hot liquid diet all day, and tonight ought to be the time I break the bank" (p. 289).

Ellen Langer's (1977) experiments with gambling demonstrate people's ready susceptibility to the illusion of control. For example, in a game of chance, research participants bet significantly more money when playing against an awkward, uncertain opponent than one who appeared confident and smooth. And compared with people assigned a lottery number, people who chose their own number demanded four times as much money if someone asked to buy it. But in such chance tasks, what difference could confidence or personal choice make? Indeed, the perception of control can be illusory. Only when the stakes involved in a chance task are high—when we have a lot to lose—do we seem to moderate our perceptions of control (Dunn & Wilson, 1990).

Biological and Environmental Constraints

Not only chance events but natural, biological constraints limit the range of human choice and control. Look again at the two sets of arrows you viewed earlier in this chapter. Try to see the two sets of arrows simultaneously pointing in opposite directions. Can you do it? Not easy, is it? Can you choose to jump a 30-foot wall?

Decide to run a 3-minute mile? Commit to memorizing the *Encyclopædia Britannica?* These would be pointless pursuits—a waste of time. Of course, such constraints are obvious. Decades of careful and productive psychological research define other, less obvious limits.

For example, neuroscientists have made enormous advances in understanding how the body and brain create positive and negative emotions, memories, and sensory experiences (some have linked our brain's biology to happiness; Edelman, 2012). Evolutionary psychologists show how nature selects traits that promote the perpetuation of our genes. Behavior geneticists demonstrate how our unique genetic blueprint contributes to individual differences in intelligence, personality, sexual orientation, and vulnerability to psychological disorder. For example, about 50 percent of most personality traits may be attributable to genetic inheritance (Seligman, 2002). The human strengths are not exempt. Consider happiness. Martin Seligman has suggested that we may inherit a genetic inclination that steers us toward a specific level of happiness or sadness.

Positive psychologist Sonja Lyubomirsky (2007) is even more direct about how key factors influence our happiness. Think of the factors affecting our happiness as three pieces of a pie. Half the pie is given over to genetic influences—some of us are more or less happy than others; this part of our pie cannot really be changed. A 10 percent sliver of the pie is linked to the environment and the things in it that affect our happiness. The third slice—which amounts to 40 percent of the pie—deals with intentional actions we can take to make ourselves happier. We can exercise, travel, meet new people, renew old friendships, seek meaningful and rewarding work, and so on. In short, we can do some things that are linked with enhancing our well-being and incrementally boosting our happiness. According to Lyubomirsky, we might not move dramatically far on a hypothetical happiness scale, but isn't moving from a 6 to a 7 or even an 8—while exercising some control—better than remaining where we started?

In his book *What You Can Change and What You Can't*, Seligman (1994) shows how the biological underpinnings of behavior make certain psychological conditions harder to change than others. Partly because of biology, a phobia is easier to change than being overweight. Depression is more modifiable than a serious psychological disorder such as schizophrenia. Similarly, genes may make it easier for some people to master certain adaptive skills and strengths than for others. Seligman's conclusion? Choose your areas of change carefully. Invest in changing traits or behaviors that are more readily modified.

And what about those environmental effects? In important respects we are products of our environment. We typically learn to repeat acts that our environment rewards and avoid acts that it does not. Modeling in the home, peer groups, and the culture leaves a lasting imprint. Culture profoundly affects our belief systems and value orientations. And behavioral and social-cultural psychologists have demonstrated the dramatic power of individual situations.

We have already seen the power of the environment in Carol Dweck's analysis of how parents and teachers shape children's self-understandings and subsequent levels of achievement. Other lines of research indicate that our current environment—where and with whom we live—affects our level of happiness. Those who live in wealthy democracies are happier than those in impoverished dictatorships (Seligman, 2002). Similarly, those who enjoy a rich social network experience a greater sense of well-being than those who live more isolated lives. It's no wonder that one of the important goals of positive psychology is to build a positive ecology, including healthy families, communal neighborhoods, and effective schools.

So, is "trying to be happier like trying to be taller," as researcher David Lykken (1999) once concluded and then strongly recanted? No. Although the study of biological and environmental influences on behavior helps define our limits, neither biology nor environment is destiny. Seligman argues that although a genetic steersman affects our sense of well-being, our actions still make a difference. Similarly, Lykken came to acknowledge that within the broad limits set by genetic inheritance, we steer our own boat: "I can proceed to do some of the positive wave-making things that I might miss out on if I let my four grandparents collectively do the steering" (1999, p. 66).

Research on biological and environmental influences provides specific direction for our efforts at fostering strengths in ourselves and others. The new understandings help us to make wiser choices in pursuing control and change. For example, when findings indicate that those who eat a balanced breakfast are, by midday, more alert and less fatigued, we have a new responsibility to eat accordingly. When research shows that those who regularly exercise are more successful in quitting smoking, losing weight, and maintaining general well-being, we'd better get moving. When studies tell us that social connections are vital to both physical and psychological welfare, wisdom requires that we give priority to close relationships. We choose our environment and then it shapes us. Ironically, knowledge of the internal and external determinants of human behavior can, in important ways, increase rather than decrease our responsibility.

Close to a century ago, Dorothy Sayers, in *Begin Here: A Statement of Faith* (cited by Yancey, 1989) used a helpful metaphor to capture the relationship between psychological determinism and human freedom. It summarizes our discussion well.

> It is true that man is dominated by his psychological make-up, but only in the sense that an artist is dominated by his material. It is not possible for a sculptor to carve a filigree brooch out of granite; to that extent he is the servant of the stone he works in. His craftsmanship is good in precisely so far as he uses granite to express his artistic intentions in a manner conformable to the stone's own nature. This is no slavery, but the freedom of the sculptor and the freedom of the stone working together in harmony. The better the sculptor understands the true nature of his raw material, the greater is his freedom in using it; and so it is with every man, when he uses his own mind and emotions to express his conscious intention (p. 30).

> Although people value their freedom, the availability of too many choices can be paralyzing. It can also fuel an illusion of control. Freedom within constraint fosters optimal functioning. Natural physical constraints limit the range of human choice. Research identifying the biological and environmental determinants of behavior not only defines our limits but gives direction to efforts for successful change and control.

Initiative and Human Values

Christine Robitschek's (1998) Personal Growth Initiative Scale (PGIS) captures the importance of choice, change, and control to personal development. But there's another key ingredient to flourishing that her scale incorporates: having clear direction. Personal growth, suggests Robitschek, is a person's active, intentional involvement in changing and developing as a person. Growth, she suggests, must be an intentional process. What do you choose, what do you change, what do you seek to control? Try it for yourself.

 ✓ **SELF-ASSESSMENT**

Personal Growth Initiative Scale

Using the scale, indicate the extent to which you agree or disagree with each statement.

1 = Definitely disagree   2 = Mostly disagree   3 = Somewhat disagree
4 = Somewhat agree   5 = Mostly agree   6 = Definitely agree

_____ **1.** I know how to change specific things that I want to change in my life.

_____ **2.** I have a good sense of where I am headed in my life.

_____ **3.** If I want to change something in my life, I know how to initiate the transition process.

_____ **4.** I can choose the role I want to have in a group.

_____ **5.** I know what I need to do to get started toward reaching my goals.

_____ **6.** I have a specific action plan to help me reach my goals.

_____ **7.** I take charge of my life.

_____ **8.** I know what my unique contribution to the world might be.

_____ **9.** I have a plan for making my life more balanced.

Source: Robitschek, Christine (1998), Personal growth initiative: The construct and its measure. *Measurement and Evaluation in Counseling and Development* Vol. 30(4), pp. 183–198. Copyright © 1998 by the Association for Assessment in Counseling and Education, a division of the American Counseling Association. Reprinted by permission of SAGE Publications, Inc.

To score your responses, simply add the numbers you circled to obtain a total score. PGIS scores range from 9 to 54. People who score higher (31.5 is the midpoint) recognize and capitalize on opportunities for personal change. More than that, they search out and create situations that will foster their growth. In contrast, people with low scores actively avoid situations that challenge them to grow.

PGIS scores seem to be strongly positively related to psychological well-being and negatively related to psychological distress (Robitschek & Cook, 1999). Individuals with higher PGIS scores are assertive and tend to have an internal locus of control. Robitschek and her colleagues developed a second version of the PGIS—the PGIS-II—that contains 16 items and four subscales (readiness for change, planfulness, using resources, and intentional behavior). Readiness for change and planfulness are cognitively oriented skills, while using resources and intentional behavior represent overt behaviors that people use. If you are interested in a more multidimensional view of your own person growth, you can find a copy of the longer scale in Robitschek et al. (2012).

Although a sense of freedom is important to personal development, the PGIS suggests that it is not enough. It is also a matter of making wise choices, making the right changes, and in the process, exercising appropriate control. And finally, human values are at the core of our personal development. Values, writes Bert Hodges (2000), "provide distant but real guides that help us to find our way, that help us in the journey of life. Values provide not only place but prospective; they indicate where we have come from and where we are going" (p. 478).

But what values? What is life's "game"? More specifically, asks Barry Schwartz (2000), "What kind of game is being a student? Is it to prepare for a career that will be financially rewarding...one that is intellectually challenging...one that provides public service?" (p. 80). What kind of game is being a businessperson? Are there limits to serving corporate interests? Should businesspeople market whatever people buy, tell people whatever they think people will believe? Should they be concerned about ethics and fairness? Should they demonstrate care for the environment? What kind of game is being a spouse or lover? Ought lovers submerge their own interests or desires to serve those of their partners? When does devotion turn into subjugation? At what point does self-actualization turn into selfishness? Even the notion of responsibility itself is a matter of values. Responsibility for what and to whom?

Most of us would agree that we have responsibility for ourselves, for others, and for our environment and future generations. Most of us, regardless of our vocational or family role, aim to live joyfully and responsibly. We want fulfilling and productive lives, but we also want to demonstrate compassion, commitment, and self-control in our interpersonal relationships. Living fully demands the ability to be oneself and at the same time to be intimately connected with others.

A meaningful, productive life, argues Mihaly Csikszentmihalyi (2003), involves two processes. *Differentiation* reflects a strong sense of personal responsibility for developing and using our unique talents—for enjoying the expression of our being in action. *Integration* is the realization that, however unique we are, we are "also completely enmeshed in networks of relationships with other human beings, with cultural symbols and artifacts, and with the surrounding environment" (p. 29). In short, to be happy, people must enjoy doing their best while at the same time contributing to something beyond themselves, ideally with actions that have effects reaching far into the future. "Responsibility," writes Robert Sternberg (2003), "includes the wisdom to be responsible for others...as well as for oneself" (p. 5).

We will revisit these responsibilities in the course of this book. For now, we can summarize that autonomy does not refer to being detached, selfish, or even "independent" but rather to the experience of choice—regulated and responsible choice. Freedom to choose is linked to responsibility when we acknowledge and meet our obligations to others as well as to ourselves. Fortunately, we not only want to be free, we also have a need to feel connected with others. We have a motive for relatedness (Deci, 1995; Ryan & Deci, 2000), a fundamental need to belong. We are naturally inclined to form bonds with others on whom we then rely and for whom we care—something we will explore more fully in Chapter 2.

Research suggests that, contrary to conventional wisdom, needs for autonomy and relatedness can fit together quite well. For example, cross-cultural research with Korean and U.S. samples has found autonomy to be more strongly linked with collectivistic attitudes than individualistic ones (Kim, Butzel, & Ryan, 1998). Even more interesting are the positive links between autonomy and relatedness that researchers have discovered in American teens. High school is a time when adolescents struggle for independence from their families. Some people have wrongly suggested that relinquishing connections with parents is an important step to maturity. But other research suggests that a chosen dependence on parents rather than strong independence from them is more positively linked to teenagers' integrity and well-being (Ryan, Stiller, & Lynch, 1994). Teens who have strong connections with their parents are happy and tend to perform well in school.

Edward Deci (1995) uses Garth Fagan's modern dance troupe to illustrate the beauty of freedom with responsibility. In a routine called "Prelude: Discipline in Freedom," the dancers soar to unbelievable heights in elegantly creative postures. They show truly amazing energy and force. Still, there is no chaos or disorder in their performance. In fact, everyone is in precisely the right place at the right time. There is freedom and flexibility, but also discipline and responsibility to others.

Personal growth is more than a matter of exercising freedom. Wise choices, the right changes, and appropriate control are also key. Our own values are at the core of our personal development. Most people would agree that we have responsibilities to ourselves, to others, to our environment, and to future generations. A productive, meaningful life requires the development of our unique talents and a commitment to something beyond ourselves. We have both a need for autonomy and a need to belong.

A Research Primer in Positive Psychology

Like other psychologists, positive psychologists are empirically minded; they believe that knowledge about human behavior must be learned through careful observation and critical evaluation. Whenever possible, positive psychologists rely on experimental research where at least one *independent variable* is manipulated by the experimenter while the outcome variable—the *dependent variable*—is measured to assess any behavioral change. True experiments always have a minimum of two groups within their research design. The *experimental group* receives some special treatment linked to the independent variable. In contrast, members of the *control group* do not receive the special treatment but otherwise have the same experience as those in the experimental group. If the two groups are similar in all respects except for the difference created by the manipulation of the independent variable, then any difference between the two groups based on the dependent variable must be due to manipulation of the independent variable.

Consider a simple experimental intervention from positive psychology. Seligman, Steen, Park, and Peterson (2005) randomly assigned participants to an experimental group or to a control group. Those in the former group were asked to write down three things that went well each day, as well as their causes, for 1 week. They were also asked to provide a causal explanation for each good thing. Members of the control group did a filler task that did not entail listing good things. Compared with the control group, the experimental group showed increased levels of happiness and decreased depressive symptoms for 6 months.

Not all research in positive psychology is experimental, which means not all conclusions based on research findings are causally based. Very often, positive psychological research entails the examination of a correlation or the relationship between two variables. Correlational relationships are generally positive or negative. A *positive correlation* indicates that both variables "covary" in the same direction: As one increases in value, so does the other. Similarly, as one decreases in value, so does the other. For example, social activity (e.g., doing things with friends) is positively linked with happiness (Weiten, Dunn, & Hammer, 2015). More activity with friends is associated with higher happiness, just as less activity with friends is linked with lower happiness. Both relationships represent a *positive correlation*. A *negative correlation* is one in which two variables covary in opposite directions. For example, think about the association between grade point average and the number of parties one attends. Students who go to fewer parties during a school term are likely to have higher grades, just as students who go to more parties during the term are likely to have lower grades (i.e., as one variable increases in value, the other falls).

The important distinction between *correlational research* and *experimental research* is that *correlation does not imply causation*. When psychologists create an intervention where a variable is manipulated and its influence on another variable is measured, the case for a causal explanation can be made. The same is not true for correlational work. Think about it: Some people study all the time and they still get low grades. Others never study and they routinely make the dean's list. Why? Very often some unknown—and unmeasured—third variable is in play. Consider the link between social activity and happiness: It turns out that extraversion (being outgoing, sociable, and gregarious) is *positively correlated* with both variables, which means that extraversion could lead to more social activity as well as higher levels of happiness. We will not know whether one, both, or neither is influential until an experiment is conducted to determine cause and effect. Again, correlation does not imply causation. As you learn about positive psychological research in this book, remember that no one study, whether it is experimental or correlational, is definitive—positive psychologists build a theory and make a case for it by relying on a variety of investigations that suggest how particular variables influence other variables in particular settings.

Overview of Positive Psychology

In carefully applying the scientific method, positive psychology seeks to assess, understand, and then build or enhance human strengths. Learning to live a good life is a worthy goal (Franklin, 2010). This book is designed to convey some of the field's most important findings. It highlights factors that do or do not promote happiness and well-being (Lyubomirsky, 2013), while helping you explore ways to apply them to your own personal growth. Here is a summary of the book's central themes and strategies:

1. We are creators of our personal and social worlds. We benefit from experiences of freedom and from being able to view ourselves as agents rather than pawns of external forces. The belief in a dynamic self capable of choice, change, and control influences the goals we choose and the energy with which we pursue

them. High-functioning people are responsible—they own their actions and answer for them.

2. We are also creatures of our worlds. Biological factors, past experience, and our present situation powerfully shape our behavior. Understanding the impact of external factors enables us to make wise choices and exercise more effective control in fostering change that promotes our well-being. To build human strengths and civic virtues, we must build healthier families, positive workplaces, communal neighborhoods, more effective schools, and socially responsible media.

3. In carefully applying the scientific method, psychology can help us sort fact from fiction. This is especially important in understanding subjective well-being and civic virtue. The methods of science that have helped us understand psychological disorder can also illuminate our understanding of the roots and fruits of human strengths. Sometimes these methods confirm conventional wisdom and commonsense ideas. In other cases these methods challenge popular assumptions. For example, we will see that research strongly supports the familiar adage "Money does not buy happiness." Yet we will also learn that spending money on others or on enjoyable experiences (e.g., sharing lunch, attending a concert) can enhance our happiness. More surprising are findings that people of different ages, genders, races, and educational levels have roughly equivalent levels of happiness. In considering research on self-respect, we will discover, as we might expect, that people with high self-esteem persist in the face of failure. On the other hand, fostering self-esteem is not an effective vaccine, as many have proposed, for social problems such as aggression.

4. Although recently given renewed emphasis, positive psychology actually has a long and rich history in the discipline. For decades investigators have sought to understand such human strengths as love, empathy, and self-control. Most of the important theoretical perspectives contribute to the understanding of positive emotions, positive character, and positive institutions. Working from different points of view, psychologists help us understand the important biological, environmental, and cognitive components of human flourishing. These perspectives complement one another, just as psychology's study complements that of other disciplines that study human strengths and civic virtues.

5. One of psychology's unique contributions to the study of human strengths is its measurement of individual differences. Scales that assess the strengths are included in every chapter of this book. They are important research tools that you can complete for yourself. Learning proceeds best when we are actively engaged, especially when we relate the new material to ourselves. The scales will help you appreciate how researchers have defined and studied specific human strengths. Remember that the scales are research instruments, not diagnostic tools. Still, if you answer honestly—not merely as you think you should

or how others might want you to—the scales will give you some idea of where you fall in the pursuit of a specific strength.

6. In each chapter, we will consider the implications and applications of basic research. We will ask, "What does the research suggest we do to foster the strengths and virtues in ourselves and in others? How do we promote human well-being and civic responsibility? How can we build a healthy social environment?" You are invited to participate in this process, to exercise your critical judgment in anticipating and interpreting the research results as well as their appropriate applications.

7. Values penetrate psychologists' work, including what they study, how they study it, the interpretation they give the results, and the applications they make. For example, positive psychology's call to attend to human strength itself reflects a value judgment. Conclusions of what constitutes a strength or a weakness, a virtue or a vice are also value judgments. The values need to be stated openly so that they can be discussed and debated. One of the important assumptions of this chapter (and of this book) is that we each not only have a need to be our own person, we also need to belong. We have a need for relatedness as well as autonomy. Thus, any prescription for human well-being needs to recognize both.

We will revisit these important themes as we pursue specific human strengths in the rest of this book. Let's begin on a highly positive note with an activity—*thinking about your best possible self*—that you can perform once a week (Kurtz & Lyubomirsky, 2008). What is a "best possible self"? Imagine what you could be like in the future, especially if everything has gone as well as it possibly could where you are concerned. Assume that you have consistently worked hard and generally succeeded at meeting the life goals you set for yourself. Your best possible self is the one in which you realize your dreams and match your potential. Here's all you need to do: Once a week for 20 minutes, sit down in a quiet place and reflect on your best future possible self. To do so, write a detailed narrative of what this future good life could be like. Highlight aspects of both your personal and professional life—just be sure to change the domain you think about each week (e.g., career aspirations, romantic relationship, exercise goals, your health, and so on).

⇒ IN REVIEW

Positive psychologists acknowledge that we are both creatures and creators of our personal and social worlds. In applying the scientific method to the study of human strengths and civic virtues, investigators from different theoretical perspectives contribute to our understanding of human flourishing. The assessment of specific strengths is one of positive psychology's significant contributions to the scientific study of well-being. Positive psychologists recognize the importance of autonomy and relatedness as well as the effects of our values in human flourishing.

Love

Attachment

Exploring Love

Building Close Relationships

Love is when the other person's happiness is more important than your own. —H. JACKSON BROWN, JR., 1991

Learning to love is really about learning to live. —HARRY HARLOW, 1970

When asked "What missing element would bring you happiness?" most people in one study said "love" (Freedman, 1978). In fact, four in five adults rate love as important to their happiness. Similarly, when they are asked to describe "the last bad thing that happened to you," the majority of American respondents describe a breakup or loss of a significant relationship (Veroff, Douvan, & Kulka, 1981). Most people just *know* that being in a loving relationship or being able to genuinely love others makes us better, more content human beings (Hojjat & Cramer, 2013).

Evolutionary psychologists argue that social bonds not only predict happiness, they also are the single most important factor responsible for the survival of our species (Berscheid, 2003; Buss, 2006). Our ancestors gained strength from numbers. Whether hunting game, erecting shelters, or defending themselves from predators, 12 hands were better than 2. Because people living in small, cooperative groups were more likely to survive and reproduce, today we carry genes that predispose social connections.

Before you read any further, try the following thought experiment:

Reflect on one of your happiest memories. What is it? Who was involved in this memory?

_____

_____

Next, think of one of your most painful experiences. Likewise, what was it? Did it involve another person or other people?

_____

_____

If your memories include a significant person or persons in your life, then this would support social evolutionary theorists' beliefs that social bonds, like love, have a tremendous influence on our overall well-being. Keep these memories in mind as we explore the bonds we form with others in our lives.

Attachment

As infants we survive only if an adult is willing to meet our basic needs. Early in life we form bonds with our caregivers. "Love begins at the beginning," suggests Deborah Blum (2002); "perhaps no one does it better, or needs it more, than a child" (p. 170).

Our most important first question is: Can I count on my caregiver to be available and responsive when needed? There are three possible responses to the question: yes, no, and maybe (Hazan & Shaver, 1994). Thinking back to your own childhood, how would you answer?

 **SELF-ASSESSMENT**

First Attachments

Read the following three paragraphs and select the one that best describes your relationship with your mother when you were a child growing up. Then select the one that best describes your relationship with your father.

____ ____ **1.** Warm/Responsive—She/he was generally warm and responsive. She/he was good at knowing when to be supportive and when to let me operate on my own. Our relationship was always comfortable, and I have no major reservations or complaints about it.

____ ____ **2.** Cold/Rejecting—She/he was fairly cold and distant or rejecting, not very responsive. I wasn't her/his highest priority; her/his concerns were often elsewhere. It's possible that she/he would just as soon not have had me.

____ ____ **3.** Ambivalent/Inconsistent—She/he was noticeably inconsistent in her/his reactions to me, sometimes warm and sometimes not. She/he had her/his own agenda, which sometimes got in the way of her/his receptiveness and responsiveness to my needs. She/he definitely loved me but didn't always show it in the best way.

Source: Hazan & Shaver, 1986. Reprinted with permission of the author.

Answers to the exercise demonstrate how nature (our inherent tendency to bond) and nurture (the responsiveness of our caregivers) shape social ties (Ainsworth,

Blehar, Waters, & Wall, 1978). Early in life their interaction yields three different attachment styles: secure, avoidant, and anxious.

Infants who experience warm, responsive parents show *secure attachment*. When they are placed in a laboratory playroom with their caregiver, the infants happily explore their unfamiliar environment. If the caregiver leaves, the infants become distressed, and when the caregiver returns, the infants run to hold the caregiver, then relax and return to playing. About 60 percent of North American infants show this pattern (Hazan & Shaver, 1994).

Babies with cold, rejecting caregivers show *avoidant attachment*. In the unfamiliar playroom, they show little distress during separation or clinging upon reunion. They react to a stranger in the same unresponsive way that they do to the parent and keep their attention focused on the toys. About 25 percent of North American infants demonstrate this type of attachment.

Infants who experience inconsistent parenting show *anxious attachment*. In the unfamiliar setting, they cling anxiously to their mother and cry when she leaves, but are indifferent or hostile when she returns. These infants tend not to explore their environment much at all. Many continue to cry after being picked up and are not easily comforted. This style, the rarest of the three, averages about 15 percent in North American samples.

From Cradle to Grave

Understandably, early care-receiving experiences affect our view of our social world. Are people trustworthy? Can they be counted on to provide protection and support? Am I a lovable person, someone worth caring for? The answers we give to these questions shape how we approach close relationships. Most important, they affect (1) our level of comfort with closeness and (2) our degree of anxiety over abandonment.

How do the emotional bonds we form with caregivers early in life lay the foundation for our adult love relationships? Psychologists argue that our adult attachments—the key close relationships in our lives—begin with the nature of our attachments in childhood (Shaver & Mikulincer, 2012).

 **SELF-ASSESSMENT**

Romantic Relationships

Which of the following best describes your current feelings, particularly as they might apply to present or potential romantic love relationships?

1. *Secure*—I find it relatively easy to get close to others and am comfortable depending on them. I don't often worry about being abandoned or about someone getting too close to me.

2. *Avoidant*—I am somewhat uncomfortable being close to others; I find it difficult to trust them completely, difficult to allow myself to depend on them. I am nervous when anyone gets too close, and often love partners want me to be more intimate than I feel comfortable being.

3. *Anxious*—I find that others are reluctant to get as close as I would like. I often worry that my partner doesn't really love me or won't want to stay with me. I want to get very close to my partner and this sometimes scares people away.

Source: Hazan & Shaver, 1990. Reprinted with permission of the author.

How closely did your self-assessment match your earlier ratings of your parents? Adult love relationships do tend to mirror early infant attachments (Myers, 2002).

- Secure adults find it easy to get close to others and are unconcerned about becoming too dependent or being abandoned. Their relationships are characterized by happiness, trust, and friendship. They seem able to accept and support their partner in spite of faults, and their relationships endure longer. About 55 percent of participants in adult attachment studies are classified as secure adults.

- Avoidant adults tend to be less invested in relationships and more likely to leave them. Some seem to be fearful ("I am uncomfortable getting close to others"), while others are dismissing ("It is very important for me to feel independent and self-sufficient"). Their relationships are marked by emotional highs and lows. They are also more likely to have brief sexual encounters without love. Approximately 25 percent of participants are avoidant adults.

- For anxious adults, love is obsession; these adults are less trusting, demand reciprocation, and are generally more possessive and jealous. They may break up repeatedly with the same person. When discussing differences, they often get emotional and angry. Studies find that around 20 percent of adults fall into the anxious category.

In comparison with their secure counterparts, avoidantly attached men and anxiously attached individuals of both sexes report lower relationship satisfaction (Tucker & Anders, 1999). People with secure attachments tend to display better mental health than those with less secure attachments (Haggerty, Hilsenroth, & Vala-Stewart, 2009). In fact, insecurely attached persons often report experiencing a variety of psychosocial challenges, including anxiety, anger, resentment, loneliness, and depression, as well as low self-esteem and self-confidence, and heightened self-consciousness (Cooper et al., 2004; Mikulincer & Shaver, 2003).

Development of Attachment

Both nature—the infant's inherent need to bond and belong—and nurture—parental responsiveness—contribute to attachment. Although many psychologists once assumed that the parents' personality shaped their caregiving style, more recent research indicates that the infant's genetically based temperament can elicit different parental responses that in turn affect attachment style. Clearly, nature and nurture interact.

Three components contribute to attachment: closeness, care, and commitment. *Close physical proximity* is the context in which infant and adult attachments unfold. The motives differ—for infants it's security, for adults, sexual attraction is added to the mix. In both types of relationships, close physical contact fosters an emotional bond. Infants and adults generally welcome physical touch, feel distress when separated, and express strong affection when reunited. We tend to judge the relationships between parents and children, and between adult lovers as the "closest," and only in those relationships is prolonged bodily contact considered normal. The intensity of our need for close contact gradually diminishes—a finding that still awaits full explanation (Hazan & Shaver, 1994).

From closeness emerges the second important characteristic of attachment: a safe haven. Proximity brings us together, and the degree to which attachment provides care, including both comfort and emotional support, grows over time. How our parents and partners regard us is very important to us. Research (Kotler, 1985) suggests that sensitive and responsive care, not passionate attraction, is the better predictor of the strength of relationships over the long term.

Over time, *commitment* makes the safe haven a base of security. With a consistently available, supportive, and reassuring caregiver, one can confidently confront life's everyday challenges. Free of relationship concerns, the child eagerly explores a new world, the adult enthusiastically engages in work and community opportunities. Commitment, suggest Cindy Hazan and Philip Shaver (1994), is the glue that holds relationships together and ensures safety and security over the long haul. Most parents are naturally committed to their children. On the other hand, adult relationships are chosen, and we must develop commitment to our life partners.

Closeness, care, and commitment make up the stuff of which attachment and, as we will see, love are made.

Can Attachment Style Change?

Before turning to more specific research on adult love relationships, let's consider an important question you may be wondering about: Can early attachment style, with all the implications for the quality of our interpersonal relationships, change? Can avoidant or anxious attachment become secure? Yes! Attachment patterns provide a dramatic example of how both nature and nurture shape the course of one's life. Yet these patterns are not fixed. Researchers suggest several routes to change. Simply reflecting, as you have in this chapter, on how beliefs about yourself and others have their roots in early experience is an important first step in altering an avoidant or anxious attachment.

Research shows that attachment styles remain more or less stable from infancy through late adolescence (Fraley, 2002). However, life events can undermine such stability. Children's attachments can shift from secure to insecure because of parent's divorce, maltreatment, parental substance abuse, and the death of parents (Waters et al., 2000). Adult attachment can become stronger or weaker based on the level of support offered by partners (Shaver & Mikulincer, 2008). Interestingly, short-term therapeutic interventions can help individuals move from insecure to secure attachment styles (Travis et al., 2001).

"Corrective" relationship experiences, argues John Bowlby (1988), also foster more secure attachments. Given that the function of attachment is to attain security, change is more likely to occur in the direction of secure than insecure attachment. We are more likely to enter relationships that promise more, rather than less, security than we have experienced in the past. And research indicates that secure bonds are more stable than either avoidant or anxious attachments. We will revisit this concern later in the chapter as we examine more specific strategies for fostering loving relationships.

⇒ IN REVIEW

> Social attachments are important to our personal happiness and have enabled our survival as a species. Our interactions with our first caregivers yield different attachment styles: secure, avoidant, or anxious. The emotional bonds formed early in life lay the foundation for later love relationships. Childhood attachments and adult romantic attachments are marked by physical closeness, caring, and long-term commitment. Both nature and nurture are crucial factors in shaping attachment style, and our patterns of relating can change.

Exploring Love

Love is challenging to define—yet we typically know it when we see it or, even better, experience it. Social psychologists define love by distinguishing between two types: passionate and companionate love (Hatfield & Rapson, 1987). *Passionate* or romantic love entails intense feelings of longing, excitement, and desire for a particular person. *Companionate* or affectionate love is marked by intimacy, mutual understanding, and care focused on helping the relationship to succeed. In general, passionate love marks the spark and start of a new loving relationship, one that is sexual, while companionate love is the important ingredient in long-term marriages and other sustained relationships.

We will first review love's important features and see how they have been incorporated in an influential model of love. Then we will explore these two types of love that psychologists have researched so extensively.

Love's Features

Some researchers have studied human traits, including the strengths, by asking respondents to identify the important features or characteristics of those traits. For example, if you were to list the characteristics of the concept EXTRAVERSION, you might write "liveliness," "vivaciousness," "sociability," and so on. What are the important features or characteristics of the concept LOVE? List up to 10 features as they come to mind. Take only a minute or two.

1. _____   6. _____

2. _____   7. _____

3. _____   8. _____

4. _____   9. _____

5. _____   10. _____

How do other respondents view love's crucial features? Beverly Fehr (1988) asked 141 men and women and found that the characteristics most often mentioned were caring (by 44 percent of respondents), happiness (29 percent), wanting to be with the other (28 percent), friendship (23 percent), feeling free to talk about anything (20 percent), warm feelings (17 percent), accepting the way the other is (16 percent), trust (15 percent), commitment (14 percent), sharing (14 percent), thinking about the other all the time (14 percent), and sacrifice (14 percent). A total of 68 features were listed by more than one respondent.

When a second group was asked to rate how central each of these 68 features was to the concept of love by using a scale from 1 (extremely poor feature of love) to 8 (extremely good feature of love), the features regarded as most central were trust (7.50), caring (7.28), honesty (7.18), friendship (7.08), respect (7.01), concern for the other's well-being (7.00), loyalty (7.00), commitment (6.92), accepting the way the other is (6.82), supportiveness (6.78), and wanting to be with the other (6.82). Among those receiving somewhat lower ratings were warm feelings (6.04), touching (5.82), sexual passion (5.81), and energy (4.29).

Love's Triangle

By using the sophisticated statistical tool of factor analysis, Arthur Aron and Lori Westbay (1996) found that the 68 prototypical features of love could be organized into three categories: passion, intimacy, and commitment. Robert Sternberg's (1986, 2006) triangular theory of love recognizes these three dimensions as the major components of love—each one can be represented as a point on a triangle. *Passion* is the often-intense motivational component of love, reflecting attraction, romance, and sexual desire. *Intimacy* involves feelings of warmth, closeness, trust, and the sharing of one's innermost thoughts and feelings. *Commitment* is the actual decision to maintain a caring relationship in spite of the inevitable challenges that arise in the course of daily life. Commitment can be of short duration (the choice to love someone) or more long-term (the decision to help a relationship endure despite obstacles).

Completing Sternberg's love scale takes a bit longer than most exercises in this book, but it will be well worth the effort. Taking and scoring it will help you better understand the research on love and will provide insight into the nature of your own close relationships.

 **SELF-ASSESSMENT**

Sternberg's Triangular Love Scale

In responding to the statements, think of one person you love or care about deeply. Then rate your agreement with each of the items by using the nine-point scale. Use intermediate points on the scale to indicate intermediate levels of feelings.

1	2	3	4	5	6	7	8	9
Do not agree at all				Moderately agree				Extremely agree

_____ **1.** I actively support my partner's well-being.

_____ **2.** I have a warm relationship with my partner.

_____ **3.** Just seeing my partner excites me.

_____ **4.** I know that I care about my partner.

_____ **5.** I find myself thinking about my partner frequently throughout the day.

_____ **6.** I am able to count on my partner in times of need.

_____ **7.** I am committed to maintaining my relationship with my partner.

_____ **8.** I have confidence in the stability of my relationship with my partner.

_____ **9.** My relationship with my partner is very romantic.

_____ **10.** My partner is able to count on me in times of need.

_____ **11.** I find my partner to be personally attractive.

_____ **12.** Because of my commitment to my partner I would not let other people come between us.

_____ **13.** I expect my love for my partner to last the rest of my life.

_____ **14.** I idealize my partner.

_____ **15.** I am willing to share myself and my possessions with my partner.

_____ **16.** I cannot imagine another person making me as happy as my partner does.

_____ **17.** I would rather be with my partner than with anyone else.

_____ **18.** I could not let anything get in the way of my commitment to my partner.

_____ **19.** I receive considerable emotional support from my partner.

_____ **20.** I will always feel a strong responsibility for my partner.

_____ **21.** I give considerable emotional support to my partner.

_____ **22.** There is nothing more important to me than my relationship with my partner.

_____ **23.** I especially like physical contact with my partner.

_____ **24.** I communicate well with my partner.

_____ **25.** I value my partner greatly in my life.

_____ **26.** I feel close to my partner.

_____ **27.** I view my commitment to my partner as a solid one.

_____ **28.** I cannot imagine ending my relationship with my partner.

_____ **29.** There is something almost magical about my relationship with my partner.

_____ **30.** I have a comfortable relationship with my partner.

_____ **31.** I adore my partner.

_____ **32.** I am certain of my love for my partner.

_____ **33.** I view my relationship with my partner as permanent.

_____ **34.** I cannot imagine life without my partner.

_____ **35.** I view my relationship with my partner as a good decision.

_____ **36.** I feel that I really understand my partner.

_____ **37.** My relationship with my partner is passionate.

_____ **38.** I feel that my partner really understands me.

_____ **39.** I feel a sense of responsibility toward my partner.

_____ **40.** I feel that I can really trust my partner.

_____ **41.** When I see romantic movies or read romantic books, I think about my partner.

_____ **42.** I share deep personal information about myself with my partner.

_____ **43.** I plan to continue in my relationship with my partner.

_____ **44.** Even when my partner is hard to deal with, I remain committed to our relationship.

_____ **45.** I fantasize about my partner.

Source: Sternberg & Whitney, 1991, pp. 82–84. Copyright © Robert J. Sternberg. Reprinted by permission.

To score yourself, first add up the numbers on the passion subscale (statements 3, 5, 9, 11, 14, 16, 17, 22, 23, 29, 31, 34, 37, 41, 45). Then add up the numbers on the intimacy subscale (1, 2, 6, 10, 15, 19, 21, 24, 25, 26, 30, 36, 38, 40, 42). Add up the numbers on the commitment subscale (4, 7, 8, 12, 13, 18, 20, 27, 28, 32, 33, 35, 39, 43, 44). Divide each of the three totals by 15 to obtain an average rating for each of the three components:

Passion = _____   Intimacy = _____   Commitment = _____

   An average rating of 5 on a subscale indicates a moderate level of the component represented by the subscale; for example, an average rating of 5 on the intimacy subscale indicates a moderate amount of intimacy in the relationship you chose to measure. A higher average rating would indicate more intimacy, and a lower average rating would indicate less intimacy. Examining your ratings for each of the three subscales will give you an idea of how you perceive your love relationship in terms of these important dimensions.

   According to Sternberg's model of love (1988), the three components—passion, intimacy, and commitment—form the vertices of a triangle. Their various combinations create seven basic subtypes of love.

Types of Love Relationships	Passion	Intimacy	Commitment
Liking	Low	High	Low
Infatuated love	High	Low	Low
Romantic love	High	High	Low
Empty love	Low	Low	High
Companionate love	Low	High	High
Fatuous love	High	Low	High
Consummate love	High	High	High

Sternberg's love triangle follows. Looking back at your scores, can you locate your specific love relationship on it?

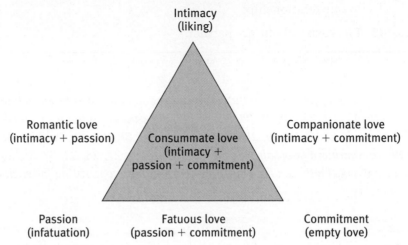

Aron, A., Aron, E. N., & Smollan, D. (1992). Inclusion of other in the Self Scale and the structure of interpersonal closeness. *Journal of Personality and Social Psychology*, *63*, 596–612. American Psychological Association. Adapted with permission.

Sternberg's description of the development of consummate love parallels the unfolding of secure attachment. The passion associated with physical closeness grows very quickly and initially dominates a relationship. Over time it declines. Proximity and passion prompt reciprocal sharing and caring, and a healthy love relationship shows a slow but steady increase in intimacy. Commitment involves both a short-term decision to love someone and a longer-term decision to maintain the love. In enduring relationships, the increase in commitment is gradual at first, accelerates, and then remains at a high level. Research demonstrates that the three-component model describes same-sex romantic relationships as well as it does opposite-sex relationships (Baumeister & Bushman, 2011).

In practical terms, the triangular theory of love can give both couples and therapists a better sense of how partners view a relationship. Differences on the triangular love scale indicate where change may be necessary to preserve and strengthen the relationship.

Romantic Love

Of the love types Sternberg identifies, psychologists have studied romantic and companionate love the most extensively. In considering the components of romantic love, let's begin by looking at mate preferences.

Mate Preferences

When you think of the ideal romantic partner, what image comes to mind? The following list of 18 traits has been used in research investigating mate preferences over several decades. Rate each of the traits in terms of their importance in choosing a mate, using the following scale:

3 = Indispensable   2 = Important but not indispensable   1 = Desirable but not important   0 = Irrelevant

_____ **1.** Ambition and industriousness

_____ **2.** Chastity (no prior intercourse)

_____ **3.** Dependable character

_____ **4.** Desire for home and children

_____ **5.** Education and intelligence

_____ **6.** Emotional stability and maturity

_____ **7.** Favorable social status or rating

_____ **8.** Good cook and housekeeper

_____ **9.** Good financial prospect

_____ **10.** Good health

_____ **11.** Good looks

_____ **12.** Mutual attraction–love

_____ **13.** Pleasing disposition

_____ **14.** Refinement, neatness

_____ **15.** Similar education

_____ **16.** Similar religious background

_____ **17.** Similar political background

_____ **18.** Sociability

Source: Buss, 1989.

David Buss (1989) reported outcomes for this trait list in a comprehensive study of hundreds of people in 37 cultures. For these international samples, both sexes rated mutual attraction–love (12), dependable character (3), emotional stability and maturity (6), and pleasing disposition (13), as most important. Chastity (2), similar religious background (16), and similar political background (17) were least important. How do your ratings compare?

Buss also found important gender differences in mate preferences. Good looks (11) and chastity (2) were more important to males; a good financial prospect (9) and ambition and industriousness (1) were more important to females. Do your scores support Buss's findings?

Evolutionary psychologists provide an intriguing explanation for these findings. They argue that nature selects behavioral tendencies that increase the likelihood of sending one's genes into the future. Obviously, mate selection becomes important. Gene survival is more likely if one has a mate who is committed to the relationship and is reliable, cooperative, and unselfish. No wonder both sexes regard mutual attraction, dependability, stability, and a pleasing disposition to be essential qualities in a mate!

Sex differences in reproductive biology may also lead to some important sex differences in mating preferences. Evolutionary psychologists point out that, compared with eggs, sperm are cheap. While a woman incubates and nurses one child, a male can spread his genes by impregnating many other females. In our ancestral history, women most often sent their genes into the future by pairing wisely, men by pairing widely (Myers, 2002). Women look for features in a mate that communicate protection and support for offspring. Thus, a good financial prospect (9) as well as ambition and industriousness (1) become important. Think about it: Because of the demands of pregnancy and child-rearing, having sexual relations with partners who have limited prospects is risky and costly for women (Buss & Schmidt, 1993). In contrast, men desire features that communicate fertility and assure paternity. Good looks (11), especially youthful features, suggest reproductive capacity, and chastity (2) helps assure paternity. Why assure paternity? Evolutionary psychologists explain that while women are always certain that they are mothers of their children, men are never certain that they are the fathers. Interestingly, research shows that men feel most jealous over their mate's having sex with someone else, while women tend to feel greater jealousy over their mate's becoming emotionally attached to someone else (Larsen & Buss, 2002).

Passion

For both sexes, mutual attraction–love (12) tops the list of important traits for choosing a mate. What does such attraction involve? Clearly "being in love" is different from "love." Ellen Berscheid and Sarah Meyers (1996) asked college undergraduates to compose three lists: people they "loved," people they were "in love with," and people they were "sexually attracted to." Only 2 percent of those in the "love" category also appeared in the "sex" list. However, the overlap of the "in love" with the "sex" list was 85 percent. Similarly, when Pamela Regan and her colleagues (1998) asked people to list the characteristics of romantic love, two-thirds mentioned sexual desire—placing it well ahead of happiness, loyalty, sharing, or commitment. Yes, passion is a key component of romantic love.

Now answer this question: If a man or woman had all the other qualities you desired in a mate, would you marry this person if you were not in love? In 1967, a whopping 76 percent of American women and 35 percent of American men said yes. Just two decades later, only 20 percent of women and 14 percent of men indicated that they would marry someone with whom they were not in love (Simpson, Campbell, & Berscheid, 1986). After spontaneously enumerating all the sparkling qualities of her close male friend, one of my recent students matter-of-factly concluded, "But there's no chemistry, no spark—we could never marry." No fire, no future.

Passionate love, writes Elaine Hatfield (1988), is a "state of intense longing for union with another." If the love is returned, one is fulfilled, even ecstatic. If not, one is despairing and anxious. To explain passionate love, Hatfield suggests that any state of physiological arousal can be experienced as one of several emotions, depending on how we interpret and label the emotion. A pounding heart and sweating palms can be interpreted as fear, anger, or surprise, depending on the environmental context. If the situation is interpreted as potentially romantic, for example with an attractive person present, we may experience the arousal as passion.

Several research findings support Hatfield's theory. In a clever field study (Dutton & Aron, 1974), young men crossed one of two bridges in North Vancouver—a solid, safe structure or a narrow, wobbly suspension walkway that was 230 feet above rocks and rapids below. As each man crossed the bridge, an attractive college woman approached to ask if he would fill out a questionnaire for her. Offering to explain her "class project" further, she left him her phone number. Far more of the men who crossed the suspension bridge than those who used the safe structure called the woman. Similarly, laboratory studies have found that men who have been aroused by exercise, humorous tapes, or an alarming situation feel more attracted to a girlfriend or even to a woman just introduced to them. A pounding heart makes the heart grow fonder.

Consider how our popular media reinforce the "pounding heart" case for love. How many action movies can you name that contain a story line involving a man and a woman who are initially strangers? These strangers usually have little in common—sometimes they even seem to be indifferent or even dislike each other—but then, after a series of harrowing experiences eliciting fear, anger, and finally euphoria, something magical happens. By the end of the movie they have fallen madly in love. Cue the movie theme and roll the credits.

Intimacy

But romantic love, according to Sternberg's triangular theory of love, is not only passionate. It is also intimate.

Intimacy, suggests Hatfield (1988) is a process in which a person attempts to get close to another—exploring similarities and differences in the way they think, feel, and behave. What most clearly fosters intimacy? A critical element seems to be self-disclosure. Self-disclosure occurs anytime a person is moved to intentionally share personal information with another individual. Designed by Lynn Miller, John Berg, and Richard Archer (1983), the Opener Scale assesses the capacity to elicit intimate disclosure from others.

 SELF-ASSESSMENT

Openers

Respond to each statement using the following scale:

1	2	3	4	5
Strongly disagree				Strongly agree

_____ **1.** People frequently tell me about themselves.

_____ **2.** I've been told that I'm a good listener.

_____ **3.** I'm very accepting of others.

_____ **4.** People trust me with their secrets.

_____ **5.** I easily get people to "open up."

_____ **6.** People feel relaxed around me.

_____ **7.** I enjoy listening to people.

_____ **8.** I'm sympathetic to people's problems.

_____ **9.** I encourage people to tell me about how they are feeling.

_____ **10.** I can keep people talking about themselves.

Source: Copyright © 1983 by the American Psychological Association. Reproduced with permission. Table 1, p. 1235, from Miller, L. C., Berg, J. H., & Archer, R. L. (1983). Openers: Individuals who elicit intimate self-disclosure. *Journal of Personality and Social Psychology, 44(6),* 1234–1244. No further reproduction or distribution is permitted without written permission from the American Psychological Association.

To score, simply add up the numbers you placed in response to the 10 items. Scores can range from 10 to 50, with higher scores reflecting a greater tendency to elicit revelations from others. Mean scores for a sample of 487 undergraduate women and 253 undergraduate men were 40.68 and 38.01, respectively.

Some people, especially women, are skilled "openers." They tend to be what Carl Rogers (1980) called "growth promoting" listeners: genuine in revealing their own feelings, *accepting* of others' feelings, and empathic—readily assuming the other's perspective. We are especially likely to disclose when distressed—when angry or anxious. Having an intimate partner with whom we can share threats to our self-image helps us survive such stresses. Research confirms that dating and married couples who reveal themselves most to each other express greatest satisfaction with their relationship and are more likely to remain committed to it.

Intimacy is an essential element of a loving relationship. Typically it grows gradually as partners reveal more and more of themselves to each other. Disclosure tends to elicit disclosure, a process appropriately dubbed the *disclosure reciprocity effect*. As one person reveals a little, the other reciprocates, and the process spirals. Over time their knowledge of each other penetrates to deeper and deeper levels. Trust builds and partners feel accepted. Dropping our masks and letting ourselves be known as we truly are, suggested Sidney Jourard (1964), nurtures love.

Companionate Love

Typically the passion of romantic love cools. Its intimacy, however, can foster a companionate love—an affection for those with whom our lives are intertwined. We may even begin to incorporate a partner into our view of ourselves.

✔ SELF-ASSESSMENT

Self and Other

Think of the person with whom you have the closest relationship. Which of the following diagrams best describes the relationship?

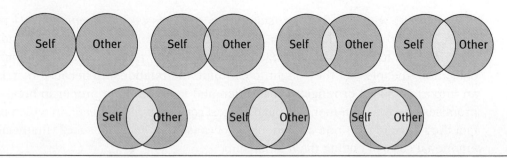

Data from: Aron, Aron, & Smollan, 1992, p. 597.

Arthur Aron and his colleagues (1992) found that the longevity of a romantic relationship can be predicted by how people choose to portray their partnership. The more overlap—that is, the more one incorporates a partner into the self—the more enduring the relationship. The more overlap, the stronger the commitment to maintaining the relationship. "Love is the expansion of two natures in such a fashion that each includes the other," claimed eighteenth-century European philosopher Felix Adler, "and each is enriched by the other."

In companionate love, commitment accompanies intimacy. Commitment, the intention to maintain a relationship, springs from different sources. Three quite different types of commitment are reflected in the following sample items from Jeffrey Adams's and Warren Jones's (1997) Dimensions of Commitment Inventory.

 **SELF-ASSESSMENT**

Commitment

Pause for a moment to think of commitment in the context of marriage. Whether you are now married or not, consider how the following statements reflect your beliefs about the nature of the marital relationship.

T F **1.** I'm dedicated to making my marriage as fulfilling as it can be.

T F **2.** I am completely devoted to my spouse.

T F **3.** I believe that marriage is for life regardless of what happens.

T F **4.** A marriage should be protected at all costs.

T F **5.** It would be particularly hard on my family and friends if my spouse and I divorced.

T F **6.** A divorce would ruin my reputation.

Source: Copyright © 1997 by the American Psychological Association. Adapted with permission. Table 1 (adapted), p. 1181, from Adams, J. M., & Jones, W. H. (1997). The conceptualization of marital commitment: An integrative analysis. *Journal of Personality and Social Psychology, 72(5),* 117–1196. No further reproduction or distribution is permitted without written permission from the American Psychological Association.

Agreement with the first two statements suggests *personal commitment*—people desire to continue a relationship because the relationship is satisfying and they are attracted to their partners. Statements 3 and 4 reflect *moral commitment* or obligation—people feel they ought to continue the relationship because marriage is an important social or religious institution and it would be improper to break one's promises or vows. Statements 5 and 6 suggest *constraint commitment*, in which people feel they have to continue a relationship because they fear the social, financial, and emotional costs of ending the relationship.

The three types of commitment not only feel different, they also have different consequences (Brehm, Miller, Perlman, & Campbell, 2002). Normally, personal commitments are more satisfying. For people in a long-distance romantic relationship, moral commitment better predicts its longevity than does personal commitment. It can keep a relationship intact even though the partners' level of satisfaction wanes.

Commitment in the context of a loving relationship can serve several important functions, including the following:

- Like intimacy, commitment leads partners to think of themselves as "us" instead of "me" and "him" or "her." Events that please one's partner produce indirect benefits for oneself. Sacrifices for one's partner become less costly.

- When people know they are in a relationship for the long term, they may be better able to tolerate times of high cost and low reward, much like long-term investors in stock tolerate periods of low earnings.

- Commitment motivates people to take more deliberate action to protect and maintain a relationship even when it is costly for them to do so. Committed people seem to respond with more self-restraint when provoked by their partner and to show more willingness to sacrifice self-interest for the good of the relationship.

When you think of your closest peer relationship—friend or romantic partner—how would you describe it? Does your partner contribute more to it than you do? Less? Or would you say that you each contribute equally?

Often casual acquaintances maintain their connections through tit-for-tat exchanges. From coworkers in a carpool taking turns driving, to neighbors rotating responsibility for hosting the annual block party, people trade similar benefits. As you reflect on your closest friendship or love relationship, is that how things go? Probably not. As relationships form, we are less concerned with instant repayment. Lovers respond to each other's needs without expecting immediate repayment. Mother Teresa stated this much more strongly: "If you really love one another you will not be able to avoid making sacrifices."

Only when the benefits are voluntary, when partners freely give and receive, do we view the relationship as true friendship or love. In fact, Margaret Clark and Judson Mills (1993) reported that tit-for-tat exchanges increased people's liking when the relationship was relatively formal, but the same social economics decreased liking when the two sought a close relationship. Such close or communal relationships are marked by reciprocal love, respect, and concern—and without any expectation of repayment for what one person does for the other.

Nonetheless, one important key to an enduring relationship is *equity*—the outcomes people receive from a relationship are proportional to what they contribute to it. Commitment is likely to be fostered if, over the long term, the relationship is perceived as fair as well as intimate. Those who perceive the other as receiving a better deal experience distress and irritation, sometimes even depression. Those who believe they are receiving a better deal may feel guilty. As you might expect, however, being overbenefitted is less troubling to most than being underbenefitted (Brehm et al., 2002).

Robert Sternberg's triangular theory identifies passion, intimacy, and commitment as the key components of love. Various combinations of these factors may yield different types of love. The key ingredients of romantic love are passion and intimacy. Although men and women express somewhat different mate preferences, they identify mutual attraction as the most important factor in choosing a romantic partner. Hatfield's two-factor theory suggests that we are likely to interpret physiological arousal that occurs in a romantic context as passion. Intimacy is fostered by mutual self-disclosure.

Companionate love, the affection we feel for those with whom our lives are intertwined, combines intimacy with commitment. Such commitment leads partners to think of themselves as "we" and enables people to endure times of high cost and low rewards in a relationship. Long-term commitment is fueled by equity in which outcomes are proportional to investments.

Building Close Relationships

What factors promote enduring, satisfying love relationships? What can partners do to maintain and enhance their relationship connection? John Harvey and Julia Omarzu (1997, 1999) provide one answer in their minding theory of relationships. First complete their minding scale.

 ✓ SELF-ASSESSMENT

Minding Scale

Respond to each of the statements using the following scale:

1 = Strongly agree   2 = Moderately agree   3 = Slightly agree   4 = Slightly disagree   5 = Moderately disagree   6 = Strongly disagree

_____ **1.** Successful romantic partners have the same opinions about things.

_____ **2.** You should avoid telling a loved one too much personal detail about your past.

_____ **3.** It is irritating when people ask you to do favors.

_____ **4.** Partners should be as much alike as possible.

_____ **5.** People will take advantage of you if they can.

_____ **6.** There is no reason to discuss your past relationships with a new love.

_____ **7.** Partners who have different opinions will have a poor relationship.

_____ **8.** It is difficult to be close to someone whose past is different from your own.

_____ **9.** Partners should spend lots of time talking together.

_____ **10.** People mainly look out for their own welfare even in close relationships.

_____ **11.** You should find out as much as you can about a new love.

_____ **12.** Even when people love you they think mainly about themselves.

_____ **13.** It is important to keep some mystery about yourself in a relationship.

_____ **14.** Romantic partners should agree about all things.

_____ **15.** The people we love are really strangers to us.

_____ **16.** Partners should give each other the benefit of the doubt no matter what.

_____ **17.** People who do nice things for you usually want something from you in return.

_____ **18.** Close partners often have different friends and interests.

Source: Copyright © 2001. From Omarzu, J., Whalen, J., & Harvey, J. H., "How well do you mind your relationship? A preliminary scale to test the minding theory of relating," in J. H. Harvey & A. Wenzel (Eds.), *Close romantic relationships: Maintenance and enhancement* (pp. 345–356). Reproduced by permission of Taylor and Francis Group, LLC, a division of Informa plc.

The minding theory of relationships suggests that certain types of perceptions and expectations are key to satisfying close relationships. First, a person seeks to build a foundation of knowledge about one's partner. Items 2, 6, 9, 11, 13, and 15 measure the knowledge component of "minding." Reverse the numbers (1 = 6, 2 = 5, 3 = 4, 4 = 3, 5 = 2, 6 = 1) you placed in front of items 9 and 11, and then sum the numbers for all six items. Scores range from 6 to 36, with the mean for 152 students being 27.73 with no gender difference. As a relationship develops, mutual self-disclosure leads partners to feel increasingly comfortable sharing their thoughts and experiences with each other. The focus is less on self-expression and more on eliciting information about the other. Moreover, as circumstances change, partners stay attuned to each other.

Second, partners must be willing and able to accept what they learn about each other. Items 1, 4, 7, 8, 14, and 18 compose the acceptance component of "minding." Reverse the number you placed in response to statement 18 and then sum the numbers for the six items. Scores again range from 6 to 36, with a mean score of 25.07. Again, there is no gender difference. This acceptance includes respect for differences in opinions, values, and habits that inevitably occur. Respect prevents partners from falling into criticism that impairs and can destroy relationships.

Third, minding theory states that the attributions partners make for each other's behaviors can support or handicap intimate relations. Items 3, 5, 10, 12, 16, and 17 assess the attributions that partners make. Reverse the number you chose in response to statement 16 and then add the numbers for the six items. Scores range from 6 to 36 with higher scores reflecting a tendency to provide more favorable attributions. The mean is 24.24, with women scoring slightly higher than men. Partners who give each other the benefit of the doubt are happier in their relationship and are more likely to remain together for longer periods of time.

In their theory, the authors make clear that these behaviors and thinking patterns must be *reciprocal* (Harvey & Omarzu, 2006). That is, both partners must be committed to pursuing knowledge, acceptance, and positive attributions for the relationship to thrive. In addition, these expectations and perceptions must have *continuity*. Over time, partners must continue to find out about each other, respect the other's individuality, and engage in positive attributions.

Specific Strategies

Our overview of the literature on love, concluding with the minding theory of relationships, suggests several principles for strengthening love. The most important and effective strategies include the following:

1. **Carve out time to talk.** Through his in-depth examination of hundreds of marriages, John Gottman (1994) is able to predict with better than 90 percent accuracy which relationships will last. In comparison with their divorced counterparts, successful couples devote an extra 5 hours per week to their marriage. What do they do? Most important, they talk. Before these couples part every morning, they find out one thing that each is going to do that day. And at the end of each workday, they have a low-stress reunion conversation.

   One sage suggested that we are born with two ears and one mouth because we need to listen twice as much as we speak. Tuning out distractions, including turning off the TV, is the first step. The second is to listen without interrupting. Of course, conversation is a two-way street. Although we think our partners know us inside and out, they are not mind readers. If we want them to understand us, we have to speak up and mean what we say. Choosing the right time to talk about important matters is also a skill to be cultivated. Bringing up a sensitive topic just before bedtime is hardly wise.

2. **Handle conflict constructively.** Minding theory recommends that we strive to accept differences in opinions, values, and habits that we inevitably have. Unquestionably some of the differences lead to conflict. A marriage lives and dies, suggests Gottman (1994), by how well disagreements and grievances are aired. Or as one notable self-help book states:

   > Marital happiness has little to do with whom you marry and everything to do with how you cope with conflict.... Simple truth #2: One zinger will erase twenty acts of kindness.... It takes one put-down to undo hours of kindness you give to your partner (Notarius & Markman, 1993, pp. 20, 28).

In dealing with conflict, respect for one's partner needs to override anger. Relationships that fail are typically marked by harsh startups in disagreement, partner criticism and contempt, hair-trigger defensiveness, and stonewalling. Instead, recommends Gottman (1994), remain calm, edit yourself (avoid uttering every angry thought when discussing touchy topics), soften your startup, speak nondefensively, validate your partner (express understanding and acknowledge that his or her perspective may have some validity), and accept influence. Successful couples, continues Gottman, know when to exit and repair by using humor, changing the topic to something unrelated, stroking ("I understand this is hard for you"), and communicating that they are on common ground ("This is our problem; we're in this together").

3. **Express admiration.** Minding theory suggests that we give partners the benefit of the doubt and strive to make relationship-enhancing attributions for each other's behavior. Such explanations attribute negative behaviors to external causes and positive behaviors to personal, internal causes. That is, a partner's negative behaviors are explained in terms of something outside the relationship; the partner's positive behaviors are viewed as reflecting his or her inherent virtues.

In *The Seven Principles for Making Marriage Work*, Gottman and Nan Silver (1999) suggest that in successful relationships, partners make at least five times as many positive statements about each other and their relationship than they do negative ones. Communicate admiration directly: "I believe you've done a good job, and I'm proud of you." Such genuine praise cements connections and also becomes a powerful source of motivation that extends beyond the relationship.

4. **Show affection.** Compared with their less successful counterparts, couples successful in relationships have three common behaviors.

- They regularly show physical affection—touching, holding, kissing—that reflects tenderness and forgiveness.

- They have one weekly date.

- They show genuine appreciation at least once a day.

Sometimes nothing needs to be said, just the expression of quiet acts of tenderness—touching or holding hands while watching TV or listening to a concert, intertwining feet while reading the Sunday newspaper, taking an evening walk regularly, giving a spontaneous kiss while doing household chores.

Romance fades in the midst of family or household responsibilities. Wise couples step back and step out to stoke their passion. They make a date to do something together on a regular basis (Shepell, 2000). They build in playtime. Taking turns organizing the details of the date adds to the enjoyment. And when they're having a really good time, they express delight. They let their partner know how they are feeling.

5. **Create shared meaning.** The willingness to grow and assume responsibility for life together, suggest Robert Sternberg and Catherine Whitney (1991), is a fundamental quality of a successful relationship. When we are stuck in a negative self-story, they observe, we do not take advantage of the gift of life. People who succeed in close relationships are willing to try new things.

Developing interests and activities that can be shared as a couple strengthens bonds. Sharing of a hobby, spending time with mutual friends, or formulating life-altering plans for the future (e.g., building a house, raising a family) serve as strategies for creating shared meaning. Annual family rituals that surround important events such as birthdays, vacations, and holidays, too, serve to build a shared identity.

Remember Hatfield's two-factor theory of passionate love? Any physical arousal in a romantic context may be interpreted as passion. Perhaps it explains why couples who engage together in novel and arousing activities—outdoor activities, new sports, travel, even card games—report greater relationship satisfaction than those who participate in more mundane activities. Surveys as well as field and laboratory experiments (even the simple 7-minute task of jointly carrying a pillow through an obstacle course without using hands, arms, or teeth) confirm the effect (Aron, Norman, & Aron, 2001).

6. **Model Michelangelo.** Our close relationships powerfully shape our well-being. When they are satisfying, our lives are enriched. In fact, close relationships affect the very core of our existence—our self-identity.

Would both you and your partner say this of each other? "My partner regards me as the person I would most like to become," "My partner thinks I have the traits and dispositions that I believe are most desirable," "I find my partner often creates situations in which my ideal self can shine." And thinking back over your relationship, to what degree have you changed as a result of being involved with your partner? Are you closer to your ideal self than before you met?

The careful minding of a relationship—including reciprocity and continuity in building knowledge, acceptance, and positive attributions—can produce the *Michaelangelo effect* (Drigotas, 2002), in which partners come closer to the people they most aspire to be. Just as Michelangelo released the ideal form buried in a block of marble, so romantic partners can foster each other's realization of their ideal selves. When acted on, positive expectations become self-fulfilling prophecies.

In modeling Michelangelo, be specific. Identify three strengths you know your partner values in himself/herself. Then write down recent instances in which he or she displayed the strengths and share it.

7. **Watch out for how you communicate in a marriage.** Gottman (2011) points to four communication patterns that serve as serious risk factors for

divorce: contempt, criticism, defensiveness, and stonewalling. *Contempt* involves one partner conveying the insulting message that the other partner is somehow inferior. *Criticism* entails ongoing communication of negative evaluations of a partner, the majority of which begin with an accusatory *you* and end with a broad condemnation (e.g., "*you* broke all of your promises to me," "*you* never think of me"). *Defensiveness* occurs when one partner refutes, denies, or otherwise invalidates the other partner's statements, which may themselves be based on contempt or criticism. Defensive communications are obstructive and often fan the flames of marital conflict. Finally, *stonewalling* is a simple refusal to listen or to acknowledge a partner's concerns, particularly his or her complaints. Although the message here is about marriage and avoiding divorce, the lessons can be extended to relationships more generally: good, open, and sincere communication is essential to maintaining our most important relationships and to sustaining the love found in them.

8. **Don't debate important issues or problems when you are hungry.** This advice sounds like a little thing but it appears in actuality to be a big thing. When people are hungry, they are usually irritable, cranky, and easily angered, a combination that can lead to heightened aggression. Bushman and colleagues (2014) measured glucose levels in more than 100 heterosexual married couples for 3 weeks. To assess anger at their spouse, each partner had a voodoo doll he or she could stick with pins (ranging from 0 to 51) each night. Later, couples were invited to a lab setting where they competed against their spouse in multi-trail game—the winner could "blast" the loser with a loud noise after each round (both were wearing headphones). The upshot? Hungrier spouses (those with lower glucose levels) were more likely to stick more pins into the voodoo dolls and to discharge both longer and louder noise blasts following competition than less hungry spouses. Just as you should pick your proverbial battles carefully with the one you love, you should also monitor whether you are hungry before having a serious talk so you don't act *hangry*.

Consummate Love?

By now, you no doubt realize that love is a complex as well as a many splendored thing. Our love for our partner, our parents, and our children or friends can be strong. But the nature of that love in each case is probably quite different. Indeed, saying, "I love you" to a lover is quite distinct from saying the same thing to one's father, mother, or brother.

Still, when we think of love, our focus tends to be on a romantic partner, which leads to a pressing and concluding question: Is a consummate love that includes passion, intimacy, and commitment actually possible? As this chapter's discussion, self-assessments, and recommended strategies suggest, the answer is yes—but it is a clear challenge for both parties in the relationship. Solid, loving relationships require effort and attention. If you are currently in a romantic relationship, ask yourself whether you are working toward consummate love, doing the things that promote passion, intimacy, and commitment. If not, then consider a course correction. On the other hand, if you are looking for love, then use the positive psychological guidelines outlined in this chapter to construct a mutually beneficial relationship for you and your next partner.

⇒ IN REVIEW

The minding theory of relationships states that building knowledge about our partners, respecting differences in habits and values, and making favorable attributions for their behavior builds lasting bonds. Carving out time to talk, handling conflict constructively, expressing admiration, practicing affection, creating shared meaning, and modeling Michelangelo are additional strategies for fostering a consummate love of passion, intimacy, and commitment.

3 Empathy

Seeing and Feeling from Another's Perspective

Dangers of Snap Judgments

Forgiveness

Cultivating Empathy

I think we all have empathy. We may not have enough courage to display it. —MAYA ANGELOU, 2013

Compassion is the keen awareness of the interdependence of all things. —THOMAS MERTON, 1968

Here is what is known as an ambiguous figure. What do you see—what's your first impression?

Do you see an old woman's face? Or, instead, do you see a young woman's profile? Both possibilities are present but we can only perceive one at a time.

Perspective matters. In fact, it can transform both attitudes and actions. Shawn Eric Eckardt knew this. As Tonya Harding's bodyguard, Eckardt engineered a debilitating attack on Nancy Kerrigan, Harding's chief competitor for the 1994 Olympic gold medal in figure skating. With her right knee battered, Kerrigan was sidelined for several months. However, when Eckardt saw the image of a sobbing Kerrigan on television, he identified with her plight, experienced remorse, and bared his soul to a friend. The series of events finally led to the arrest of the attackers.

W. E. Hill, 1915.

Or consider the case of Carl Lee Hailey in John Grisham's novel *A Time to Kill*. Hailey, a poor black farmer in the Deep South, was given little chance of escaping death row. His crime? He had shot his daughter's drunken rapists as they departed from a preliminary courtroom hearing. After several brutal assaults, they had left 10-year-old Tonya Hailey for dead. There was little question that their punishment was precisely what they deserved.

Still, with an inexperienced defense attorney, a biased judge, and an unsympathetic jury, Hailey faced an uphill fight—a nearly impossible task. In the middle of jury deliberations, however, Wanda Womack asked her fellow white jurors to engage in a simple role-play. Imagine, she said, that the victim was your daughter, that the two assailants were black, that they repeatedly raped her while cursing her for being white. They kicked her in the mouth, knocked out her teeth, broke both jaws, crushed her nose. "Now be honest with yourself," implored Wanda, "wouldn't you kill if you got the chance?" By secret ballot, all 12 agreed that they would have killed the rapists. Carl Lee Hailey was acquitted.

Seeing and Feeling from Another's Perspective

Perceiving another's situation can elicit strong emotions and sometimes even that elusive feeling called *empathy*. Psychologist Edward Bradford Titchener (1909) coined the word to refer to the tendency of observers to project themselves into the scene of a painting. Most psychologists now define empathy as a person's ability to understand and share the feelings—and perhaps perspective—of another person.

Ezra Stotland (1969) demonstrated that assuming the perspective of another in need fosters feelings of empathy. His research participants watched someone undergo what they believed was a painful medical treatment. Observers who were instructed to imagine how the "patient" felt showed greater physiological arousal and reported stronger empathic feelings than those who were merely asked to watch the patient's movements.

Empathy involves the capacity to imagine the way the world looks through another's eyes. As we consider another's world, our heart vibrates with its emotional impact. By putting ourselves in another's shoes, we come not only to see what another sees but to feel what another feels. Compassion, a term closely linked to *empathy*, comes from the Latin *cum passio*, meaning "suffer with," or "suffer alongside the other." In contemporary terms, compassion refers to feelings that arise when one is confronted with another's plight, feelings which trigger a motivation to help in order to relieve whatever distress is present.

The following self-test, designed by Mark Davis (1980), captures the "seeing" and "feeling" components of empathy. Taking the test will help you appreciate the nature of empathy as many psychologists have studied it and will give you a rough idea of how your current level of empathy compares with others'.

 **SELF-ASSESSMENT**

Components of Empathy

For each item, indicate the degree to which the statement is self-descriptive using the following scale:

0	1	2	3	4
Does not describe me well				Describes me very well

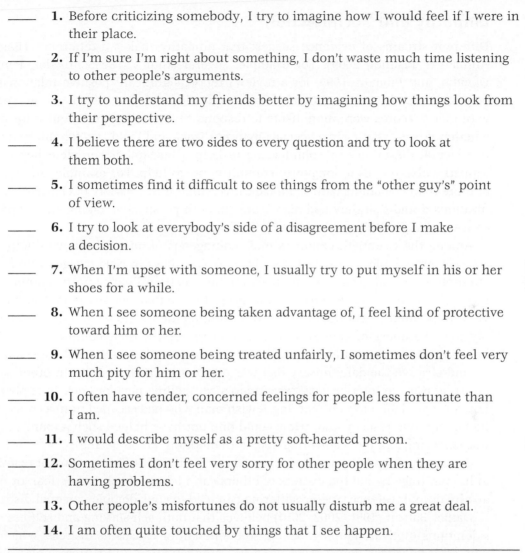

_____ **1.** Before criticizing somebody, I try to imagine how I would feel if I were in their place.

_____ **2.** If I'm sure I'm right about something, I don't waste much time listening to other people's arguments.

_____ **3.** I try to understand my friends better by imagining how things look from their perspective.

_____ **4.** I believe there are two sides to every question and try to look at them both.

_____ **5.** I sometimes find it difficult to see things from the "other guy's" point of view.

_____ **6.** I try to look at everybody's side of a disagreement before I make a decision.

_____ **7.** When I'm upset with someone, I usually try to put myself in his or her shoes for a while.

_____ **8.** When I see someone being taken advantage of, I feel kind of protective toward him or her.

_____ **9.** When I see someone being treated unfairly, I sometimes don't feel very much pity for him or her.

_____ **10.** I often have tender, concerned feelings for people less fortunate than I am.

_____ **11.** I would describe myself as a pretty soft-hearted person.

_____ **12.** Sometimes I don't feel very sorry for other people when they are having problems.

_____ **13.** Other people's misfortunes do not usually disturb me a great deal.

_____ **14.** I am often quite touched by things that I see happen.

Source: Davis, 1980. Reprinted by permission of the author.

Items 1 through 7 assess one's ability to step outside the self and assume another's perspective. In scoring your responses, first reverse the numbers before statements 2 and 5 (i.e., 0 = 4, 1 = 3, 2 = 2, 3 = 1, 4 = 0). Then add the numbers in front of all seven items to obtain a total score. Average scores are 17 or 18; higher scores indicate a greater capacity for perspective taking.

Items 8 through 14 assess one's capacity to experience feelings of warmth, compassion, and concern for another. Reverse the numbers before statements 9, 12, and 13 (i.e., 0 = 4, 1 = 3, 2 = 2, 3 = 1, 4 = 0). Then add the numbers for all seven items to obtain a total score. Average scores are approximately 20; higher scores reflect greater empathic concern.

Empathy and Social Action

Different streams of evidence suggest that empathy makes a difference (Batson, Ahmad, & Lishner, 2009). For example, several studies (see Schroeder, Penner, Dovidio, and Piliavin, 1995, for a review) report significant positive relationships between empathy, as measured by Davis's questionnaire, and social action. People with higher scores were more likely to respond to an unexpected request for help, whether it was assisting in a Special Olympics Track and Field Day for children with intellectual disabilities or volunteering to help a researcher complete her study. Empathy also relates to long-term commitments to help. For example, an analysis of more than 400 adults with significant involvement in a variety of charitable organizations found that they had high scores in both perspective taking and empathic concern (Unger & Thumuluri, 1997).

Among the twentieth century's most courageous *altruists* (those who help selflessly) were people who risked their lives to save Jews in Nazi-ravaged Europe. In attempting to understand the motives for their extraordinary efforts, Samuel and Pearl Oliner conducted extensive interviews of more than 400 rescuers. Many interviewees pointed to feelings of empathy as guiding their actions. In some cases, simply the awareness of another's peril or misery evoked their compassion. Merely knowing others were suffering was sufficient to arouse them—"I could not stand idly by and observe the daily misery that was occurring" (1988, p. 168). In other cases, empathy was the interviewees' reaction to a compelling plea for help. In explaining how she cared for a ragged, starving Jewish man who had escaped from a concentration camp, one rescuer said, "How could one not have helped such a man? . . . He was shivering and I was shivering, too, with emotion" (1988, p. 189).

Of course, empathy is not the only response to human suffering. Our gut reactions to human tragedy and the distress of others can include shock, anger, fear, or even apathy or ambivalence. Seeing suffering can lead to considerable personal distress.

Daniel Batson (1991, 2002, 2010) believes that both self-serving and selfless considerations motivate helping. Seeing someone suffer causes us distress, which we may seek to relieve by escaping the distressing situation. But suffering also elicits empathy, particularly when we feel attached to the victim. Such "other" orientation lifts us above self-centered need and reflects genuine compassion. We help even if escape is possible.

Controlled laboratory experiments have been especially helpful in sorting out how these different reactions to human suffering affect behavior. In one study, Batson and his colleagues (1981) evoked empathy in some research participants by telling them that they were very similar in attitudes and values to "Elaine," a young woman they observe receiving what they believe are electric shocks in a study on task performance under stressful conditions (Elaine was actually a confederate working with the experimenters and she never received any real electric shocks). In the course of the experiment, Elaine explains that a childhood fall against an electric fence has left her acutely sensitive to shock. To express sympathy, the experimenter suggests that the observers might take Elaine's place and receive her remaining shocks. The research team then tells some of the observers that their part in the experiment is complete and they have finished observing Elaine's suffering. They can escape the distressing situation. Others are told that they will continue to see the victim suffer. In short, these observers have no escape. Results indicated that those who felt empathic concern helped regardless of whether escape was available or not. Those who felt no empathy were more likely to choose escape when it was made available.

⇒ **IN REVIEW**

> Individuals may perceive even a simple stimulus quite differently. Judgments of others are very much in the eye of the beholder. By putting ourselves in others' shoes we come to see what they see and to feel what they feel. Research suggests that empathy is an important source of prosocial action. In fact, laboratory studies indicate that it may promote genuine altruism.

Dangers of Snap Judgments

Although our perceptions are almost automatic, they are not always accurate (Kahneman, 2011). Try the following puzzles.

Does this shape appear to be a spiral? Now cover half the figure and you'll see that it's really a series of concentric circles.

Seckel, A. (2002). *More Optical Illusions.*
New York: Carlton Books.

Are the lines in the following figure straight, or are they distorted? Check them with a ruler.

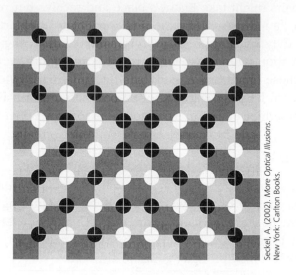

Seckel, A. (2002). *More Optical Illusions*. New York: Carlton Books.

Finally, are all the lines in this pattern the same length? Measure them.

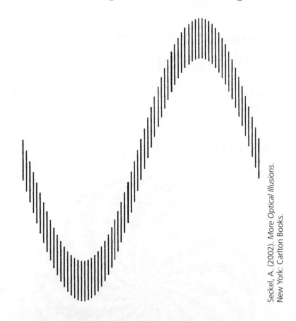

Seckel, A. (2002). *More Optical Illusions*. New York: Carlton Books.

Things are not always what they seem.

We make snap judgments quickly and easily (Fiske, 2014), doing so because we can't read other people's minds (Uleman & Saribay, 2012). Here are some impressions of students from recent classes. Take a look. What are your impressions? Do they match the ones reported here?

1. *Behavior:* For each of the first 3 days of an early-morning introductory psychology course, a male student arrives 10 minutes late. *Impression:* This tardy student seems irresponsible, inconsiderate, and unmotivated.

2. *Behavior:* An international student sits near the back of class. He needed even questions addressed specifically to him to be repeated. *Impression:* This unmotivated student has probably never learned to study. He needs to get on track.

3. *Behavior:* In the week before the first test, a student comes to my office several times for help in understanding the course material. On the day of the test she arrives late and performs poorly. *Impression:* Although she craves attention, she lacks both the ability and the motivation to succeed.

4. *Behavior:* A student who sits in the front row of the class appears to be emotionless. She is attentive but never says a word. Always entering and leaving class alone, she ignores greetings as well as good-byes. *Impression:* She is aloof and socially awkward, and probably socially inept as well.

5. *Behavior:* The highest-scoring student in class majors in another subject. Often smirking, he rarely makes eye contact and never contributes to the class discussion. *Impression:* He is here merely to meet a course requirement. Rather arrogant, he finds the subject matter neither challenging nor interesting.

In each case, the student's life situation proved these snap judgments and impressions to be terribly wrong. The tardy student turned out to be a single father whose kindergartner climbed on the school bus just as class started. From the bus stop the father rushed to join the class. The international student? He had recently learned that his father had terminal cancer and he had no money to return home for a good-bye visit. The privately tutored student was knocked off her bike on the way to class. Although severely shaken and late, she had studied hard and did not want to postpone the test. The "aloof" student's course journal at semester's end movingly described years of childhood sexual abuse she had not previously disclosed. The tragic experience had devastated her emotional and social life. And how about the "arrogant" student? He was painfully shy. He appeared in an elective class the following semester eager to minor in psychology.

People are not always what they seem at first glance. This is not to say that negative judgments are always erroneous or that people never contribute to their own failure, merely that life situations are unique and shape people's actions more than we know. Snap judgments are the strongest competitor to empathy. We tend to think that people's behavior and their life outcomes necessarily reflect their inner traits. Because the impact of a situation on people's behavior is less apparent, sometimes even buried in the past, it often is ignored, even though it may be an important contributor to a person's behavior. Too often we focus on the person and presume the presence of (often unsubstantiated) personality traits while ignoring or even discounting the (usually unknown) influence of the situation on his or her actions (Ross, 1977). It takes time and effort to consider the situational context.

"At its simplest, empathy means feeling the same thing that another person's feeling," suggests psychologist Martin Hoffman (cited in Glass, 2001, p. 72). "At its most sophisticated, it's understanding his [sic] entire life situation." Compassion often requires that we look beneath the surface when we are seeking genuine understanding and insight.

But the demands and pressures of daily living often force snap judgments. We are people with important jobs to do. We intend to do them well and want not to be interrupted. We have classes to meet, appointments to keep, books to read, papers to write, clothes to wash, and rooms to clean. Our calendars are filled, our watch alarms set. Workaholics always have an edge, observes Lewis Smedes (1982, p. 30): "We deserve to be excused because we are so virtuous."

Timothy Miller suggests that the first step to empathy is to overcome our tendency to make snap judgments. "Most blanket condemnations," he writes, "of a person's character, intelligence, intentions, or social value are non-compassionate. It doesn't matter whether they are spoken or remain private" (1995, p. 101).

Practice empathy with the following Critical Thinking activity, and then consider the effects of your preconceptions and expectations on your empathy levels.

CRITICAL THINKING

Practicing Empathy

Read the following frustrating situations, allowing yourself first automatic, noncompassionate reactions. Then follow them, suggests Miller, with more empathic reflections that take into account the person's possible life situation.

Frustrating/Annoying Situation	Noncompassionate Thoughts	Compassionate Thoughts
1. Your pizza order gets lost, and you have to call again to get it delivered.		
2. A fellow student always reminds you of his latest accomplishments.		
3. A neighbor's barking dog wakes you early in the morning.		
4. A telemarketer calls to sell you discounted car insurance.		
5. A friend fails to meet you at the airport as she promised.		

Preconceptions and Expectations: Is It a Just World?

Do you agree with the following statements? Are they true or false?

T   F   **1.** Basically, the world is a just place.

T   F   **2.** By and large, people deserve what they get.

T   F   **3.** People who get "lucky breaks" have usually earned their good fortune.

T   F   **4.** People who meet with misfortune have often brought it on themselves.

T   F   **5.** Students almost always deserve the grades they receive in school.

Source: Selected items from Rubin & Peplau, 1975.

Do you tend to agree or disagree with these statements? Do you believe the world is a just or fair place—or not?

Another reason why we rush to judgment, suggests psychologist Melvin Lerner (1980), is a deep-seated belief in a just world. We need to believe that the world is a place where people generally get what they deserve. From early childhood we are taught that good is rewarded and evil is punished. Success comes to those who do what's right and suffering to those who don't. Hard work will pay off; laziness will not.

According to Lerner, people do care about justice for others as well as for themselves. This concern may motivate people to help those in distress, if only to eliminate what they perceive as a threat to their belief in a just world (i.e., "if bad events befall others, then—uh-oh—perhaps they can also happen to me"). However, the desire for a just world may also lead them to rationalize injustice. When the British marched German civilians through the Bergen-Belsen concentration camp after World War II, one German responded: "What terrible criminals these prisoners must have been to receive such treatment."

We may come to believe that those who are rewarded must be good, and those who are punished must be evil. Especially when we feel powerless to change things, it's a short step from believing that people get what they deserve to believing that people deserve what they get.

Perceived Dissimilarity

Empathy—and avoiding making a rush judgment—seems to flow from the awareness that we are all made of the same basic stuff. Samuel and Pearl Oliner's interviews with the rescuers of Jews in Nazi Europe repeatedly indicated that it was the perception of human kinship that motivated the rescuers. In general, the rescuers experienced feelings of connection to diverse people and groups. They tended to see others as similar to themselves; nonrescuers were more likely to emphasize their distinctiveness. Using extensivity ratings to assess the degree to which one's perception of similarity reaches beyond one's immediate family to include acquaintances, unfamiliar groups, and finally all of humanity, the Oliners were able to identify rescuers and nonrescuers 73 percent of the time.

Common Fire: Leading Lives of Commitment in a Complex World (Daloz, Keen, Keen, & Parks, 1997) relates the stories of more than 100 humanitarians. Although a variety of motives contributed to their helping others, every single person shared one experience in common. Early in life, these future humanitarians came to know someone very well whom they previously thought was very different from themselves. By working or studying or traveling together, they came to understand that the person was more like them than not. The experience transformed their understanding of who is "us" and who is not.

Perceived dissimilarity and, with it, the apparent inability to assume another's perspective, have opposite effects on behavior. Imagining the absence of empathy helps us understand how criminal psychopaths, child molesters, spouse or partner abusers, rapists, and torturers can engage in their horrifying acts.

⇒ IN REVIEW

Snap judgment is a major obstacle to empathy. Our strong tendency to see people's behavior as reflecting their traits often leads us to overlook their life situations. Time pressures, the belief in a just world, and perceived dissimilarity also short-circuit compassion.

Forgiveness

Empathy for suffering victims is one thing. Empathy for the perpetrators of suffering is another matter, especially if we have been their targets. Did anyone ever bully you, push you around, or even intentionally ignore you? How easy is it to forgive? Should we forgive? This Transgression Narrative Test (TNT) by Jack W. Berry and his colleagues (2001) provides a brief measure of whether we are apt to forgive those who harm us.

 SELF-ASSESSMENT

Likeliness to Forgive

Below are a number of situations in which people might find themselves. People respond in different ways to these situations in terms of what things they will forgive. Read each situation and imagine that it has happened to you. Using the scale, indicate how you think you would respond to the situation.

1 = Definitely not forgive   2 = Not likely to forgive   3 = Just as likely to forgive as not   4 = Likely to forgive   5 = Definitely forgive

_____ **1.** Someone you occasionally see in a class has a paper due at the end of the week. You have already turned this paper in, and your classmate says that he or she is under a lot of time pressure and asks you to lend him or her your paper for some ideas. You agree, and your classmate simply retypes your paper and hands it in. The professor recognizes the paper, calls both of you to her office, scolds you, and says you are lucky she doesn't put you both on academic probation. Imagine yourself in such a situation and rate how likely you are to forgive the person who borrowed your paper.

_____ **2.** A fairly close friend tells you that he or she needs some extra money for an upcoming holiday. You know a married couple who needs a babysitter for their 3-year-old for a couple of nights and you recommend your friend. Your friend is grateful and takes the job. On the first night, the child gets out of bed after your friend has fallen asleep watching television and drinks cleaning fluid from beneath the kitchen sink. The child is taken by ambulance to the hospital and stays there for 2 days for observation and treatment. The married couple will not speak to you. Imagine yourself in such a situation and rate how likely you are to forgive your friend.

_____ **3.** A friend offers to drop off a job application for you at the post office by the deadline for submission. A week later, you get a letter from the potential employer saying that your application could not be considered because it was postmarked after the deadline and they had a very strict policy about this. Your friend tells you that he or she met an old friend, went to lunch, and lost track of time. When he or she remembered the package it was close to closing time at the post office and he or she would have had to rush frantically to get there. He or she decided that deadlines usually aren't that strictly enforced, so he or she waited until the next morning to mail the package. Imagine yourself in such a situation and rate how likely you are to forgive your friend for not mailing the application on time.

_____ **4.** After high school graduation, you start a new job, and it turns out that a former classmate from high school works there, too. You think this is great; now you don't feel like such a stranger. Even though the classmate wasn't part of your crowd, there's at least a face you recognize. You two hit it off right away and talk about old times. A few weeks later you are having lunch in the cafeteria and you overhear several of your coworkers, who do not realize you are nearby, talking about you and laughing; one even sounds snide and hostile toward you. You discover that your old classmate has told them about something you did back in school that you are deeply ashamed of and did not want anyone to know about. Imagine yourself in such a situation and rate how likely you are to forgive your old classmate for telling others your secret.

_____ **5.** A distant cousin you haven't seen since childhood calls you one day and asks if he can stay with you while he looks for work and an apartment. You say it will be fine. He asks you to pick him up at the bus station that night and you do so. Your cousin is just as you fondly remember him; you reminisce for several hours. The next morning you give him some advice on job and apartment hunting in the area, then you go about your own business. That night you come home and witness an angry argument in front of your residence between your cousin and a neighbor. Your cousin is obviously very drunk, cursing, and out of control. You ask what's happening, and without really taking the time to recognize you, your cousin throws a bottle at you, cutting the side of your head. The police arrive and with some scuffling, take your cousin away and take you to the emergency room where your cut is stitched up. The next afternoon, your cousin calls from the police station. He says he is really sorry about the whole scene and that it was not like him; he was upset about being turned down for three jobs that day. Imagine yourself in such a situation and rate how likely you are to forgive your cousin.

To obtain a total score, add up the numbers you used to respond to the five situations. Scores range from 5 to 25, with higher scores reflecting a greater disposition to forgive. A sample of 88 undergraduate students at an urban, mid-Atlantic state university obtained a mean score of 13.3.

Fostering Forgiveness

Forgiveness entails making a deliberate decision to stop feeling resentful toward or wishing to avenge a wrong done to you by a person or group. The essence of forgiveness, suggests Michael McCullough and his colleagues (2000), is a motivational change, one that occurs regardless of whether the offender really deserves your forgiveness. When people forgive, they become less driven to harm their transgressors. In fact, they become more motivated to act in ways that will benefit them.

Forgiveness seems to be positively linked with physical health, psychological well-being, and favorable relationship outcomes (McCullough et al., 2009). Forgiving people are less anxious and report less depression, hostility, and anger than those who are less forgiving. People with a strong drive to forgive (or who are not vengeful when hurt by others) are less likely to be dependent on nicotine or to have substance abuse problems.

Of particular interest is research relating forgiveness to physical well-being. Charlotte vanOyen Witvliet and her colleagues (2001; Witvliet & McCullough, 2007), for example, tested the physiological responses of undergraduates as they imagined responding to their real-life offenders in both unforgiving and forgiving ways. During these imagery trials, the students experienced less physiological stress, lower levels of negative emotion, higher levels of positive emotion, and more perceived control when they imagined empathizing with the humanity of the offender and granting forgiveness. The implication is clear: Those who adopt forgiving responses may reap psychological and physiological benefits, at least in the short run. Other studies indicate that engaging in forgiving imagery actually lowers blood pressure and reduces heart rate; the reverse is true when participants dwell on grudges or discuss past violations they have yet to forgive (Lawler et al., 2003; Witvliet et al., 2001). Finally, a propensity to forgive is also linked with high-quality social support, which is associated with positive mental and physical health (House, Landis, & Umberson, 1988).

What about you? Can you forgive and forget transgressions in order to promote prosocial relations with someone who has offended you? Take the following scale, the Transgression-Related Interpersonal Motivations Inventory (TRIM-18), which assesses the motivation to forgive.

 **SELF-ASSESSMENT**

TRIM-18

*For the following questions, please indicate your current thoughts and feelings about the person who hurt you; that is, we want to know how you feel about that person **right now**. Next to each item, write the number that best describes your current thoughts and feelings.*

Strongly disagree	Disagree	Neutral	Agree	Strongly agree
1	2	3	4	5

_____ **1.** I'll make him/her pay.

_____ **2.** I am trying to keep as much distance between us as possible.

_____ **3.** Even though his/her actions hurt me, I have good will toward him/her.

_____ **4.** I wish something bad would happen to him/her.

_____ **5.** I am living as if he/she doesn't exist, isn't around.

_____ **6.** I want to bury the hatchet and move forward with our relationship.

_____ **7.** I don't trust him/her.

_____ **8.** Despite what he/she did, I want us to have a positive relationship again.

_____ **9.** I want him/her to get what he/she deserves.

_____ **10.** I am finding it difficult to act warmly toward him/her.

_____ **11.** I am avoiding him/her.

_____ **12.** Although he/she hurt me, I am putting the hurts aside so we can resume our relationship.

_____ **13.** I am going to get even.

_____ **14.** I have given up my hurt and resentment.

_____ **15.** I cut off the relationship with him/her.

_____ **16.** I have released my anger so I can work on restoring our relationship to health.

_____ **17.** I want to see him/her hurt and miserable.

_____ **18.** I withdraw from him/her.

Scoring instructions. The TRIM-18 has three subscales: Avoidance Motivations, Revenge Motivations, and Benevolence Motivations.

Avoidance Motivations: Add up the scores for items 2, 5, 7, 10, 11, 15, and 18. Higher scores indicate a motivation to avoid contact with the transgressor (scores can range from 7 to 35).

Revenge Motivations: Add up the scores for items 1, 4, 9, 13, and 17. Higher scores indicate a motivation to seek revenge on the transgressor (scores can range from 5 to 25).

Benevolence Motivations: Add up the scores for items 3, 6, 8, 12, 14, and 16. Higher scores indicate a desire to forgive the transgressor and preserve the relationship (scores can range from 6 to 30).

Review your three scores on the TRIM-18. How high was your avoidance score? Avoiding someone who hurt you is an understandable reaction as long as you don't end up ostracizing the person. *Ostracism* involves interpersonal rejection, where one person intentionally ignores, neglects, or excludes another person (Williams, 2001). Ostracism hurts: People who are socially rejected by another (or others) endure social pain, experience anger, and feel alone, and their self-esteem suffers (Williams et al., 2002). In a sense, ostracizing another person—even one who wronged you and is deserving of such treatment—creates feelings in the person that are akin to the ones you experienced. If revenge is your goal, then avoiding the offender in a serious way can be effective, but do you really want to generate anguish for another person? Being benevolent and forgiving is probably a better course of action for you to take.

Now that you have some sense of whether you are willing to forgive the person who hurt you, why not try one more exercise, a Forgiveness Journal, that will enable you to explore your thoughts and feelings about this individual?

Forgiveness Journal

Many—perhaps most—of us live with the memory of hurt received from someone. Often that person had been close to us. Should we and can we forgive? In Forgiveness Is a Choice, *Robert D. Enright (2001) suggests that you tell the story of the person who hurt you. In an effort to foster compassion, your journal might address the following questions:*

1. What was life like for the offender when he or she was growing up? Because most hurts occur at the hands of people close to us, we usually know something of their life history. Try to enter the offender's world and describe three or four things about his or her past that may have contributed to the person's vulnerability. Be careful not to confuse *forgiving* with *excusing*. The person's hardships should not become your own.

2. At the time of the hurtful event, what was life like for the person? Try to imagine what he or she may have been thinking and feeling. Was he or she under considerable pressure or perhaps vulnerable?

3. Tell the story of your relationship with the person more broadly than just describing the offense itself. How long had you known the person? Had you shared good times? Try to think of at least three times the person showed good judgment or strong character.

4. Write down any impressions of how the offender may be worse off now than are you as a result of the painful event. What is life like for him or her because of what happened?

5. What is the person like apart from the offense? Forgiving does not necessarily mean that you must welcome the person back as a boyfriend or girlfriend, employer, or close friend. Merely try to see the person as a member of the human community with intrinsic value. Review your answers to the previous questions and describe what makes the person human.

6. Has your view of the person changed in any way as a result of answering these questions? Is there anything you must still do to deepen or broaden your story of the person?

⇒ **IN REVIEW**

> Empathy for those who have injured us is a special challenge. However, forgiveness is positively linked to well-being. Retelling the story of the person who has harmed us can be an effective route to forgiveness.

Cultivating Empathy

Why cultivate empathy? Let's first consider the many benefits that come from developing compassion.

Benefits of Empathy

Both philosophers and psychologists have claimed that empathy is the bedrock of human morality. We might cultivate it for no other reason than as a tool for doing our moral duty. But compassion is more than a duty. In many respects, it is the most natural thing in the world. Most of us come hardwired for empathy. Newborns cry in response to the sound of another infant's cry. It is no mere echo either, but a vigorous, intense, spontaneous cry—one that draws our attention and encourages us to offer comfort. In hospital nurseries, one newborn's distress can evoke a chorus of crying. Children often display rudimentary forms of compassion and helping—for example, offering a toy to a distraught sibling—before their second birthday. Time and again, people asked to reflect on their motives for rescuing Jews during the Holocaust refused to see themselves as heroic: "I insist on saying that it was absolutely natural to have done this," or "I did nothing unusual; anyone would have done the same thing in my place," or "Well, where else could they go? I had to take them in."

In shifting our attention to others, compassion keeps us from becoming preoccupied with ourselves and thus enables us to live with more purpose and freedom. "Nothing makes you happier," suggests Mother Teresa, "than when you really reach out in mercy to someone who is badly hurt" (Myers, 1992, p. 194). Reflecting on what she learned in her work in Calcutta with the Missionaries of Charity, one volunteer wrote: "One lesson is that you become less vulnerable when you concern yourself with other people's vulnerability rather than your own. We've found that when we're fully involved with helping others, we haven't really got time to worry about our own fears—and so they fall into perspective."

Neal Plantinga captures the same simple truth: "The more self-absorbed we are, the less there is to find absorbing. To have no real involvement in others, no identification with them, no interest—in other words, to lack compassion—is to shrink one's world down to the cramped precincts within one's own skull. And there is not enough there for one long solo trip in a car … let alone for a lifetime" (1987, p. 17).

CRITICAL THINKING

Happiness and Helpfulness

Try a simple test. List 10 people you know well, using just their initials or nicknames.

1. _____

2. _____

3. _____

4. _____

5. _____

6. _____

7. _____

8. _____

9. _____

10. _____

*Beside each name write an **H** if that person tends to be happy, an **N** if he or she is not happy.*

*Go through the list again, writing an **S** if that person tends to be selfish, that is, shows a stable tendency to devote time and resources primarily to his or her own interests and welfare and is unwilling to be inconvenienced by others. Write a **U** if the person tends to be unselfish.*

*Examine your list. Is there any pattern between the assignment of **H**'s and **N**'s and the assignment of **S**'s and **U**'s?*

Most people perceive happy people as being unselfish. Likewise, unhappy people are more likely to be characterized as selfish. Bernard Rimland (1982), who first suggested this little exercise, notes that these relationships provide an interesting paradox: Selfish people are those who are devoted to bringing themselves happiness. As judged by others, however, these selfish people are far less likely to be happy than those who are devoted to making others happy.

As with forgiveness, empathy-induced altruism also boosts physical and psychological well-being (Batson, 1991, pp. 222–223). One survey of more than 1700 women regularly involved in prosocial action found that they experienced a "high" while helping and a sense of "calm" afterward. Similarly, fostering heart patients' interest in the welfare of others, and in doing things for others, not only made them feel better, it actually led to reduced coronary artery blockage. The "helper's high," suggests Robert Cialdini (cited in Elias, 2002, p. 4A) lowers the output of stress hormones and strengthens the immune system.

Indeed, the old adage "It is better to give than to receive" seems true. Compassionate people live longer. Following 423 older couples over a 5-year period, University of Michigan psychologist Stephanie Brown and her colleagues (2003) found that giving support and assistance was a better predictor of longevity than was receiving it. People who reported giving day-to-day help were half as likely to have died by the study's end. To make sure that "givers" were not healthier at the outset of the study, the researchers controlled for a host of factors linked to longevity, including age, gender, smoking, and drinking.

Fostering Empathy

How do we foster empathy? How do we nurture social compassion in ourselves and in our children? This chapter's brief overview of the relevant psychological research suggests several specific answers:

1. **Put on new glasses.** If indeed we make snap judgments about people's behavior, it helps to practice doing the opposite, especially when others irritate us. What factors in her situation might contribute to her not calling as she promised? What might be happening in his life that makes it difficult for him to communicate and makes him seem unfriendly? What factors might be leading a person to exaggerate and distort what really happened?

2. **Turn on the receptors.** Practicing compassion requires active listening, not only to those closest to us, but also to distressed people we rarely talk with in our daily lives. "To spend time talking with street people," writes Alfie Kohn (1990, p. 162), "to learn how they fear falling asleep in the wrong places lest someone steal what little they have, how they drink to blot out the hopelessness, how fiercely loyal friendships blossom in alleys and parks—this is to turn an abstract problem (homelessness) into real human beings."

3. **Learn from stories and films.** Narratives put a human face on social problems and provide a helpful channel of communication for ourselves and our children. Films that transport us into the experience of specific individuals and families are particularly effective in fostering empathy. Many years ago, two film series—*Roots* and *Holocaust* (both still available on video)—elicited great empathy for African-American and Jewish suffering. More recently, the portrayal of Alzheimer disease in *Still Alice* and the coverage of AIDS through the eyes of some who have it in *Dallas Buyer's Club* have fostered empathy for those suffering these horrific illnesses.

4. **Broaden the range of our experiences.** "How can you truly know the poor," challenged Mother Teresa (1995, p. xxxi), "unless you live like them?" One of the most encouraging developments on college campuses throughout the country has been the explosion in service learning. Students who participate in the programs subsequently demonstrate more citizen involvement, social responsibility, cooperation, and leadership (Andersen, 1998; Putnam, 2000). After volunteering in a homeless shelter, one student wrote: "My work in the shelter was emotional learning. I was forced to not-so-gently confront my assumptions, the barriers in my mind between us and them. When a former high school classmate needing a free lunch appeared among the homeless, I realized what a narrow line separated my life from hers. I am recommitted to a career in the helping profession where caring becomes a vocation, not just an avocation" (Mother Teresa, 1995, p. 183).

5. Role-play. Assuming the role of those closest to us, if only for a brief time, can enhance mutual understanding. Read this heartwarming note to advice columnist Ann Landers (1990):

> I want you to help me say thank you to my wife. We both have full-time jobs, and there's plenty to do to keep this household running. Last night we fell asleep knowing there was one more load of laundry to move from the washer to the dryer. I woke about 12:15. I knew my wife needed those clothes in the washer to wear to her job the next day, so I figured I'd just toss them in the dryer. When I got there, the dryer was full, and so was the clean clothes basket. I started to fold and stack underwear and socks to make room for the next load. Ann, there were at least 100 pieces to handle from just one load, and I'm sure my wife does at least four or five loads every week. Well, 35 minutes later, while standing on that cold cement floor, I had a much deeper appreciation for what my wife does several times a week with never a complaint. I decided not to sign my name, because there are probably thousands of women out there who would fit this description, and I'd like each one to think this thank-you is from a grateful mate.
> —A Lucky Guy, Canton, Ohio

6. See similarities. To foster compassion, we need to see that kinship extends beyond our immediate family, group, and country to every member of the human race. As Robert C. Roberts (1982, p. 110) notes, vulnerability to suffering, weakness, and death are things we have in common with absolutely every human being. In this respect we have fellowship with anybody who comes along. I, too, am vulnerable to disease and early death. I, too, may suffer unhappiness in my work and perhaps the pain of lost employment. I, too, may experience family discord and rejection by loved ones. Coming to such awareness is hardly easy, but it is essential to the development of empathy and self-understanding.

7. Perform random acts of kindness. Aristotle observed, "We become just by the practice of just actions, self-controlled by exercising self-control, and courageous by performing acts of courage." And we become compassionate by exercising compassion. Our actions powerfully shape our attitudes (Wilson, 2011). We can become the people we want to be.

8. Raise helpful children. Several child-rearing practices strengthen compassionate habits, including the following:

a. Be a responsive parent. Parents who establish warm, nurturing relationships with their children teach them to approach life with trust and the sense that the world is a benevolent, safe place. As a result, the children themselves are more caring. To teach children empathy, one must show children empathy (Borba, 2001).

b. Build the child's emotional vocabulary. Parents help foster empathy when they tune in to their child's feelings, recognize what's causing the emotion, and name the feeling. As children acquire emotional literacy, they become more capable of experiencing and understanding other people's concerns and needs (Borba, 2001).

c. Let children know how you feel. Children are clearly affected by parents' accounts of their personal reactions to others. Compassion-modeling parents regularly take into account another's perspective ("Boy, I guess that waitress must have had a long, hard day to forget to bring our drinks, huh?") and behave accordingly.

d. Give reasons. Parents and teachers need to explain the reasons for rules and, more specifically, the impact that hurting and helping have on others. ("When you share your paper dolls with Katie, she gets to have fun, too, and that makes her happy.") Undergraduates raised in homes characterized by a rational rather than a punitive approach to discipline are later more likely to be involved in social service and political activism (Kohn, 1990, p. 90).

e. Provide hands-on experience. Children do not have to leave school to experience a different world. For years, all students in kindergarten through fifth grade at Swansfield Elementary School of Columbia, Maryland, have learned compassion first-hand at the school's Disabilities Awareness Day (Peterson, 1992). The entire school spends the day with people with disabilities, including individuals with their service dogs and wheelchair users who play basketball. Such contact is a way to promote understanding while reducing negative snap judgments.

f. Introduce cooperative learning. Research has shown that Elliot Aronson's (Aronson & Bridgeman, 1979; Aronson & Patnoe, 2011) "jigsaw" technique sharpens youngsters' general empathic capacity. Jigsaw is a group learning experience that requires everyone's cooperative effort in order to be successful. Students in, for instance, a history class may be divided into small groups of five or six each. In a unit on France, one student might be assigned to become the expert on France's culture, another on its government, another on its economy. First, the various "experts" meet to research their assignment. Then each expert returns to the home group to teach to the class what he or she has learned. Students quickly learn that they are dependent on each other: Each has a piece of the puzzle. The only way to master the material is to pay attention to what every group member has to say. Students learn to listen attentively as well as to put themselves in each other's shoes in order to ask questions in a clear and nonthreatening manner. Self-confident students have to listen carefully to learn from the more reticent, who in turn learn that they have something important to contribute to their peers. Research findings suggest that the strategy changes "those people" to "we people" and that the newly discovered empathy spills over into other relationships.

g. Encourage a compassionate self-image. Hands-on experiences not only promote learning by doing but also encourage children to think of themselves as compassionate, caring people. Thus, a self-fulfilling prophecy is set in motion. Prompting children with enough justification to perform a good deed may increase their pleasure in performing such deeds on their own. Furthermore, when children are generous, an unanticipated compliment—for example, "It's great that you were willing to take an hour out to help your little brother"—is likely to strengthen an empathic self-image and promote continued generosity.

9. Helping others helps us. Helping others feels good, thus our actions enhance our own well-being. We benefit—mentally and physically—when we empathize with others and constructively act on our feelings (Dillard et al., 2008; Omoto et al., 2009). Engaging in volunteer work, for example, is associated with enhanced psychological well-being (Piliavin & Siegl, 2008). One study found that women who helped others following the 9/11 terrorist attacks in the United States displayed a larger reduction in distress over time than a comparable sample of women who did not offer aid (Wayment, 2004). So, consider whether you can fit a volunteering opportunity into your life—you and those you help will be glad you did.

⇒ **IN REVIEW**

Empathy can enable us to live with more purpose and freedom and with better physical and psychological health. Promoting empathy begins with a conscious effort to surmount its obstacles. Informing ourselves of others' life situations helps cultivate empathy. Active listening, then, is an important part of empathy. Sharing others' experiences, even vicariously through role-playing, also helps. Responsive, nurturant parents provide models of empathy. Providing children with hands-on experiences builds bonds with people in need and helps children build a self-image that includes being compassionate.

Self-Control

The Power of Immediate Rewards
Controlling Our Internal States
Fostering Self-Control
Taking a Long View: Grit

I count him braver who overcomes his desires than him who conquers his enemies, for the hardest victory is over self. —ARISTOTLE (384–322 B.C.)

Homer's Odysseus knew the power of human desires and impulses. He recognized what he should do but he questioned his ability to do it. To avoid destroying himself, Odysseus took preemptive action. To sail past the Sirens, whose sweet melodies lured men to the rocks and shipwreck, he plugged the ears of his crew with wax and then tied himself to the mast of his ship.

Consider a contemporary example:

> In a cocaine addiction center in Denver, patients are offered an opportunity to submit to extortion. They may write a self-incriminating letter, preferably a letter confessing their drug addiction, addressed to an important person. They deposit the letter with the clinic and submit to a randomized schedule of laboratory tests. If a laboratory test finds evidence of cocaine use, the clinic sends the letter to the addressee. An example is a physician who addresses a letter to the State Board of Medical Examiners confessing that he has administered cocaine to himself in violation of the laws of Colorado and requests that his license to practice be revoked. Faced with the prospect of losing career, livelihood, and social standing, the physician has a powerful incentive to stay clean (Schelling, 1992, p. 167).

What about you? Do you have any "guilty pleasures" that you try to keep under control? Perhaps you worry that you spend too much time playing video games or watching TV, so you "ration" your time carefully. Some people find themselves overly focused on exercising. Keeping fit is important but you shouldn't overdo it, nor should you focus on physical fitness to the extent that it keeps you from carrying out other important responsibilities. Many students, for example, wonder if they are studying enough for their classes, an activity that certainly requires a lot of self-control. Sometimes our best intentions—say, to study for that upcoming exam—are undermined by the availability of other pleasurable opportunities, such as connecting with our friends via social media. The availability of such options to satisfy our longing for instant gratification is a real challenge for our self-control.

The Power of Immediate Rewards

Sometimes we are our own worst enemies. Many of us have been guilty of the following:

- Sleeping in rather than going to work or class
- Partying the night before a test or even a final exam
- Charging purchases to credit cards without having money to pay the cards off
- Watching television rather than exercising or studying
- Taking an expensive vacation instead of saving for college
- Blowing a diet with a high-calorie dessert
- Consuming excessive amounts of alcohol that damages our brains and livers
- Smoking, vastly increasing our vulnerability to cancer, emphysema, and other ills
- Obsessively checking our cell phones for updates or messages instead of attending to lecture or class discussion

What do these self-control failures have in common? In each case, small, immediate rewards prove more powerful than large but delayed rewards (Logue, 1995). Where behaviors linked to our long-term health are concerned, many of us have a tendency to underestimate the risks associated with our pleasurable habits, even if we recognize them in other people (Weinstein, 2003).

The Marshmallow Test

Think back to when you were only 4 years old. Imagine that a man takes you into a room and places one of your favorite treats—a marshmallow—on the table in front of you. He then says, "You can have this marshmallow now if you want, but if you don't eat it until after I run an errand, you can have two."

What would you do? Do you think you could wait?

Some years ago Walter Mischel and his colleagues (e.g., Mischel, Ebbesen, & Zeiss, 1972) presented the marshmallow dilemma to preschoolers at Stanford University. The children found the task real and utterly involving. Most, of course, wanted the double treat and decided to wait. However, as the time passed for the experimenter to complete his errand, their patience was tested. The delay became increasingly frustrating. Children showed significant differences in their ability to wait the seemingly endless 15 minutes it took for the experimenter to return.

The importance of kids' ability to delay gratification in the marshmallow test became apparent as the years passed (Goleman, 1995). Researchers who revisited the children as adolescents found important differences. Compared with the impulsive children, those who resisted temptation at age 4 were, as adolescents, more confident, trustworthy, and dependable. They were better at handling stress. They were more likely to welcome challenges and to persevere in the face of difficulty. More than a decade after they had been put to the test, they were still better able to delay gratification in pursuit of larger rewards.

Even more surprising was that when the children were again tested as high school graduates, those who had patiently waited for the extra marshmallow proved to be superior students. Compared with those who had succumbed to temptation, they showed a stronger ability to concentrate and were more persistent in pursuing their goals. Most astonishingly, they had dramatically higher college-placement test scores. In fact, those who had waited the longest for the marshmallows scored more than 200 points higher than those who had immediately grabbed for one. Compared with their IQ at age 4, passing the marshmallow test was a much better predictor of college preparation success (Goleman, 1998).

The advantage persisted further into adulthood (Mischel, 2014; Mischel et al., 2011). Followed into their late twenties, those who resisted temptation were more socially competent. Compared with their counterparts, they developed more stable interpersonal relationships and were more dependable in the workplace (Goleman, 1998). This deceptively simple test of whether children can delay gratification has shed considerable insight into the dynamics and consequences of self-control (or its absence) (for other views, see Duckworth, Tsukayama, & Kirby, 2013; McGuire & Kable, 2013).

How about you? Are you more prone to favor the here and now rather than what's to come? To what extent do you reflect on the future consequences of your current behavior? The following scale measures our tendency to consider the distant outcomes of our current behaviors.

✔ SELF-ASSESSMENT

Consideration of Future Consequences Scale

For each statement, use the scale to indicate whether or not the statement is characteristic of you.

1 = Extremely uncharacteristic   2 = Somewhat uncharacteristic   3 = Uncertain
4 = Somewhat characteristic   5 = Extremely characteristic

_____ **1.** I consider how things might be in the future and try to influence them with my day-to-day behavior.

_____ **2.** I often engage in a particular behavior to achieve outcomes that may not result for many years.

_____ **3.** I only act to satisfy immediate concerns, figuring the future will take care of itself.

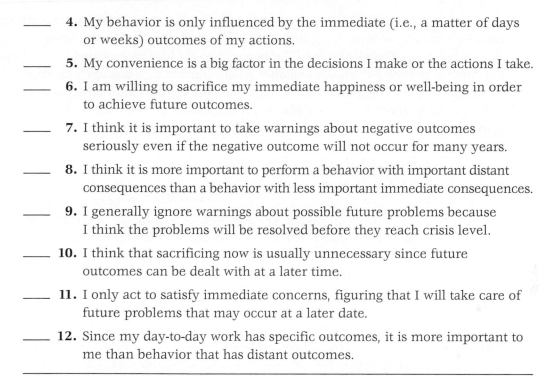

_____ **4.** My behavior is only influenced by the immediate (i.e., a matter of days or weeks) outcomes of my actions.

_____ **5.** My convenience is a big factor in the decisions I make or the actions I take.

_____ **6.** I am willing to sacrifice my immediate happiness or well-being in order to achieve future outcomes.

_____ **7.** I think it is important to take warnings about negative outcomes seriously even if the negative outcome will not occur for many years.

_____ **8.** I think it is more important to perform a behavior with important distant consequences than a behavior with less important immediate consequences.

_____ **9.** I generally ignore warnings about possible future problems because I think the problems will be resolved before they reach crisis level.

_____ **10.** I think that sacrificing now is usually unnecessary since future outcomes can be dealt with at a later time.

_____ **11.** I only act to satisfy immediate concerns, figuring that I will take care of future problems that may occur at a later date.

_____ **12.** Since my day-to-day work has specific outcomes, it is more important to me than behavior that has distant outcomes.

Source: Copyright © 1994 by the American Psychological Association. Reproduced with permission. Appendix, p. 752, from Strathman, A., Gleicher, F., Boninger, D. S., & Edwards, C. S. (1994). The consideration of future consequences: Weighing immediate and distant outcomes of behavior. _Journal of Personality and Social Psychology, 66(4)_, 742–752. No further reproduction or distribution is permitted without written permission from the American Psychological Association.

To score yourself, first reverse the numbers you gave in response to statements 3, 4, 5, 9, 10, 11, and 12 (i.e., 1 = 5, 2 = 4, 3 = 3, 4 = 2, 5 = 1). Then add up the numbers in front of all 12 items. Total scores can range from 12 to 60, with higher scores reflecting greater consideration of future consequences. Students in an introductory psychology course at the University of Missouri obtained a mean score of 42.5.

Do scores on the Consideration of Future Consequences Scale make a difference? The researchers found that high scorers were more conscientious, hopeful, and optimistic. They demonstrated more concern for their health, smoked fewer cigarettes, and consumed less alcohol. Those with higher scores were also more likely to be environmentally conscious, as measured by such markers as recycling, driving a fuel-efficient car, and using a water-saving showerhead.

Self-Control: Master Virtue?

Learning to delay gratification is both a mark of maturity and a key to a productive and socially responsible life. Working toward a college degree and a meaningful career represents a classic example of the benefits of delaying gratification.

Health psychologists tell us that we would all live longer if we did just three things: exercise regularly, stop smoking, and eat the right foods (Twenge & Baumeister, 2002). But it's not easy. The pleasures of the moment might lead us to spend the night on the couch watching TV, smoking cigarettes, and consuming a box of chocolates.

Studies of the marshmallow kids and research with the Consideration of Future Consequences Scale both highlight the importance of self-control to academic achievement and job success. June Tangney and Roy Baumeister (2000) found that high scores on their trait measure of self-control were linked to success across many activities, including higher college grades. Underachievement in school and work can often be traced to failure to see a task through to the end. (Think for a moment: Do you tend to finish those tasks you start?) The ever-present lure of procrastination—a temptation as enticing as chocolate, video games, or surfing the Internet—can also undo us (Twenge & Baumeister, 2002). Self-control even pays off for college and professional football players. Coaches rated players with more self-restraint as having better football ability, as being more highly motivated, and as showing stronger leadership (Goleman, 1998).

Self-regulation or self-control—the terms are often used interchangeably—is also important to happy and stable interpersonal relationships. The capacity to delay gratification has been linked to stronger family cohesion, more secure attachments to others, and better anger management (Tangney & Baumeister, 2000). In contrast, people who fail at self-control bring unhappiness not only to themselves but also to those people who are close to them. Neglecting the future consequences of one's actions underlies most antisocial conduct. Indeed, deficient self-control may be the major contributing factor to criminality (Gottfredson & Hirschi, 1990).

Self-control, suggest Roy Baumeister and Julie Exline (1999), is the master virtue. In fact, Baumeister and his colleagues (1994) argue that instilling strong self-control should be the single most important objective of socializing children. They recommend "that parents regard the inculcation of self-control as the premier goal in child-rearing" (p. 259). This is more important, they suggest, than cultivating self-esteem, creativity, obedience, sociability, or even love for parents.

Willpower, a form of self-control, apparently can be depleted after people exercise it (Baumeister, Bratslavsky, Muraven, & Tice, 1998). To test this possibility, college students took part in a study supposedly on taste perception. Members of one group were asked to eat a few radishes within 5 minutes while not touching some nearby chocolate chip cookies and chocolate candies. Students in a second group were invited to eat some of the cookies and candies but told not to eat the radishes. A third (control) group was told nothing of the sweets or vegetables. While waiting for the next part of the study, all of the students were asked to spend some time solving some puzzles (they did not know that the puzzles were unsolvable). As expected, Baumeister and colleagues found that the radish eaters quit trying to solve the puzzles more quickly than everyone else; they also made fewer attempts compared with the students in the other two groups. Why? The researchers assumed that exercising willpower to avoid eating the enticing cookies and candies was more draining than avoiding the radishes or, in the case of the control students, not eating either of the food groups. Baumeister and colleagues argue that the radish eaters had less willpower available to motivate them to keep working on the frustrating puzzles. Thus, we should be mindful that sometimes serious self-control (a good thing) may sap our resolve and have unlooked-for behavioral consequences (a not-so-good thing).

Is willpower always decreased? Not necessarily. Baumeister (2002b) suggests that willpower may be like a muscle—regularly exercising it can increases its strength, even if, like all muscles, it becomes fatigued after a "workout." Regularly exercising our self-control, then, can build it up so that we can fend off many temptations.

Let's turn to an arena where many people struggle to exercise willpower and self-control: Online activity. How much time do you spend online, whether you are checking in on social media or just surfing around? Could you be addicted to the Internet?

 **SELF-ASSESSMENT**

Internet Addiction Test

Answer the following questions using this scale:

0 = Does not apply   1 = Rarely   2 = Occasionally   3 = Frequently
4 = Often   5 = Always

_____ **1.** How often do you find that you stay online longer than you intended?

_____ **2.** How often do you neglect your household chores to spend more time online?

_____ **3.** How often do you prefer the excitement of the Internet to intimacy with your partner?

_____ **4.** How often do you form new relationships with fellow online users?

_____ **5.** How often do others in your life complain to you about the amount of time you spend online?

_____ **6.** How often do your grades or school work suffer because of the amount of time you spend online?

_____ **7.** How often do you check your email before [attending to] something else that you need to do?

_____ **8.** How often does your job performance or productivity suffer because of the Internet?

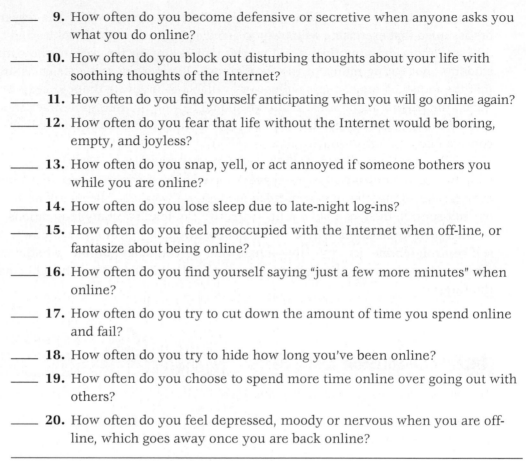

_____ 9. How often do you become defensive or secretive when anyone asks you what you do online?

_____ 10. How often do you block out disturbing thoughts about your life with soothing thoughts of the Internet?

_____ 11. How often do you find yourself anticipating when you will go online again?

_____ 12. How often do you fear that life without the Internet would be boring, empty, and joyless?

_____ 13. How often do you snap, yell, or act annoyed if someone bothers you while you are online?

_____ 14. How often do you lose sleep due to late-night log-ins?

_____ 15. How often do you feel preoccupied with the Internet when off-line, or fantasize about being online?

_____ 16. How often do you find yourself saying "just a few more minutes" when online?

_____ 17. How often do you try to cut down the amount of time you spend online and fail?

_____ 18. How often do you try to hide how long you've been online?

_____ 19. How often do you choose to spend more time online over going out with others?

_____ 20. How often do you feel depressed, moody or nervous when you are off-line, which goes away once you are back online?

Source: From Young, K., _Caught in the net._ Copyright © 1998 John Wiley & Sons. Reprinted by permission.

Total up all the scores for each item. The higher your score, the higher your level of addition to the Internet.

20–49 points: You are an average user. You may surf the Web a bit too long at times, but you have control over your usage.

50–79 points: You are experiencing occasional or frequent problems because of the Internet. You should consider their full impact on your life.

80–100 points: Your Internet usage is causing significant problems in your life. You should evaluate the impact of the Internet on your life and address the problems directly caused by your Internet usage.

What does your Internet addiction score suggest to you? Is this an opportunity for you to work to exercise more self-control? If your score is higher than you like, how will you begin to curtail your online time? If you score is relatively low, think about why you have been able to exercise willpower in this behavioral arena where so many people struggle.

> Self-control often requires that we ignore immediate rewards in favor of larger, delayed rewards. Compared with the children who failed the marshmallow test, the children who passed it demonstrated more personal and social competence in adulthood. Consideration of the future consequences of one's behavior seems to be associated with better health, more job success, and stronger interpersonal relations. Self-control may be the master virtue.

Controlling Our Internal States

How did some of the kids in the marshmallow test manage to reap the double treat? Some covered their eyes so that they wouldn't have to look. Others talked or sang to themselves. A few even tried to go to sleep. By using distraction, they maximized their reward (Mischel, 1974).

Hot "Go" Versus Cool "Slow"

Self-control may be best understood in terms of the operation of "hot" versus "cool" systems (Metcalfe & Mischel, 1999). A hot, emotional system signals "go." It is simple, reflexive, fast, and fully developed at birth. It seeks immediate rewards—the quick gratification of our needs and impulses. In contrast, a cool, thinking system signals "slow." It is complex, reflective, flexible, and develops with age. It applies the brakes to our automatic reactions. It considers the future consequences of action and thereby enables self-control.

The hot/cool system analysis helps us to understand why the use of distraction strategies was the best predictor of successful delay in the marshmallow test. Those who attended to the rewards, thus activating the hot emotional system, were unable to wait. Those who focused their attention elsewhere, thereby activating the cool system, passed the test.

In one clever variation on the original study (Mischel, 1974), investigators found that merely instructing the children to think differently about marshmallows affected their capacity to delay. They told some of the kids to think of the marshmallows they were waiting for as puffy, round clouds—in other words, to focus on the cool, abstract qualities of the rewards. Other children were told to think about how sweet and chewy the marshmallows would be in their mouth, that is, to focus on the hot, pleasurable aspects of the rewards. The results? The children who thought about the rewards in hot terms were able to wait only 5 minutes on average. Those who thought about them in cool terms were able to wait an average of 13 minutes.

Clearly, self-control includes managing our thoughts and feelings as well as our behavior. Rather than shaping our external environment to meet our needs, sometimes we must shape our internal world to fit our environment. To what degree do you believe you have control over your own internal states? The following scale assesses the extent to which people believe they can absorb the impact of aversive events on their emotions, thoughts, and physical well-being. Try it for yourself.

 SELF-ASSESSMENT

Perceived Control of Internal States Scale

Use the following scale to indicate your level of agreement with each statement:

1 = Strongly disagree   2 = Disagree   3 = Neutral   4 = Agree   5 = Strongly agree

_____ **1.** I don't have much control over my emotional reactions to stressful situations.

_____ **2.** When I'm in a bad mood, I find it hard to snap myself out of it.

_____ **3.** My feelings are usually fairly stable.

_____ **4.** I can usually talk myself out of feeling bad.

_____ **5.** No matter what happens in my life, I am confident of my ability to cope emotionally.

_____ **6.** I have a number of good techniques that will help me cope with any stressful situation.

_____ **7.** I find it hard to stop myself from thinking about my problems.

_____ **8.** If I start to worry about something, I can usually distract myself and think about something nicer.

_____ **9.** If I realize I am thinking silly thoughts, I can usually stop myself.

_____ **10.** I am usually able to keep my thoughts under control.

_____ **11.** I imagine there will be many situations in the future where silly thoughts will get the better of me.

_____ **12.** I have a number of techniques that I am confident will help me to think clearly and rationally in any situation I might find myself.

_____ **13.** Even when under pressure I can usually keep calm and relaxed.

_____ **14.** I have a number of techniques or tricks that I use to stay relaxed in stressful situations.

_____ **15.** When I'm anxious or uptight, there does not seem to be much that I can do to help myself relax.

_____ **16.** There is not much I can do to relax when I get uptight.

_____ **17.** I have a number of ways of relaxing that I am confident will help me cope.

_____ **18.** If my stress levels get too high, I know there are things I can do to help myself.

Source: Copyright © 2000. From "Development and validation of a scale to measure perceived control of internal states," *Journal of Personality Assessment, 75*, 308–337, by Pallant, J. F. Reproduced by permission of Taylor & Francis LLC (http://www.tandfonline.com)

To score your scale, first reverse the numbers you gave in response to statements 1, 2, 7, 11, 15, and 16 (1 = 5, 2 = 4, 3 = 3, 4 = 2, 5 = 1). Then add up the numbers in front of all 18 statements. Scores can range from 18 to 90, with higher scores reflecting more perceived control of one's internal states. A sample of 250 adults representing all ages and educational levels obtained a mean score of 64.08 (Pallant, 2000).

Although we may not be able to control the occurrence of negative events in our lives, we can learn to control our thoughts, feelings, and reactions during stressful encounters, which helps us deal with stress more effectively. People who perceive that they have the skills and ability to control their internal states appear less likely to succumb to the negative effects of major life stressors.

Research with the Perceived Control of Internal States Scale has found that people with higher scores experience less depression and anxiety as well as fewer physical symptoms; possess higher self-esteem; feel they are more effective in dealing with their external environment; hold more optimistic expectations; and in general show more satisfaction with life. People with a high sense of control are less likely to view stressful situations as threatening (Pallant, 2000). In situations requiring action, they are less likely to be hampered by a hot "go" system clouding their decision-making process. Their confidence provides a significant advantage in choosing the most appropriate coping strategy and executing it effectively. In contrast, low-control people are more likely to see aversive events as threatening and are less likely to cope adaptively.

Misregulation

Of course, perceived control does not guarantee *effective* emotional regulation. People may misregulate—that is, exercise control in a manner that fails to bring about a desired outcome—in various ways. For example, socializing with friends is sometimes an effective way to improve a bad mood. In other cases, the strategy backfires. Sad people who talk with others to lift their depression may find they feel no better; they have only made others feel worse. Similarly, talking about one's anger and life's unfairness may merely elicit anger in the listener (Tice & Bratslavsky, 2000).

The marshmallow study suggests that use of distraction to take one's mind off a distressing problem can sometimes be a useful means of controlling thoughts and emotions—but not always. In one variation, the researchers told some children to think fun thoughts: "If you want to, while you're waiting, you can think about Mommy pushing you on a swing." When the children were led to think pleasant, distracting thoughts, they were able to wait a long time. However, other kids who were instructed to think sad thoughts ("Think about the last time you fell off the swing") were actually less able to resist temptation. Distraction didn't work. Children thinking sad thoughts could not wait as long.

If the distractions are themselves troubling, then we are merely exchanging one source of distress for another. Depressed people tend to think negative thoughts in their efforts to distract themselves from their depression, which only compounds their depression. In general, negative thoughts increase stress and frustration, thus lowering resistance to temptation. Put another way, experiencing unpleasant emotions often causes people's ability to regulate their emotions to break down (Baumeister, Zell, & Tice, 2007).

Sometimes we misregulate by giving emotional regulation priority over other forms of self-control. Seeing a movie or going out with friends is hardly an effective strategy for dealing with the anxiety associated with procrastination. Indeed, many people admit to a variety of maladaptive coping responses, including eating, drinking, smoking, shopping, and gambling to "feel better" (Tice & Bratslavsky, 2000).

Underregulation

Some people feel that they *could* control their emotions but don't think they should. In fact, the conventional wisdom in many Western cultures seems to support the idea that healthy people must freely express their emotions.

On entering a social psychology class, many students agree: "To be mentally healthy, people need an opportunity to act out and thus to vent their aggression." They are unaware that venting is typically ineffective in lifting a negative mood. In fact, findings suggest that venting prolongs and sometimes even increases negative affect (Lohr et al., 2007).

Expressing angry aggression amplifies it. One possible reason is that venting one's anger prevents people from effectively distracting themselves. Rather, venting focuses attention on precisely the wrong thing, namely, on one's distress and what is producing it. In addition, the physical feedback involved in emotional expression that comes from facial muscles, posture, and the rest of the body plays a role in prolonging the negative mood (Baumeister et al., 1994).

Irresistible Impulses?

Are we sometimes helpless victims of our internal states? Are some impulses irresistible? Or do we acquiesce and permit our self-control to lapse?

Self-regulation failures often involve our active participation. Although we may feel overwhelmed and that our strength is depleted, the irony is that we still take an active role in indulging ourselves.

When completely stressed out, for example, some people go on an eating binge. But doing so demands that they actively seek food, put it in their mouth, chew it, and swallow it. They may have felt overwhelmed and weak, but while they eat they are anything but helpless. Similarly, given the many restrictions on when and where smokers can light up, they often need to be genuinely creative to indulge in uncontrolled smoking. Loss of self-control is more a matter of giving in than of being overwhelmed. "Self-regulation failure," suggests Baumeister and his colleagues (1994), "seems to involve a relinquishing of control because the exertion of controlling oneself is too unpleasant, and not because the impulse is too powerful" (p. 249).

American soldiers who were heroin addicts in Vietnam often recovered immediately and without treatment for addiction when they returned home (Peele, 1989). Some even used heroin in the United States without resuming their addiction. Similarly, drinking binges among alcoholics may be due more to beliefs and expectations of being unable to resist than of actual physiological dependency. American Jews often drink but rarely become alcoholic. Why? This may be due to a cultural emphasis on personal responsibility that does not exempt drinkers (Peele, 1989).

In the Malay Peninsula of Southeast Asia, people who become wildly destructive, attacking anyone and anything in their path, are described as "running amok." Within the culture, stress, sleep deprivation, and extreme heat were thought to be important causes of this "irresistible" behavior. Close examination, however, indicated that the targets of aggression were hardly arbitrary. And when the government instituted severe penalties for running amok, the problem declined dramatically (Tice & Bratslavsky, 2000).

Interestingly, research participants whose self-control had been "depleted" on a first experimental task did manage to show self-control on a second task if they were offered substantial amounts of money for doing well (Muraven, 1998). In fact, when offered 25 cents an ounce for drinking Kool-Aid laced with vinegar, one participant drank 40 ounces for a cool reward of $10. When they were offered only 1 cent per ounce, the control-depleted participants decided not to exert their self-control and drank fewer ounces of vinegar Kool-Aid compared with a control group.

Procrastination: A Special Case of Misregulation

Bruce Tuckman (1991) defines procrastination as "the tendency to put off or completely avoid an activity under one's control" (p. 474). Procrastination illustrates the important role that emotional distress plays in self-control. Whether it's working on a difficult project (a course paper, an oral presentation) that elicits worry and anxiety, or a too-simple task (mowing the lawn, cleaning your room) that leads to boredom, putting the work off provides ready escape, however temporary, from a bad mood. The marshmallow test illustrates how self-control sometimes demands that we wait for a long-term goal. Procrastination shows how, at other times, self-control requires that we get moving.

✔ SELF-ASSESSMENT

Procrastination Scale

Respond to each statement using the following scale:

4 = That's me for sure.   3 = That's my tendency.   2 = That's not my tendency.
1 = That's not me for sure.

_____ **1.** I needlessly delay finishing jobs, even when they're important.

_____ **2.** I postpone starting in on things I don't like to do.

_____ **3.** When I have a deadline, I wait until the last minute.

_____ **4.** I delay making tough decisions.

_____ **5.** I keep putting off improving my work habits.

_____ **6.** I manage to find an excuse for not doing something.

_____ **7.** I put the necessary time into even boring tasks, like studying.

_____ **8.** I am an incurable time waster.

_____ **9.** I'm a time waster now, but I can't seem to do anything about it.

_____ **10.** When something's too tough to tackle, I believe in postponing it.

_____ **11.** I promise myself I'll do something and then I drag my feet.

_____ **12.** Whenever I make a plan of action, I follow it.

_____ **13.** Even though I hate myself if I don't get started, it doesn't get me going.

_____ **14.** I always finish important jobs with time to spare.

_____ **15.** I get stuck in neutral even though I know how important it is to get started.

_____ **16.** Putting something off until tomorrow is not the way I do it.

Source: Tuckman, 1991. Copyright © 1991 SAGE Publications Inc. Reprinted by permission.

To obtain your total score, first reverse the responses (4 = 1, 3 = 2, 2 = 3, 1 = 4) for items 7, 12, 14, and 16. Then add up the numbers for all 16 items. Scores can range from 16 to 64, with higher scores reflecting a greater tendency to procrastinate. The average score for college undergraduates appears to be about 40, right at the midpoint of the scale.

The majority of us admit to procrastinating at least some of the time (Tice & Baumeister, 1997). A substantial minority acknowledge that such behavior is self-defeating. Not everyone, however, thinks it's a problem. In fact, some claim, "I do my best work under pressure." Others more modestly ask, "If one puts in the same amount of work, what difference does early or late make?"

In examining procrastination among college students, Diane Tice and Roy Baumeister (1997) found that while procrastinators seemed to benefit from their care-free, casual attitude in the early phases of a project, their advantage did not last. Overall, total stress and even illness levels proved higher for procrastinators than for those who started on time. And what about quality of work? Procrastinators ended up doing infe-rior work. Postponing seems to lead to compromises and sacrifices in quality. Tice and Baumeister (1997) concluded that "procrastination is not a neutral or innocuous form of time management, let alone a helpful or beneficial one (as some people claim)" (p. 457). So, people may believe that waiting until the last minute doesn't matter, but research shows that indeed it does—and the consequences are negative, not neutral.

Procrastination provides a fascinating puzzle in self-control. We know what we want to do, in some sense can do, at times even try to do; yet we don't do it (Sabini & Silver, 1982). Why? Psychologists' efforts to answer this question provide three important insights into the challenges of self-control more generally. And identify-ing the causes of this self-control failure also points us to a possible cure.

First, Baumeister and Tice's findings with college students suggest that, like many other forms of self-defeating behavior, procrastination is marked by short-term benefits and long-term costs. Investing ourselves in a task, like writing a course paper, can elicit anxiety over eventual performance evaluation, depression over not meeting ideals, or just plain boredom (Baumeister et al., 1994). Better to postpone. Putting it off provides a quick fix for a bad mood. Tasks that we find painful or difficult to understand are espe-cially likely to elicit distress and thus are also likely candidates for delay. Baumeister argues for transcendence—stepping back to see beyond the immediate here and now to long-term goals. Transcendence is an important key to overriding current distress.

Second, we sometimes procrastinate when we don't know what to do. We have failed to identify a long-range goal. But even more often, we sometimes procrastinate when we fail to set short-term goals. Think about it. A course paper is a monumental task. However, breaking it down into subtasks makes it manageable. A literature search, then an outline, next an introduction, finally a rough draft. Amazing! A course paper! Part of some procrastinators' problems might be the inability to break a large task down into smaller, manageable units. They may simply not know what to do, which means that asking for concrete guidance ("What steps should I take?") is a way to loosen the behavioral logjam.

Third, we tend to procrastinate when we set unrealistically high goals. Ironically, perfectionists are particularly susceptible to delay. Creating a masterpiece, locating the perfect job, finding just the right birthday present, meeting the ideal partner—all lead to delays in writing, job hunting, gift buying, and marriage. If we delay long enough, we can congratulate ourselves for our high standards and never despair over having made a wrong choice.

Implementation plans, suggests Peter Gollwitzer (1999), help people get started. Such plans tell when, where, and how to begin. We link a specific situation to a specific response: "When situation x arises, I will perform response y." We might finally launch a long-delayed exercise program when we use a simple implementation plan: "I will ride the exercise bike tonight while watching the evening news." One of our friends took up fitness swimming seriously only after spending substantial pool time just "splashing around."

Gollwitzer and Veronika Brandstätter (1997) asked university students to name two projects—one easy, the other difficult—that they intended to complete during a holiday break. When the students were asked whether they had formed intentions on when and where to get started, some said they had. After the break, the researchers checked on who had completed their projects. For difficult projects, two-thirds of the participants who had formed plans had actually carried them out. Those without plans mostly failed to complete their projects. For the easy projects, formulating plans had little effect on whether a project was completed. In short, plans seem most important when starting is difficult.

Gollwitzer and Brandstätter next gave participants a task that was difficult to implement. Prior to the holiday break, they were asked to write a report on how they spent December 24. The report had to be written and mailed to the researchers no later than 48 hours after that day. Presumably, participants believed the researchers were studying how people spend the holidays in modern times. Half the participants were instructed to form implementation plans, indicating when and where they intended to write the report during the critical 48 hours. The other half were not. Who completed the task? Three-quarters of those who did and only one-third of those who did not have implementation plans actually wrote the reports.

For those who normally let things slide, plans trigger action. With a plan in place, the critical time and situation "initiate" the action immediately, even without our conscious intent.

⇒ IN REVIEW

Self-control involves regulating our own thoughts, feelings, and behaviors. Perceived control of internal states is linked with successful coping and less depression and anxiety. Misregulation of emotion is a frequent cause of self-control failure. Procrastination provides one familiar example. Like other forms of self-defeating behavior, it is marked by short-term benefits and long-term costs. We are most apt to procrastinate when we fail to set clear objectives or when we have unrealistically high goals. Implementation plans help people get started.

Fostering Self-Control

How do we develop the capacity for self-control that is essential to our well-being? In answering this important question, we will first examine a helpful theory and its applications. Then we will consider a specific plan for addressing problems in self-regulation.

Self-Regulation Theory

Self-regulation theory assumes that behavior is directed from within the person. More specifically, self-regulation consists of three components: standards, monitoring, and strength (Carver & Scheier, 1981).

Standards are the targets of self-regulation. To control your emotions effectively, you first need to identify clearly what feelings or expressions are appropriate. Having no standards or having unrealistic or conflicting standards creates self-management problems. Having both short-term and long-term goals for reaching your standards is also important. People who lack either type of goal typically experience failure in self-control. Being explicit about setting rewards and punishments in meeting established standards seems to be an effective strategy for fostering self-control. So, if engaging in regular exercise is your goal, you might contract with yourself: "If I run my scheduled 2 miles before evening, I get to watch my favorite television program tonight. If I don't meet my objective, I watch no television until at least tomorrow."

Effective self-regulation also requires monitoring yourself—comparing your behavior to the standards. People seem to vary in their self-consciousness. How many of the following are true of you?

T   F   **1.** I generally pay attention to my inner feelings.

T   F   **2.** I'm constantly thinking about my reasons for doing things.

T   F   **3.** I sometimes step back in my own mind in order to examine myself from a distance.

T   F   **4.** I'm quick to notice changes in my mood.

T   F   **5.** I know the way my mind works when I work through a problem.

Source: Copyright © 1999. From "Alternative factor structure for the Revised Self-Consciousness Scale," *Journal of Personality Assessment, 72,* 266–282, by Martin, A. J., & Debus, R. L. Reproduced by permission of Taylor & Francis LLC (http://www.tandfonline.com)

To monitor ourselves effectively, we need to either hone our self-consciousness or develop some alternative way of acquiring knowledge of our responses. For people who have difficulty monitoring themselves—those who would have very few "true" responses to the questions above—some form of external monitoring, such as recording progress on the calendar, may help. Involving family or friends provides another helpful means of external, unbiased monitoring.

Sometimes even a mirror helps. Stacey Sentyrz and Brad Bushman (1998) found that people eat less unhealthy food when they see their own reflections. The researchers asked college students to test full-fat and no-fat cream cheese spreads on bagelettes. Students in a mirrored room ate less of the full-fat spread than did students in a room with no mirror. Sentyrz and Bushman then asked grocery shoppers to try full-fat, reduced-fat, and fat-free margarine. Those snacking over a mirrored tabletop ate less of the fatty type. A looking glass prompts self-focused attention. We don't like to catch ourselves violating our own standards (Duval & Wicklund, 1972).

Strength represents the third important component of self-regulation. We need to have the capacity to make desired changes—to alter our behavior to conform to our standards. For example, we need the strength to override the inappropriate emotions that foster procrastination.

Self-control seems to be a limited resource. Coping with stress and attempting to control negative emotions depletes limited willpower reserves. In everyday life, people are more likely to commit impulsive crimes, have addiction relapses, and engage in eating binges when they are tired or are under heavy work pressures.

From all this we can learn that it's best not to try to control many things at once. If we make multiple New Year's resolutions, we are likely to fail. Moreover, we should keep in mind that demands such as adapting to a new environment (a new school) or unusual work pressures (a new job or an unexpected work assignment) may severely tax self-control efforts in other spheres. Conversely, relaxation, rest, sleep, meditation, and positive emotions seem to replenish one's strength.

Like a muscle, self-control is also strengthened by exercise. Setting up small but frequent challenges for self-improvement seems to foster greater capacity for self-discipline. Students given various self-control drills over a period of 2 weeks (improving posture, regulating moods, monitoring eating) subsequently showed more stamina in self-regulatory capacity (Muraven, Baumeister, & Tice, 1999). More significantly, success in overcoming alcohol addiction is followed by higher success in quitting smoking (Breslau et al., 1996).

Cultivating better control over our attention or focus is a special challenge that meditation can help us address (Baumeister et al., 1994). Although it is not easy to take time to meditate once or twice a day, the investment may pay important dividends. At first, the effect may seem to be contrary. In early attempts to meditate, we may seem to have little control over our mind and attention. But practice makes our efforts more fruitful.

Remember that careful pursuit of accurate self-knowledge is an important part of self-management (Baumeister et al., 1994). Most of us think we already do this. Research indicates, however, that we don't (Dunning, 2011; Wilson, 2002). Rather, we seem to prefer hearing positive things about ourselves, regardless of whether they are accurate or not! It can be daunting to make a realistic list of our strengths and virtues, as well as our weaknesses and vices. Nonetheless, this exercise promotes effective self-control.

A Well-Defined Plan

To change a problem behavior—procrastination, smoking, a sedentary lifestyle, overeating, nail biting, poor dental hygiene, or some other troubling habit—psychologists argue that you need a well-structured plan and strong motivation (Insel & Roth, 2002).

To tackle one of your problem behaviors, implement the following steps:

Step 1 – Which Behavior Do You Want to Change? Unless you have a behavior that requires immediate medical intervention, it is usually best to choose a simple behavior to change. As you gain experience with the behavior change process, you will be better able to successfully change more challenging behaviors.

Which behavior do you want to change? _____

Step 2 – What Are the Benefits of Changing This Behavior? Identifying the benefits of your new behavior will help increase your motivation to change this behavior.

Examples:

- I will be happier.
- I will have more time to spend with my family and friends.
- My life will be less stressful.
- I will enjoy a higher quality of life.

Identify personal benefits you anticipate from this behavior change:

1. _____
2. _____
3. _____
4. _____
5. _____

Step 3 – What Are Your Behavior Change Goals? Realistic and achievable goals are the foundation for a successful healthy behavior change. A long-term goal identifies the desired overall behavior change, whereas short-term goals allow the task to be broken into smaller, more manageable steps. As short-term goals are accomplished, the long-term goal is achieved.

Long-term goal: Identify the overall target for behavior change.

Example: I will manage my time to allow one hour per day for enjoyment.

What is your long-term goal?_____

Short-term goals: Identify short-term goals that will create a step-by-step plan to achieve your goal.

Examples:

- I will make time for enjoyment a priority.
- I will create a "to do" list each day.
- I will arrange my "to do" list by priority.
- I will estimate the time needed to complete each task.
- I will make a "do-able" list for each day.

What are your short-term goals?

1. _____

2. _____

3. _____

Step 4 – Are You Ready to Change? It is difficult to accomplish a successful behavior change if you are not ready to commit to a change.

If you answer "no" to any of the questions in the following Target Behavior Test, you might consider altering your environment or priorities, consider choosing another behavior which appeals to you more, or set a more achievable goal that allows you to answer "yes" to all questions in the Target Behavior Test.

How Ready Are You?		
1. Changing this behavior is important to me.	☐ Yes	☐ No
2. I have a positive attitude about my ability to successfully change this behavior.	☐ Yes	☐ No
3. I am likely to be healthier or live in a healthier environment if I change this behavior.	☐ Yes	☐ No
4. If necessary, I am able or willing to spend the money necessary to help change this behavior.	☐ Yes	☐ No
5. I am willing to devote the time necessary to change this behavior.	☐ Yes	☐ No
6. I have chosen a target behavior that I will be able to measure or count.	☐ Yes	☐ No

7. I have selected an achievable goal. (e.g., "I will lose one pound per week by increasing my level of exercise" is probably a realistic goal. "I will lose twenty pounds this month" is probably an unrealistic goal and may be unsafe.) ☐ Yes ☐ No

8. I can identify others who will provide support for my behavior change. ☐ Yes ☐ No

Step 5 – What Are the Helpers and Hurdles to This Behavior Change?

Identifying strategies is a three-part process. First, list ideas for possible strategies to achieve your goal. Next, consider the obstacles that might keep you from reaching your goal. Finally, consider ways to overcome such obstacles.

Examples of Helpers:

- I will schedule fun things so they become part of my daily routine.
- I will join a fitness program and arrange for a personal trainer.
- I will purchase only heart-healthy foods.
- I will change jobs to allow more time with family and friends.

A. List your helpers:

1. _____

2. _____

3. _____

Identify hurdles that can potentially hinder you in your behavior change process.

Examples of Hurdles:

- Unexpected things may happen that will interfere with my scheduled fun time.
- I may not be able to afford the membership and personal trainer.
- Sometimes I don't seem to have enough willpower.
- Financially, I need to keep my job because it pays very well.

B. List your possible hurdles to achieving your goals:

1. _____

2. _____

3. _____

List ways to overcome the hurdles you have just identified. Being prepared to overcome obstacles will increase your likelihood of achieving success.

Examples of solutions to overcome hurdles:

- I will adjust other priorities rather than eliminate my free time.

- I will search for less expensive options for exercise.

- I will arrange for positive social support and remember past success when faced with obstacles.

- I will cut back on other expenditures and make my health change a top priority.

C. List your solutions for overcoming your hurdles:

1. _____

2. _____

3. _____

Step 6 – What Will Be Your Best Helper? Select the strategy or strategies that you believe will be most successful, one that you are willing to commit to.

Record your selected helper: _____

Step 7 – How Can You Alter Your Surroundings to Support Change? The people and things that are around you can greatly influence your behavior. You are more likely to succeed by creating supportive surroundings. Examine your support system (work atmosphere, home environment, family, and friends) and alter these surroundings to eliminate obstacles and increase positive support for achieving your goals.

A. How will you create a work atmosphere or home environment in which there are fewer hurdles and greater desire to engage in the new behavior?

_____

_____

Example: Share work and home responsibilities with others.

B. How Will You Build a Support Network for Yourself?

_____

_____

Examples:

- I will spend time with other people who share similar interests.

- I will ask a family member or friend to provide relief from child care so I have time for relaxation each day.

- I will ask my supervisor to positively acknowledge my successful efforts to manage my work efficiently.

C. Enlist the support of a few friends. Try using the following contract for behavior change.

Contract for Behavior Change

I, _____, pledge to meet the following goal: _____

My friend, who has signed this contract below, agrees to support me in the following ways:

1. _____

2. _____

3. _____

We will meet on _____ (date) to discuss my behavior change progress and to confirm support for my behavior change efforts.

_____   _____

Your Signature   Date   Signature of Supporting Friend   Date

Step 8 – What Will Be Your Reward? Choose enjoyable, positive rewards to motivate yourself to a successful behavior change. Make sure you reward yourself for the attainment of your short-term goals as well as your long-term goals. Rewards can be both external and internal, e. g., positive thoughts about efforts and success.

Hints about rewards:

- Take care to reward yourself with external rewards and positive thoughts about your efforts and successes.

- Reward yourself as quickly as possible when you are successful.

- Adjust your rewards as necessary.

- When you first begin to change your behavior, reward yourself each time you are successful; after your target behavior is well-established, reward yourself less frequently.

- Practice thinking positively about your decision to change, courage to change, determination to persist, and how you have succeeded in past efforts to make changes, despite challenges.

List rewards appropriate for accomplishing your short-term goals:

1. _____

2. _____

3. _____

List the reward for accomplishing your long-term goal:

1. _____

Examples of rewards:

- I will rent a videotape and invite friends to my home to watch it with me.

- I will take a relaxing bicycle ride with a friend.

- I will tell myself how well I am doing and think about how I feel better, physically and mentally.

- I will treat myself to a massage.

Step 9 – Work Your Plan and Record Your Progress. It is time to actually begin your behavior change. As a brief review:

1. Consider the benefits of your behavior change.

2. Be clear about your goals.

3. Use helpers that you believe will be successful.

4. Plan to encounter and overcome hurdles.

5. Alter your environment to support your lifestyle changes.

6. Be sure to reward yourself.

7. Have fun.

Record your progress as you work through your behavior change.
Record-keeping can help you to be successful. By observing your progress you can discover reasons for success or failure.

Use the following behavior tracking chart, or your own custom-designed chart, to document your progress.
Update your chart regularly and use it to identify not only your progress, but also the situations that promote the behavior and those that discourage the behavior.

Behavior Tracking Chart

| Date | What I planned to do | What I did | Why it happened the way it did | | How I can overcome this obstacle in the future |
			What helped me	What got in my way	
(Example) 10/20/15	Make a "to do" list	Made my "to do" list	Made my list before I went to bed last night	—	—
(Example) 10/21/15	Make my leisure time a priority	Gave up my leisure time to care for my ill child	—	My child became ill and caring for my child became a priority	I will ask a friend or relative to stay with my child while I enjoy my leisure time.

Step 10 – What Can You Do to Make Adjustments for Next Time? If, after reviewing your tracking system, you determine your success is not occurring as you had hoped, review your goals, barriers, and social support network and make appropriate adjustments. Remember, persistence is important. However, if the behavior change process is all work and no fun and you are beginning to dread the change or feel like quitting, it is probably time to alter your approach.

> **Example: I feel guilty about having time to relax and therefore do not enjoy my time. Until I have given myself enough time to rethink relaxation time, I will participate in activities that have a dual purpose—relaxation and quality family time.**

Most people are not successful in their first attempt to modify health behaviors. Learning from failures and being persistent are two qualities of people who are ultimately successful! If you slip, keep trying. Remember that behavioral change takes time. Four out of five people will do some backsliding when they try to change a behavior (Insel & Roth, 2002). Only one in four succeed the first time around. Insel & Roth note that if you retain your commitment to change even when you lapse, you are further along than before you made the commitment. Try again. And again, if necessary. If the behavior is something you know you'd be better off changing, it is worth the effort.

Taking a Long View: Grit

As you've probably noticed many times, people vary in terms of how hard they work to succeed at various challenges; some people accomplish much more than others, even when everyone is similar to one another on some key dimension, such as intelligence. Those who succeed in such circumstances often have higher levels of a trait known as "grit" (Duckworth et al., 2007). *Grit* is characterized by perseverance and passion for reaching long-term goals. Why not complete the Grit Scale in order to assess your own level of "grittiness"? To do so, go to the following link < https:// sasupenn.qualtrics.com/SE/?SID = SV_9H6iT93yv4rozeB > and complete the Grit Scale. Once you have your score, continue reading.

What is your Grit Score? People with higher scores on the Grit Scale tend to work harder than others and possess more stamina, which allows them to persevere and to achieve their goals. Grit is positively related to conscientiousness, which means that people who have a lot of grit are often orderly, punctual, and usually dependable or reliable (Duckworth et al., 2007; MacCann, Duckworth, & Roberts, 2009). Higher scores are also positively associated with higher grade point averages among college students (Duckworth et al., 2007). A study of children taking part in a national spelling bee found that the grittier ones advanced further in the competition than did those who had lower grit scores—even though those with more grit were not smarter nor were they better spellers (Duckworth et al., 2011). They just worked harder at preparing for the contest. Finally, novice teachers who show grit outperform their peers, and they are also less likely to leave their teaching jobs before the first year ends (Robertson-Kraft & Duckworth, 2014).

If your grit score was not as high as you'd hoped, don't despair. Duckworth believes that grit can be learned (Hanford, 2012), which means that it is very much like other beneficial forms of self-control. Some positive psychologists view grit as a mark of a favorable character or even an example of a moral virtue. If nothing else, it represents a good example of social-emotional competence that pays obvious dividends across time.

Self-regulation requires setting clear standards, carefully monitoring behavior, and building the strength to make desired changes. Changing a problem behavior requires a well-structured plan in which we clearly specify a target behavior and identify the advantages of change. A start date, a daily schedule, and the availability of social support facilitate our ability to enact the plan, as can developing a "gritty" outlook. Anticipating obstacles and careful tracking of progress increase the likelihood of successfully changing a behavior.

Wisdom

Emotional Intelligence

Successful Intelligence

Understanding Wisdom

Learning Wisdom

Intelligence enabled people to build a nuclear bomb. Wisdom keeps them from using it and even makes them consider the folly of building it in the first place. —ROBERT J. STERNBERG, 1997

People can be intelligent but not wise. Smart people often do foolish things. In fact, they can make a total mess of their own lives and the lives of their family and friends. Living wisely requires more than the academic aptitude assessed by traditional IQ tests. Such tests overlook important human traits, including emotional and practical intelligence. Wisdom entails some skill at perspective taking, at "[taking] stock of life in large terms" (Peterson & Seligman, 2004, p. 106) by effectively marrying knowledge to experience—through example or advice—and in so doing enhancing one's own well-being and often the well-being of others. As Baltes and Staudinger claim, "Wisdom is expertise in conduct and meaning of life" (2000, p. 124). Because other strengths contribute to wisdom, its development represents a lifelong challenge.

Emotional Intelligence

When researchers examined the factors that distinguish successful from unsuccessful managers in the workplace, they found that the most important differences related to the managers' interpersonal relations (Lombardo et al., 1988). Those who had been terminated were judged to be insensitive and arrogant. The employees who worked under these supervisors perceived them as overly ambitious and emotional, as demanding but unsupportive. Unlike their successful counterparts, the managers who messed up seemed to lack what some psychologists call *emotional intelligence* (Mayer, Salovey, Caruso, & Cherkasskiy, 2011). Emotional intelligence (EI) allows individuals to perceive, assess, and express emotion correctly and adaptively; to comprehend emotion and emotional knowledge; and to effectively regulate one's own emotions and those of others (Salovey, Mayer, Caruso, & Yoo, 2009).

The following scale attempts to assess this strength. Try it for yourself.

Measuring Emotional Intelligence

Use the following scale to indicate the extent to which each item applies to you:

1 = Strongly disagree   2 = Disagree   3 = Neither agree nor disagree
4 = Agree   5 = Strongly agree

_____ **1.** I know when to speak about my personal problems to others.

_____ **2.** When I am faced with obstacles, I remember times I faced similar obstacles and overcame them.

_____ **3.** I expect that I will do well on most things I try.

_____ **4.** Other people find it easy to confide in me.

_____ **5.** I find it hard to understand the nonverbal messages of other people.

_____ **6.** Some of the major events of my life have led me to reevaluate what is important and not important.

_____ **7.** When my mood changes, I see new possibilities.

_____ **8.** Emotions are some of the things that make my life worth living.

_____ **9.** I am aware of my emotions as I experience them.

_____ **10.** I expect good things to happen.

_____ **11.** I like to share my emotions with others.

_____ **12.** When I experience a positive emotion, I know how to make it last.

_____ **13.** I arrange events others enjoy.

_____ **14.** I seek out activities that make me happy.

_____ **15.** I am aware of the nonverbal messages I send to others.

_____ **16.** I present myself in a way that makes a good impression on others.

_____ **17.** When I am in a positive mood, solving problems is easy for me.

_____ **18.** By looking at their facial expressions, I recognize the emotions people are experiencing.

_____ **19.** I know why my emotions change.

_____ **20.** When I am in a positive mood, I am able to come up with new ideas.

_____ **21.** I have control over my emotions.

_____ **22.** I easily recognize my emotions as I experience them.

_____ **23.** I motivate myself by imagining a good outcome to tasks I take on.

_____ **24.** I compliment others when they have done something well.

_____ **25.** I am aware of the nonverbal messages other people send.

_____ **26.** When another person tells me about an important event in his or her life, I almost feel as though I have experienced this event myself.

_____ **27.** When I feel a change in emotions, I tend to come up with new ideas.

_____ **28.** When I am faced with a challenge, I give up because I believe I will fail.

_____ **29.** I know what other people are feeling just by looking at them.

_____ **30.** I help other people feel better when they are down.

_____ **31.** I use good moods to help myself keep trying in the face of obstacles.

_____ **32.** I can tell how people are feeling by listening to the tone of their voice.

_____ **33.** It is difficult for me to understand why people feel the way they do.

Source: Schutte et al., 1998. Copyright © 1998 Elsevier. Reprinted by permission.

To obtain a total score, first reverse the numbers that you have placed in response to items 5, 28, and 33 (1 = 5, 2 = 4, 3 = 3, 4 = 2, 5 = 1), and then add the numbers in front of all 33 items. Total scores range from 33 to 165, with higher scores suggesting greater emotional intelligence. The authors reported means of 131 and 125 for females and males, respectively.

The researchers recommend caution in interpreting results from this scale. They emphasize that the scale provides only a rough measure of one's emotional intelligence. Thus, it should not be used in making important life decisions such as selecting people for employment. Rather, like many of the self-report scales in this book, it provides a helpful introduction to a new and important concept. Hopefully, it also helps you reflect on your strengths and weaknesses as you set and pursue life goals.

Research with the scale in the United States suggests that higher scores are associated with measures of psychological well-being such as greater optimism and less depression and impulsiveness. Scores also predict first-year higher-education achievement, but curiously, are unrelated to the SAT or ACT scores that measure academic aptitude in U.S. secondary school students. This suggests that emotional intelligence and academic intelligence may be different concepts. Higher levels of emotional intelligence are positively associated with better health (Schutte, Malouff, Thorsteinsson, Bhullar, & Rooke, 2007), more satisfactory romantic relationships (Malouff, Schutte, & Thorsteinsson, 2014), and the maintenance of general positive mood and higher self-esteem when encountering negative information (Schutte et al., 2002).

A Model of Emotional Intelligence

Peter Salovey and John Mayer's important model of emotional intelligence (Salovey, Mayer, & Caruso, 2002) highlights four important components:

1. *Emotional perception and expression:* This component involves the ability to identify your own emotions and to recognize them in others. If you see the fleeting look of fear in another's face, you will understand much more about that person than if you miss the signal. This component also includes the capacity to express both positive and negative emotions accurately. If we always turn our attention away from our unpleasant emotions, we will learn little about emotional life.

2. *Emotional facilitation of thought:* Although emotions can disrupt thinking, they can also be harnessed for more effective problem solving and decision making. They energize us and help us attend to what is important. Sometimes mood changes enable us to appreciate multiple points of view. For example, when our perspective shifts from skeptical to accepting, we think about a problem more deeply and creatively.

3. *Emotional understanding:* This component involves the ability to label emotions with words, to understand the causes and consequences of the various emotions, and to recognize the relationships between them. Understanding complex and sometimes contradictory feelings and how they change over time is an important dimension of emotional intelligence.

4. *Emotional management:* People use a broad range of techniques to regulate their moods. Sometimes this means reducing troublesome feelings in ourselves or others. More often, effective emotional regulation calls for harnessing emotions, as when persuasive speakers "move" their listeners. Emotional self-regulation includes the ability to reflect on our feelings and disclose them appropriately to others.

Using their Multifactor Emotional Intelligence Scale, Salovey, Mayer, and David Caruso (2002; see also Salovey et al., 2009) report several significant results. For example, emotional intelligence seems to be linked with:

- Higher levels of prosocial behavior and lower levels of aggression in adolescents and college students
- Lower levels of substance abuse by adolescents, including cigarette smoking and alcohol consumption
- Higher ratings of leadership effectiveness in the workplace
- Higher ratings of employees' performance in the handling of consumer complaints. (Interestingly, emotional intelligence was negatively associated with the speed of addressing complaints. Dealing effectively with customers' feelings, speculate the researchers, probably requires time.)

- Having more friends and less conflict with close friends than people lower in emotional intelligence have

- Higher levels of life satisfaction and psychological well-being

Daniel Goleman (2002) has argued that emotional intelligence may be the distinguishing feature of good leaders. They are not brighter or tougher. Rather, they are good at perceiving, understanding, and managing emotions. In the aftermath of September 11, 2001, New York City Mayor Rudy Giuliani connected with the country's unspoken feelings in response to a reporter's question of how many died in the collapse of the World Trade Center. "We don't know the exact number," Giuliani said, "but whatever the number, it will be more than we can bear."

Whether they head a country, a city, a company, or a classroom, great leaders inspire people, suggests Goleman, by touching their emotions. They bring out the best in others. They listen empathically, they build relationships, they resolve disputes. They get others to laugh so that they enjoy what they do. Their successful management of emotion may be simple yet subtle. In work settings, employees higher in EI receive larger merit increases and tend to be viewed as more sociable and as contributing to a pleasant professional environment by peers and supervisors (Lopes et al, 2006).

⇒ **IN REVIEW**

> Wisdom involves more than academic intelligence. Some psychologists suggest that emotional intelligence is distinct from academic aptitude and is an important key to a productive life. The major components of emotional intelligence include the capacity to perceive, express, understand, and manage emotions. Research findings suggest that this capacity is an important human strength that allows for more effective functioning in many realms.

Successful Intelligence

Robert Sternberg (1996, 2011, 2012) believes that the aptitude that IQ tests assess contributes to productive living, but that aptitude is not enough. To be successfully intelligent, he suggests, one must think well in three different ways: *analytically*, *creatively*, and *practically*.

On September 11, 2001, window washer Jan Demczur demonstrated successful intelligence (Goleman, 2002). Trapped in a stalled elevator in New York's besieged World Trade Center with five other men (mostly executives), Jan, carrying his bucket and squeegee on a pole, engineered an escape. In analyzing the nearly hopeless situation, he figured that the men could use his pole to get out. Working together, they pried open the elevator door, only to find a thick wall with a giant number "50" facing them. But again Jan met the challenge. Under his direction, the men used the sharp edge of the squeegee handle to scrape away the wall. Taking turns at the tedious task, the six men used analytical, creative, and practical intelligence and finally bored through three layers of drywall to freedom.

Tacit Knowledge

The core element in practical intelligence is *tacit knowledge* (Sternberg, 1996; Sternberg & Horvath, 1999), that is, wisdom that is implied, understood, but rarely stated out loud. It is a matter of "knowing how" more than "knowing what." This knowledge is procedural—intimately related to action—and it is instrumental to the attainment of everyday goals. People typically acquire tacit knowledge without direct instruction from others, although observing models certainly helps.

CRITICAL THINKING

"Knowing How" at School and Work

You can get a sense for tacit knowledge by trying the following exercise. Identify one or two things it takes to succeed at your school or at your work that you would never read in textbooks or in your job description:

_____

_____

_____

_____

_____

Tacit knowledge can be expressed in terms of "if–then" conditionals. For example, if you need to deliver bad news to your boss, and if the boss's golf game was rained out the day before, and if the staff seems to be walking on eggshells, then it is better to wait until later to deliver the bad news to avoid spoiling the boss's week (Sternberg, 1996).

Adaptation, Shaping, Selection

Sometimes practical intelligence requires that we change or *adapt* ourselves to an existing environment. Other times it demands that we shape an environment to make it more compatible with ourselves or others. Still other times it calls for us to *select* a new environment.

Consider the following situations to understand and appreciate the differences between adapting, shaping, and selecting.

Real-World Problems

In each of the following cases, one option represents adaptation—an attempt to adjust to the environment. A second option represents shaping—trying to accommodate the environment to yourself. A third option represents selection—deciding to leave the environment and find a new one. Consider the limited information that is given and choose the solution that you think is best. In each case, Sternberg (1986) suggests you pose the following questions:

1. Given who you are, could you alter yourself in order to make your responses more adaptive?

2. If that is not possible, can you see ways of changing the situation so that it is more suitable for you?

3. If neither alternative is possible, might it be better to find a new environment altogether? If so, what alternative environments might be available to you?

Again, there are no right or wrong answers. The right answer depends on the individual, the situation, and the interaction between them. Your goal should be to identify the choice that is right for you. Thinking about the options, and about how your personality and abilities interact with the situation, may foster more practically intelligent decisions in situations such as those presented here. For each item, choose a, b, or c.

1. The nation of Dragonia is characterized by its authoritarian structure, elitist culture, brutal repression of dissent, and general intolerance. Life in this undeveloped third-world nation is predictable, monotonous, and gray. The small class of elites holds the bureaucratic and military positions while an army of second-class citizens wrests a living working in urban factories and on collectivized farms. You are a young person of high birth who has just completed your education at a prestigious institution of higher learning in Europe. Upon returning to Dragonia, do you:

    a. accept the calling of your birth, resolving to perform your duties to the best of your ability?
    b. renounce the culture of elitism and seek to build a more just order?
    c. decide you cannot live amid such hypocrisy and moral depravity and move to a large cultural metropolis elsewhere, where you can live in relative freedom and obscurity?

2. Aunt Gertrude gives you a shirt for Christmas that is not quite your style. Poor Aunt Gertrude is always giving the most hideous gifts, and this one is no exception: an ugly, red, plaid, 100-percent polyester nightmare. In this delicate situation, do you:

   a. exchange the shirt for a nice oxford cloth button-down?
   b. take Aunt Gertrude aside to discuss in private the nature of the gifts that in the future you would like to receive?
   c. hang the shirt in the back of the closet and resolve to wear it at the next Halloween party you attend?

3. Your best friend, Jill, always cheats when the two of you play tennis. She reflexively calls any ball out that falls even remotely near a line. In the face of this inexplicable ridiculousness, do you:

   a. refuse to play tennis with her (after all, you have plenty of other tennis partners who do not cheat)?
   b. decide that tennis is only a game to be enjoyed, and knowing in your heart that you are a better player, elect to tolerate her foolishness?
   c. take Jill aside, tell her with all the tact you can muster that this type of behavior is abominable, and make her promise to play squarely?

4. The cafeteria at your place of work serves virtually inedible food. Everyone in the company agrees that the food is horrible, but nobody can agree on a solution. Do you:

   a. buy their fruit and yogurt, which are rather difficult to ruin?
   b. petition for a new, improved food service?
   c. eat at the diner down the street?

5. Imagine you are a high school math teacher. One morning, you discover that the eraser for the blackboard is missing. In light of this calamity, do you:

   a. send one of the students to look for another one?
   b. wipe the board clean with your hand?
   c. decide to use the opaque projector instead?

The alternative approaches to each problem reflect adaptation, shaping, and selection. Compare your answers with the following key to assess whether your specific choices reflect adaptation, shaping, or selection.

1. a. *Adaptation*   3. a. *Selection*   5. a. *Shaping*
   b. *Shaping*   b. *Adaptation*   b. *Adaptation*
   c. *Selection*   c. *Shaping*   c. *Selection*
2. a. *Selection*   4. a. *Adaptation*
   b. *Shaping*   b. *Shaping*
   c. *Adaptation*   c. *Selection*

Source: Sternberg, 1986, pp. 316, 318–319. Reprinted by permission of the author.

In these cases, did you primarily adapt, shape, or select? Do you believe your choices are "wise" ones? If we only adapt, our own personal needs remain unmet and constructive social change never occurs. If we only shape, we ignore others' needs and generate unnecessary social conflict. If we only select, we undermine long-term commitments that ensure social stability. Wisdom, argues Robert Sternberg, demands that we balance adaptation, selection, and shaping. Most of all, wisdom involves balancing diverse interests.

⇛ IN REVIEW

> Successful intelligence, suggests Robert Sternberg, requires that we think analytically, creatively, and practically. Tacit knowledge is an important component of successful intelligence. It involves "knowing how" more than "knowing what" and is crucial to achieving important life goals. Successful intelligence sometimes requires that we adapt to our environment, at other times that we shape our environment, and at still other times, that we select a new environment.

Understanding Wisdom

Academic aptitude, emotional intelligence, and tacit knowledge contribute to wisdom. But are they enough?

A cunning terrorist may be analytically intelligent in assessing the advantages and disadvantages of various targets and even practically intelligent in delivering his attacks (Sternberg, 2002a). An unscrupulous businessperson may possess sufficient emotional intelligence to sell a worthless product and thus betray a trusting public. An evil tyrant may use her tacit knowledge to control land and resources that are not her own. Terrorists, traitors, and tyrants may be successful but, we would all agree, are not wise. One way to understand wisdom is to consider its exemplars.

CRITICAL THINKING

Wisdom's Exemplars and Characteristics

When you think of wise people, not friends or family members, but people who are well known—living or not—who comes to mind? Name three.

1. _____

2. _____

3. _____

Now pause for a moment and reflect: Why did you select those particular people? Take a few minutes to identify a few characteristics of an especially wise person.

1. _____
2. _____
3. _____
4. _____
5. _____
6. _____

When undergraduate students were asked to provide exemplars of wisdom, the top nominees included the following: Ghandi, Confucius, Jesus Christ, Martin Luther King, Jr., Socrates, Mother Teresa, Solomon, Buddha, the pope, Oprah Winfrey, Winston Churchill, the Dalai Lama, Nelson Mandela, and Queen Elizabeth (Paulus et al., 2002). (Think for a moment: What names do you think undergraduates would offer today? Would the list contain some of these names but also some newer ones?) When asked to provide exemplars for intelligence and creativity, the students generated very different lists. Curiously, only one name occurred as an example of both wisdom and intelligence: Oprah Winfrey. There was no overlap between the exemplars of wisdom and those of creativity.

After Robert Sternberg (1985) asked some respondents to identify the characteristic behaviors of wise people and had others sort the 40 top behaviors into as many or as few piles as they wished on the basis of which behaviors are "likely to hang together" in a person, he identified the six patterns below. How does your list compare?

1. *Reasoning ability:* Has the capacity to look at a problem and solve it, has a logical mind, has a huge store of information, is able to apply knowledge to particular problems.

2. *Human understanding:* Understands human nature through dealing with a variety of people, displays concern for others, is a good listener, and considers advice.

3. *Learns from experience:* Attaches importance to ideas, learns from others' mistakes.

4. *Superior judgment:* Thinks before speaking or acting, is sensible, acts within his or her own physical and intellectual limitations.

5. *Efficient use of information:* Is experienced, mature; seeks out information, especially details.

6. *Accurate perspective:* Is intuitive, is able to see through things and read between the lines, offers solutions that are on the side of right and truth.

Both lists of wise people and wise characteristics recognize the importance of analytical ability (having the capacity to look at a problem and solve it), emotional intelligence (understanding human nature, being a good listener), and tacit knowledge (applying knowledge to particular problems), but there is more.

All the exemplars of wisdom are people who have looked beyond their immediate self-interest. No terrorists, tyrants, or traitors taint our list. Why? Because such people pursue outcomes that are good for themselves but bad for others. Characteristics of wisdom include "concern for others" and choosing "solutions that are on the side of right and truth." In contrast, self-interest entails pursuing goals, opportunities, and advantages without regard for the needs of others. It is marked by a "me first" mentality.

The Balance Theory of Wisdom

The essential goal of wisdom, suggests Sternberg, is to serve a common good. Wise people balance (a) intrapersonal, (b) interpersonal, and (c) extrapersonal interests. In Sternberg's words, wisdom is "not simply about maximizing one's own or someone else's self-interest, but about balancing various self-interests (intrapersonal) with the interests of others (interpersonal) and of other aspects of the context in which one lives (extrapersonal), such as one's city or country or environment or even God" (2001, p. 231). Carefully considering the common good, the wise person uses tacit and explicit knowledge to adapt to existing environments, sometimes to shape them, and at still other times to select new environments.

How is wisdom expressed in everyday life? Sternberg poses the example of a teacher who has been instructed by her principal to spend almost all of her time teaching in a way that will maximize students' scores on a statewide assessment test. The teacher believes that the principal is essentially forcing her to abandon the true education of her students. What are the critical factors affecting her choice of a wise course of action?

1. *Balancing goals and interests:* People vary not only in the extent to which they seek a common good but also in what they view to be the common good. The teacher may believe that it is not in the children's best interests to engage only in rote memory tasks for a state-mandated test. The principal may see the children's interests differently. Moreover, both teacher and principal see their own integrity and reputation at stake. Finally, what students learn has implications for their parents and their community. The teacher is left with the responsibility of deciding what is in the best interest of all parties concerned.

2. *Balancing short- and long-term interests:* The teacher may believe that, in the long run, good education involves more than rote memorization. However, she may also recognize that performance on the state assessment test affects the students' immediate well-being as well as that of the principal and school.

3. *Balancing responses to the environmental context:* The teacher may adapt to the environment by doing what the principal has instructed. She may shape the environment by doing precisely what she believes she should do, or by trying to find some balance that meets both the principal's and her own goals. Finally, she may decide she cannot live with the principal's teaching philosophy: She may select another teaching position elsewhere.

4. *Accept boundaries on our abilities to predict our future feelings:* Instead of living in the moment, we often project how we will feel in the future—how good we will feel when vacation arrives, how sad we will feel when summer ends. The problem is that our ability to engage in such *affective forecasting* (Wilson & Gilbert, 2003, 2005) is very limited, so much so that we routinely misjudge how much pleasure or displeasure we will experience when a future event comes to pass. One reason for our inability to make such accurate self-assessments is that we focus too much on the good or bad event itself, neglecting contextual influences because we forget that events do not occur in isolation—our lives are filled with a variety of situations, events, and people who vie for our feelings and influence our thoughts (Wilson et al., 2000); no event occurs in isolation. In this context, wisdom entails remembering that no event—no matter how favorable or unfavorable, happy or sad—is apt to trigger quite the intensity of feelings we expect. Moderating expectations might just lead to somewhat more accurate forecasts, more favorable outlooks, and potentially the occasional (happy) surprise.

5. *Acquiring and using tacit knowledge:* As we saw earlier, people vary in the extent to which they have acquired tacit knowledge and in how fully they use it. The teacher may have fairly sophisticated tacit knowledge of how to teach, which means she could decide to teach in a way that represents a compromise between her own views and those of the principal. Or she may have little tacit knowledge of teaching, thus have no choice but to do what the principal says. Clearly the teacher's knowledge about how to balance the various interests of the involved parties will shape her course of action.

Apply what you've learned about Sternberg's balance theory to the following challenge.

CRITICAL THINKING

A Challenging Case

Identify the critical issues in another of Sternberg's (2002a) challenging examples:

Charles and Margaret are both engineers and have been married for five years. Three years ago Charles was offered a job in Europe. Margaret agreed to quit her job in the United States and move to Europe with Charles. The job was an excellent career move for Charles. Soon after the move, they had a baby. After the birth, Margaret decided to start working again and, with effort, found a very exciting job that paid well and promised real security. Meanwhile Charles was offered a transfer back to the U.S. Margaret feels she needs another year or two in her new job to meaningfully advance her career. She is also tired of moving. She has already given up a lot of time following Charles around. Charles knows that his wife's job is as important as his own, but he thinks returning to the U.S. would help both their careers in the end. What should Charles do?

Source: Sternberg, 2002a. Reprinted by permission of the author.

In responding to this challenge, try to apply Sternberg's balance theory of wisdom. Include responses to the following questions:

1. Whose interests should Charles take into account?

2. How might the short- and long-term interests of each party be different?

3. How might Charles' actions reflect adaptation or shaping of the environment? What would it mean for him to select a new environment?

4. How might tacit knowledge or emotional intelligence be relevant to understanding and resolving this difficult situation?

_____

_____

_____

_____

_____

_____

_____

_____

_____

_____

_____

In contrast to the problems posed on the typical intelligence test, these real-life dilemmas have multiple solutions, each associated with liabilities and assets. Most important, values are integral to the balance theory of wisdom (Sternberg, 2001). Values penetrate the consideration of interests, the identification of the appropriate response to the environment (i.e., to adapt, shape, or select), and even one's understanding of the common good. Obviously there will be great differences of opinion. Still, argues Sternberg, we can surely reach agreement on certain universal values, such as respect for human life, social justice, and enabling people to reach their full potential.

Is it possible for people to agree on what constitutes a "wise" judgment? This is a question that Paul Baltes and his colleagues at the Max Planck Institute for Human Development have attempted to answer.

Studying Wisdom

Baltes and his colleagues define wisdom simply as good judgment and advice about important but uncertain matters of life (see Baltes & Smith, 1990). It is a definition not far from that in Webster's dictionary (Goldman & Sparks, 1996, p. 1025): "Good judgment that comes from knowledge and experience in life."

Baltes's research team has attempted to move the study of wisdom from the theoretical to the empirical. In the laboratory, they ask their German participants to "think aloud" about difficult life dilemmas. They are simply asked to discuss the problem and offer advice. Here is an example. How would you respond?

CRITICAL THINKING

Another Challenging Case

A 15-year-old wants to get married right away. What should she consider and do?

_____

_____

_____

_____

_____

_____

_____

_____

_____

Source: Copyright © 2000 by the American Psychological Association. Adapted with permission. Appendix A (adapted), p. 135 and Appendix B, p. 136, from Baltes, P. B., & Staudinger, U. M. (2000). Wisdom: A metaheuristic (pragmatic) to orchestrate mind and virtue toward excellence. *American Psychologist, 55*(1), 122–136. No further reproduction or distribution is permitted without written permission from the American Psychological Association.

Baltes and his colleagues have hypothesized five components to wise judgment:

1. *Factual knowledge about matters of life:* This includes knowledge about human nature, interpersonal relations, and social norms.

2. *Procedural knowledge:* This involves strategies for dealing with life's problems and weighing goals, methods of handling conflict, and ways of offering advice.

3. *Lifespan contextualism:* Knowledge about the different roles and contexts of life (e.g., family, friends, work, recreation) and how these may change over the life span.

4. *Recognition and management of uncertainty:* The awareness that human knowledge is limited, the future cannot be fully known in advance, and life is unpredictable. The recognition that there may be no perfect solution.

5. *Relativism regarding solutions:* The acknowledgment of individual and cultural differences in values and life priorities.

In their studies, Baltes and his colleagues asked some research participants to read the responses others had given to the life dilemmas and to provide a global judgment of their wisdom. Other participants were trained to rate the responses on one of the five wisdom criteria. Results indicated that the global wisdom judgments were highly correlated with other participants' ratings on each of the five criteria. Such findings support the notion that wisdom can be reliably identified and assessed.

This is one of Baltes's examples of a low-wisdom response:

A 15-year-old wants to get married? No, no way, marrying at age 15 would be utterly wrong. One has to tell the girl that marriage is not possible. (After further probing) It would be irresponsible to support such an idea. No, this is just a crazy idea.

This is one of Baltes's examples of a high-wisdom response:

Well, on the surface this seems like an easy problem. On average, marriage for 15-year-old girls is not a good thing. But there are situations where the average case does not fit. Perhaps in this instance, special life circumstances are involved, such as the girl having a terminal illness. Or, the girl may have just lost her parents. And also, this girl may live in another culture or historical period. Perhaps she was raised with a value system different from ours. In addition, one has to think about adequate ways of talking with the girl and consider her emotional state.

Among the important findings of the Max Planck studies of wisdom are the following (Baltes, Glück, & Kunzmann, 2002; Kramer, 2000):

1. Only about 5 percent of subjects tested achieved high scores in wisdom. Mean performance for all those tested was about three out of a possible seven on any given criterion.

2. Wisdom seems to increase sharply during adolescence and young adulthood. Although it remains relatively stable during middle adulthood and young old age, peak performances are more likely when people are in their fifties and sixties.

3. Age combined with professional experience seems to give some people an advantage in wisdom. Wise people tend to come from the human service professions, from leadership positions, or to have had some exceptional intrapersonal or interpersonal experiences, such as preparing their autobiography or being resisters during the Third Reich. Even specific professional specialization made a difference in reasoning on a wisdom task; for example, clinical psychologists performed better than nonclinical psychologists.

4. Wisdom is positively related to certain thinking styles. For example, those who like to evaluate and compare, or who show higher tolerance for ambiguity and willingness to go beyond existing rules, do better on the wisdom tasks.

5. Openness to experience—being imaginative, independent, and preferring variety over routine—is one of the strongest personality predictors of wisdom.

6. The opportunity to talk with another (even an imaginary inner dialogue with a person of choice) about difficult life dilemmas improved performance on wisdom tasks. Older adults profited more from actual interaction than did younger adults.

7. Instructions to take an imaginary journey around the world on a cloud thinking about life in different cultures improved performance on two of the five wisdom criteria.

⇒ IN REVIEW

A study of wisdom's exemplars and defining characteristics suggests that this human strength includes analytical ability, emotional intelligence, and tacit knowledge. In addition, wise people look beyond their immediate self-interest and are committed to the values of truth and justice. Balance theory argues that wisdom includes a careful balancing of one's own short- and long-term interests with those of others and with one's own values and other situational factors. Wise judgments seem to require strong factual and procedural knowledge as well as an understanding of life's uncertainty, of its diverse social roles, and of important value differences.

Learning Wisdom

What does the research on wisdom teach us about its development? Are certain attitudes and actions conducive to its acquisition? Here are a few tips:

1. *Expect to work at acquiring wisdom.* The capacity for sound judgment and judicious action is an acquired strength. The idea that intellectual potential can be developed is an important belief that fosters the growth of genius over time (Dweck, 2002). Wisdom is not a fixed trait. What is true of intelligence is even

more true of wisdom: Making wise judgments is not just a product of genetic good fortune, it's also a result of effort, experience, and self-regulation. Expect to follow a long process of self-development and self-discovery in working toward wisdom.

2. *Be open to experience.* This may be the most influential factor in the development of wisdom (Kramer, 2000). Be adventurous and inquisitive about many different things. Reflect on life's dilemmas and challenges and play with ideas. Develop interest, perhaps even sophistication, in art, music, and literature.

3. *Stay keenly aware of the limits of human knowledge and intuition.* Tolerate ambiguity and learn to accept the unpredictability of life. There are often different ways of looking at a problem, and life's complexity and uncertainty sometimes means there may be no perfect solution.

   In positions of power, we are especially vulnerable to three errors in intuition: thinking that we know more than we do, believing we are all-powerful, and feeling that we will always be protected (Sternberg, 2002b). Be aware of the human capacity for such self-deceptions, and give up illusions of omniscience, omnipotence, and invulnerability.

4. *Seek to understand significant problems from many different points of view.* Discussing life's important challenges with others enables you to uncover and critique your own values as well as those of others. Interaction with others we respect enables us to identify and correct errors in social judgment and consider alternative courses of action. By going public with our decision-making processes, we better understand how knowledge may be used for good or ill, and that the end to which knowledge is put, matters.

5. *Master wisdom by studying its exemplars.* Study the classic works of literature and philosophy and reflect on the collective wisdom of the ages and its application to the present. Seek out contemporary role models as well. This will help you understand the tacit knowledge that allows us to adapt to our specific environments.

6. *Learn to strike an appropriate balance between knowing when to adapt and when to select a new environment.* Suppose, hypothesizes Sternberg (1996), you go to work for a computer company because you are eager to write software for educators, but you find that your new job involves stealing ideas from competitors. Wise people don't adapt; they leave. Wise people also recognize a third option—to shape the environment. You don't leave your job because of a single aggravating coworker, you don't abandon your family because the kids behaved badly, and you don't divorce after your first big fight. Instead you hang in there and find ways to shape the environment in the best interests of all. You need to effectively balance the need for stability and continuity with the need for change.

7. *Work at mastering the steps of effective problem solving.* Sternberg (1996) has identified five key skills in successfully intelligent people. Work on these areas as you strive for wisdom:

a. Recognize the existence of a problem before it gets out of hand.

b. Define problems correctly and decide which ones are worth solving.

c. Carefully formulate long-range strategies for solving problems.

d. Think carefully about allocating resources for the immediate and long-term future, and choose allocations that will maximize return.

e. Monitor and evaluate your decisions so that you can correct errors as you discover them.

8. *Balance your own interests with those of others.* Demonstrate warmth and compassion (Kramer, 2000), and develop your emotional intelligence so that you can understand and manage human feelings. Effective living and self-fulfillment mean more than being conventionally successful. It is important to learn to manage ourselves. Learning to delay gratification protects us from impulsiveness. Discovering and pursuing the common good puts us more at ease with ourselves and with others.

CRITICAL THINKING

Exercising Some Everyday Wisdom and Creativity

We explored the place of wisdom in a variety of interesting, problem-focused situations, where people are asked to reflect and to tie together disparate elements in order to make wise choices. But what happens in everyday settings? How can we recharge our mental batteries in order to sharpen our attention, think more creatively, and enhance our sense of well-being?

Doing so turns out to be much easier than you might imagine: Get outside and experience nature. Some intriguing experimental evidence shows that spending even small amounts of time outdoors in green spaces—parks, gardens, a forest or the woods, leafy neighborhoods, even your own backyard—has a beneficial, restorative effect on people, causing them to be more cognitively attentive and emotionally functional (Berman et al., 2012). One simple study had undergraduate students spend 30 minutes either walking around an arboretum or sauntering through the downtown area of a medium-sized city (Berman, Jonides, & Kaplan, 2008). Both groups of students then returned to the lab and completed some stress and short-term memory measures. The upshot? The students who had walked around the arboretum had lower stress levels and elevated attention levels compared with those who wandered downtown. Using what's known as Attention Restoration Theory (ART), investigators argue that natural environments are less mentally demanding and distracting than busy urban settings. Other research finds similar (though less strong) results by having people look at slides of nature versus cityscapes.

Think about it: All of us know that green and leafy spaces are pleasing and encourage relaxation. But why don't we take more advantage of them? Why don't we display wisdom by exerting the effort to spend some time in a green space—even only a few minutes—each and every day? For many of us, that wouldn't be a huge challenge. We just need to resolve to do it.

Some more recent but related research demonstrates that taking a walk, too, can have benefits, especially where boosting creativity is concerned. We all know that regular exercise—running, swimming, cycling—has health and memory benefits. However, some new research suggests that walking for exercise also promotes higher levels of creativity (Reynolds, 2014). Although walking outdoors might be more enjoyable, it turns out that putting yourself through your paces on a treadmill indoors has a similar impact on creativity (Oppezzo & Schwartz, 2014). The point is simple: Walking encourages the free flow of ideas coupled with the benefits of physical exercise. So, when you are stuck, go for a walk to get back on your mental track to creative thinking.

⇒ **IN REVIEW**

Developing wisdom is clearly not an easy task! Yet it is not an elusive goal, either. By following specific guidelines, we make progress on the long path to living wisely. For example, we cultivate wisdom by being open to experience as well as by accepting the inherent ambiguity and unpredictability of life. We can seek to understand significant problems from multiple points of view, check our judgments against those of others, and reflect on the collective wisdom of the ages. Mastering tacit knowledge and learning the steps of effective problem solving are also important ingredients in making wise judgments. Wise people effectively balance the need for stability and continuity with the need for change, and they are keenly aware of the human capacity for self-deception. Wise people look for ways to restore their creativity by spending time connecting with nature or getting regular exercise.

Commitment

I haven't failed. I've found 10,000 ways that don't work. —Thomas Edison, 1902

When people ask, "Why are you doing that?" we typically answer in terms of our underlying motives. Some psychologists refer to our motives as "strivings" (Emmons, 1999). In this chapter, you will first be asked to give some thought to your own personal strivings and factors that influence your level of perseverance. Then we will examine the central role of commitment in attaining goals, including some ways to foster commitment. The term *commitment* refers to our level of dedication to some cause or personal activity.

Strivings

Here are some examples of common strivings:

- Gaining others' acceptance
- Earning a college degree
- Becoming independent
- Seeking novel and stimulating experiences
- Avoiding feeling lonely
- Avoiding feeling inferior to others
- Helping others to feel good about themselves
- Securing a meaningful and satisfying career
- Trying not to become dependent on others

Note that these strivings are phrased in terms of what we are "trying" to do, regardless of whether we are actually successful. For example, a person might be "trying to get others to like me" without succeeding.

Strivings can be fairly broad, such as "trying to make others happy," or more specific—"trying to make my partner happy." Also, strivings can be either positive or negative. That is, they may be about something we try to obtain or keep or about something we try to avoid or prevent. For example, we might be trying to gain attention from others, or we might be trying to avoid calling attention to ourselves.

Note that this way of describing oneself is different from the usual style of employing trait adjectives (friendly, intelligent, honest). In the following self-assessment, do not use trait adjectives. You may have never thought of yourself in this way, so think carefully before writing anything down.

SELF-ASSESSMENT

What Are Your Strivings?

Provide a list of at least 10 of your strivings. Keep your attention focused on yourself. Do not mentally compare the things that you typically seek with what other people pursue. Think of yourself and your motives alone. Be as honest and as objective as possible.

Take your time with this task; spend some time thinking about your motives before you begin.

I typically try to _____.

I typically try to _____.

I typically try to _____.

I typically try to _____.

I typically try to _____.

I typically try to _____.

I typically try to _____.

I typically try to _____.

I typically try to _____.

I typically try to _____.

I typically try to _____.

I typically try to _____.

Source: Adapted from Emmons, 1999, pp. 181–182.

Approach versus Avoidant Goals

To what degree does your list include positive (approach) rather than negative (avoidant) goals? That is, to what extent do your strivings reflect movement *toward* desirable outcomes, and to what degree do they reflect movement *away from* undesirable outcomes? For example, trying to "earn a job promotion" reflects an approach goal; trying to "avoid failure" is an avoidant goal. Attempting to "cope with stress" represents a positive striving; trying to "avoid letting anything upset me" is a negative one. For a person trying to lose weight, "to jog three times a week" involves a desirable outcome, whereas "to stay away from sweets" means avoiding an undesirable one. Although the goals seem similar, framing—the ways in which particular wording can trigger a positive or a negative expectation—makes a difference.

Compared with people with predominantly positive goals, people with mostly avoidant goals are more distressed and anxious (Emmons, 1996; Emmons & Kaiser, 1996). They have a lower sense of subjective well-being (Elliot, Sheldon, & Church, 1997) and suffer more physical distress (Elliot & Sheldon, 1998). People with avoidance strivings are also less likely to achieve their goals (Coats, Janoff-Bulman, & Alpert, 1996). Failure may focus our attention on avoiding negative outcomes in the future. However, it may also create a cycle of negativity in which we expect, and therefore achieve, less success.

To reach a positive goal, we need identify only one route (Schwarz, 1990). To avoid an undesired outcome, we must identify and block numerous possibilities. "Getting closer to someone" requires us to identify only a single path to the goal (Emmons, 1999). "Avoiding offending others" requires continuous monitoring of everyone's reactions. The most effective weight-control methods rely more on approach goals, such as exercising, than on avoidance goals, such as dieting (Coats et al., 1996).

Positive and negative strivings even affect the quality of our interpersonal relations. People are less satisfied with their marriage when their spouse is more concerned with avoiding negative outcomes than with achieving positive ones (King & Emmons, 1991). One reason for this lower level of satisfaction may be that in avoiding negative outcomes, we discourage social support from others (Emmons, 1996).

Reasons for Striving

Some gardeners strive to grow roses (which can be a challenge) for the sheer pleasure of it. Others do so to earn a living. Most golfers pay to play the game. Some professional golfers play only for the pay. One person may find a daily 5-mile run to be exhilarating. Another may run 2 miles every day—despite the joint pain involved— just to keep his weight under control. In other words, what one person finds to be an end in itself another sees merely as a means to an end.

Psychologists make an important distinction between *intrinsic motivation* and *extrinsic motivation* (Ryan & Deci, 2000). Intrinsically motivated behaviors (e.g., dancing for pleasure) are inherently enjoyable and satisfying. Extrinsically motivated actions (e.g., dancing for money in a club) are a means to an end; that is, our behavior enables us to obtain some reward (income) or avoid a punishment (debt).

This distinction has practical importance. Educators, employers, and coaches all recognize it. Children who find challenge and satisfaction in their studies persevere. They learn more and are fun to teach. Employees who enjoy their work not only produce a better product, they require less supervision and management than those who are not engaged by their labors. And athletes who relish the game practice on their own. Consider your own reasons for striving in the following exercise.

✔ **SELF-ASSESSMENT**

Four Kinds of Strivings

In reality, intrinsic and extrinsic motivations are ends of a continuum. People may be motivated to pursue a goal for at least four different reasons (Ryan & Deci, 2000). You will best understand these reasons by examining your own strivings. For each of at least (There are 12 lines of striving earlier) 10 strivings you identified earlier, indicate the major reason for your striving (write the identifying word next to it).

Extrinsic: *You strive for this goal because somebody else wants you to or thinks you ought to, or because you'll get something from somebody if you do. Stated differently, you probably wouldn't strive for this goal if you didn't get some kind of reward, praise, or approval for it.*

Introjected: *You strive for this goal mostly because you would feel ashamed, guilty, or anxious if you didn't. Rather than striving because someone else thinks you ought to, you feel that you ought to strive for that something.*

Identified: *You hold this striving because you really believe that it's an important goal to have. Although this goal may once have been taught to you by others, you now endorse it freely and value it wholeheartedly.*

Intrinsic: *You strive purely because of the fun and enjoyment that striving provides. While there may be other good reasons for the striving, the primary reason is simply your interest in the experience itself.*

Source: Adapted from Emmons, 1999, p. 187.

If you are like most people, your strivings probably reflect a mix of these four reasons.

Like extrinsic motivation, "introjected" motivation is more constrained. We feel less ownership of our goals, even somewhat coerced. In extrinsic activity, we experience external pressure. With introjected activity, we sense internal pressure.

Like intrinsic motivation, "identified" motivation is undertaken willingly and with a clear sense of choice. Although the identified activity may not be pleasurable (e.g., changing a child's diapers), it is consistent with a person's deeper beliefs. Freely chosen goals flow from developing interests or from core values.

Levels of extrinsic or intrinsic motivation also reflect personal investment. When intrinsically motivated, we pursue goals naturally and persistently. Your ratings of four kinds of strivings give you an idea of how your intrinsic motivation and extrinsic motivation levels balance. The following scale focuses only on your levels of intrinsic motivation, identifying key ingredients.

 **SELF-ASSESSMENT**

Intrinsic Motivation: Feelings I Have

Please read each of the following items carefully, thinking about how it relates to your life, and then indicate how true it is for you. Use the following scale to respond:

1	2	3	4	5	6	7
Not at all true			Somewhat true			Very true

_____ **1.** I feel I am free to decide for myself how to live my life.

_____ **2.** I really like the people I interact with.

_____ **3.** Often, I do not feel very competent.

_____ **4.** I feel pressured in my life.

_____ **5.** People I know tell me I am good at what I do.

_____ **6.** I get along with people I come into contact with.

_____ **7.** I pretty much keep to myself and don't have a lot of social contacts.

_____ **8.** I generally feel free to express my ideas and opinions.

_____ **9.** I consider the people I regularly interact with to be my friends.

_____ **10.** I have been able to learn interesting new skills recently.

_____ **11.** In my daily life, I frequently have to do what I am told.

_____ **12.** People in my life care about me.

_____ **13.** Most days I feel a sense of accomplishment from what I do.

_____ **14.** People I interact with on a daily basis tend to take my feelings into consideration.

_____ **15.** In my life I do not get much of a chance to show how capable I am.

_____ **16.** There are not many people that I am close to.

_____ **17.** I feel I can pretty much be myself in my daily situations.

_____ **18.** The people I interact with regularly do not seem to like me much.

_____ **19.** I often do not feel very capable.

_____ **20.** There is not much opportunity for me to decide for myself how to do things in my daily life.

_____ **21.** People are generally pretty friendly toward me.

The scale measures the degree to which you experience fulfillment of three fundamental needs. Autonomy *is feeling that you are in charge of your own actions. Items 1, 4, 8, 11, 14, 17, and 20 assess your feeling that you have a voice in determining your own behavior. Reverse the numbers you wrote in response to items 4, 11, and 20 (1 = 7, 2 = 6, 3 = 5, 4 = 4, 5 = 3, 6 = 2, 7 = 1), and then add up the numbers in front of the seven items that compose the subscale. The total can range from 7 to 49, with higher numbers representing a stronger sense of autonomy in your everyday life. Scores above the midpoint of 28 suggest that you generally have feelings of being in charge of your actions; scores below the midpoint indicate that you do not.*

Competence is your sense of effectiveness in dealing with your environment. Items 3, 5, 10, 13, 15, and 19 assess your experience of competence. Reverse the numbers you gave in response to items 3, 15, and 19 before adding up the numbers in front of all six items. This time, scores can range from 6 to 42, with higher scores reflecting a greater sense of effectiveness in dealing with your world. This time the midpoint is 24. Higher scores suggest feelings of competence. Lower scores indicate that you struggle with a sense of effectiveness.

Relatedness reflects the level of satisfaction you have in your interpersonal relationships, including your feeling that others genuinely care about you. Items 2, 6, 7, 9, 12, 16, 18, and 21 assess your feelings of relatedness. Reverse the numbers you gave in response to items 7, 16, and 18 before adding them to items 2, 6, 9, 12, and 21 to obtain a score. Scores can range from 8 to 56, with higher scores reflecting a stronger sense of relatedness. Scores above the midpoint of 32 indicate that you experience considerable satisfaction in your interpersonal relationships. Lower scores indicate that you are somewhat dissatisfied with your relationships.

Adding up the scores on the three subscales gives a measure of overall intrinsic motivation in your life; that is, the degree to which your need for autonomy, competence, and relatedness are being met. Total scores can range from 21 to 147 (with 84 the midpoint). Higher scores reflect greater intrinsic motivation.

Source: Johnston & Finney, 2010.

> Our strivings include both approach and avoidant goals. Compared with approach goals, avoidant goals are linked with more distress and prove harder to achieve. Intrinsically motivated behaviors are inherently enjoyable and satisfying. In contrast, extrinsically motivated activities are only a means to an end. Intrinsic motivation meets fundamental needs for competence, relatedness, and autonomy.

Commitment in Our Strivings

Now that you have given some thought to your strivings, consider how *committed* you are to your goals. Try the following exercise.

CRITICAL THINKING

What Is Commitment?

If you were asked to list the characteristics of the concept of extroversion, *you might list liveliness, vivaciousness, sociability, and so on. When you think of the concept of* commitment, *what three characteristics come to mind?*

1. _____

2. _____

3. _____

When Beverly Fehr (1988) asked her research participants to identify commitment's essential features, the terms they identified most frequently were "perseverance," "responsibility," and "living up to your word." Words such as "liking" and "contentment" were near the bottom of the list, even falling behind "feeling trapped." The most common theme among the set of features was one of making a decision and following through on it. Commitment means consciously and deliberately getting beyond the urge to do only what is immediately satisfying. Commitment entails a longer view, one that requires both vision and dedication.

Route to Competence, Relatedness, and Autonomy

Consider the following examples:

> Here we stand arm-in-arm in our oldest child's backyard on a beautiful summer evening, surrounded by friends and family. Candles are twinkling, tables are piled high with food, and big band music is playing out of speakers on the patio. It is our fortieth

wedding anniversary party, and as our daughter toasts our love and our commitment to each other and everyone raises their glasses above their heads, I catch the sight of a tear glimmering in the corner of my wife's eye. We didn't make it this far because it was easy. We made it through forty years of marriage because we vowed that we would. That meant never backing out, even when it was hard or uncomfortable or painful. We learned to compromise, and we discovered that difficult situations can make you stronger and more patient. Staying committed to your goals and dreams doesn't guarantee you'll have an easy road, but you'll be working toward something important with every step you take in that direction. Tonight, the smile on my wife's face is all I need to tell me it has been worth it.

Source: http://orkut.google.com/c15443841-t400237084d229cfe.html.

It was a couple of months after I decided to be a full-time freelance writer and the first time I submitted an unsolicited manuscript. I studied the magazine's guidelines carefully, and I was certain they were going to accept my article for their "Personal Experiences" department. Two months passed before they sent me a short explanation of why they couldn't use my article. I was devastated. I wanted to stop writing, thinking myself crazy for having decided to pursue a writing career in the first place. Then my son reminded me of something I had totally forgotten. He said, "Mom, you only lose when you quit trying." As I buried the rejection letter, I felt the spark of determination burn in my blood. I won't be a loser. I won't quit writing. I became determined to be more competent in writing my articles, in marketing my skills, and in interacting with the publishing world. I believe that a man is not measured by how tall he stands, but by how many times he stood up when life made him buckle to the ground. We can stay crumpled in the middle of the road, grieving. Or we can use the pause to calibrate our compass and build strength to avoid stumbling again. It's our choice. Adversities are inevitable. We can quit and lose—or we can keep trying and win. And, by the way, the article that was rejected? I pitched it to another magazine and it's getting published next month.

Source: Ruby Bayan, http://www.oursimplejoys.com/inspiration/thanks-for-adversities.html.

One inch at a time. That is how I climb and that is how I live. Sure, the summit is my goal, but without each carefully calculated move, I could never make it to the top. Each small step and giant reach presents a unique challenge. As I move up the cliff, I recognize characteristics of the rock and adapt learned techniques to advance further toward the goal. My father taught me perseverance by his example. I remember him going back to college when I was a little boy. He worked all day, attended classes in the evening, and then came home to study. I don't know how he did it, but somehow the yard work got done and he kept the car maintained. I never have asked him how he did it, but he did. When I was just 10 years old, my father got his degree. It took him many years, but he reached his goal and then moved on to other challenges. As I reach the summit, I look back down and enjoy the moment. Then I gather my gear and start planning my next climb. One inch at a time.

Source: www.forbetterlife.org/values/value_perseverance.php.

As these everyday examples illustrate, our strivings in relationships, in work, and even in leisure activity are not always joyful or exciting. Clearly, they are not always intrinsically motivating. If they were, there would be no need for commitment. We face conflict, encounter obstacles, and even experience failure. Alternative strivings often look attractive.

The most absorbing of activities at times contain stressful elements. Surgeons, mountain climbers, and scientists make heavy sacrifices for their skills and run risks—both material and psychological—in the exercise of their skills (Brickman, 1987). Patients die, climbers fall, experiments fail. And what about a "lonely" profession like writing? A writer has to "live in her head" quite a bit and then bring what happens there out into the world, either on paper or online. Rejection is always possible, even for things that are accepted for publication; someone might not like what a writer thinks and decide to let her know it. Teaching, too, can be a challenge because every class is different—or should be. A good or great teacher commits to a career full of ongoing refining of technique and adding new information and revising the old material in each course.

Even the development of skill in activities that are intrinsically motivating demands hard work and effort that is not always enjoyable. In challenging times, commitment keeps us on course. It runs interference against all those things that might distract us from our striving and thereby increases the probability of success. Commitment is essential to us in meeting our need for competence.

Commitment also enables community. The freedom of early childhood to do only what's inherently satisfying is quickly replaced by pressures to assume a variety of social responsibilities. By the time we reach adulthood, much of what we do we have to do. Every day we find ourselves engaged in activities that are necessary but not exciting. From washing dishes to changing diapers, from cleaning the home or apartment to taking out the trash and doing the laundry, from helping a neighbor paint her house to nursing a sick child back to health, we fulfill social obligations. As the poet T. S. Eliot (1998) famously wrote in 1915, "I have measured out my life with coffee spoons."

Imagine a society in which people never pledged loyalty. Imagine, suggests Lewis Smedes, that the best we could get from anyone was "I'll try to be there if I can, but don't count on it" (1987, p. 12). Every functioning social unit—from two roommates sharing an apartment to international organizations keeping peace—depends on commitment. Commitment makes social life possible. Commitment serves our need for relatedness, our need to belong.

Does commitment also serve our need for autonomy? At first glance, commitments seem constricting. A year before his death, Irish actor Richard Harris reflected on his promise to play Professor Albus Dumbledore, the wise old wizard, in all the Harry Potter movies. "I hate that kind of commitment," he complained. "I hate the idea that my life in any way is sort of restricted." Twice divorced, he quickly added, "That's why my marriages broke up. I hate commitment, and I'm totally unreliable anyway" ("Star of 'Camelot,'" 2002, p. D9).

However, it is important to remember that commitment is always chosen, never coerced. Thus, it does meet our need for autonomy. Commitment frees us from the whims of our own fluctuating moods—of being buffeted by the everyday ups and downs of life. Making a decision and following through on it also frees us from manipulation by others. We are least vulnerable to social pressure when we make our commitments public. Indeed, by choosing our commitments carefully and consciously, we take charge of our future. And by exercising our freedom to choose our loyalties, we develop a much clearer sense of self.

In Robert Bolt's (1960) brilliant play *A Man for All Seasons,* Thomas More, the second-most-powerful man in England, privately challenges King Henry VIII's decision to divorce his wife, Catherine of Aragon. As a result, More loses his position and finally his life. Why? His strong personal commitment shaped his self-identity. While he is in prison, his daughter Margaret visits. She pleads with her father to voice allegiance to the king in spite of her father's beliefs. But More objects: "When a man makes a promise, Meg, he takes himself into his own hands, like water. And if he opens his fingers then, he need not hope to find himself again" (p. 140).

Linking the Negative with the Positive

Commitments have both positive and negative elements (Brickman, 1987). Sometimes the positive element of enthusiasm (something valuable, even enjoyable) is evident; at other times the negative element of persistence (an obligation) dominates.

The following scale measures people's tendency to make or avoid commitments. Items reflecting persistence and items reflecting enthusiasm contribute equally to a total commitment score. Try it for yourself.

 SELF-ASSESSMENT

Commitment Scale

Check each statement that is true for you.

____ **1.** I will do anything to keep a promise.

____ **2.** I am easily distracted.

____ **3.** I know what the top priority in my life is.

____ **4.** I will suffer for what I love.

____ **5.** I feel I have made much progress toward fulfilling my life's goals.

____ **6.** I do not stop until the job is done.

____ **7.** The things that I am involved with often make me a different person than I was before.

_____ **8.** I do not mind making sacrifices for something I believe in.

_____ **9.** My life is exciting to me.

_____ **10.** It is hard for me to make up my mind.

_____ **11.** I am committed to a few special things in my life.

_____ **12.** I do things as a matter of principle.

_____ **13.** Even when I am unhappy, I hardly ever quit until things are finished.

_____ **14.** I see my life as having a definite purpose and meaning.

_____ **15.** I sacrifice for what I believe in.

_____ **16.** There are many things that would tempt me to abandon my current life.

_____ **17.** I do my best even if the situation seems hopeless.

_____ **18.** I am willing to make commitments in my life.

_____ **19.** When I get going on something, I cannot quit until it is done.

_____ **20.** I find things lose their excitement over time.

_____ **21.** I never get into anything halfway.

_____ **22.** I will give up other things I want to do in order to do something that really matters to me.

_____ **23.** I value the things I love more than I value my freedom.

_____ **24.** I often have doubts about what I am doing.

_____ **25.** I give everything I have to whatever I do.

_____ **26.** I start more things than I finish.

_____ **27.** I feel I have a mission in life.

_____ **28.** I am committed to my work.

_____ **29.** I believe in meeting deadlines.

_____ **30.** I usually find a point in activities that seem pointless.

Source: Brickman, 1987, p. 11.

In scoring the scale, give yourself one point each if you did not check items 2, 10, 16, 20, 24, and 26. Give yourself a point for each of the other items you did check. Total scores range from 0 to 30. The midpoint of the scale is 15, with lower scores reflecting a tendency to avoid commitments and higher scores reflecting more willingness to make them.

Commitments seem to last when we come to want to do what we feel we must do (Brickman, 1987). In terms of our earlier discussion of intrinsic and extrinsic motivation, what is introjected (we feel internal pressure) becomes internalized (we embrace it). Obligation merges with enthusiasm when we find that the object of our commitment has lasting value or meaning. Let's see how this might apply to our life's work.

Commitment to Work

For most adults, work involves nearly half of waking life (Wrzesniewski, Rozin, & Bennett, 2003). For the overwhelming majority of us, it is an obligation—we must work to earn a living. However, our actual work experience may range from daily drudgery to genuine joy. We may count the minutes to our next paycheck or secretly wonder why we are being paid for doing what we most enjoy. Closely linked to the enjoyment of our work is the sense that it brings fulfillment—the firm belief that, because of our work, we are better people and the world is a better place (Wrzesniewski et al., 2003).

 ✔ **SELF-ASSESSMENT**

Job, Career, or Vocation?

Read each of the following paragraphs and consider how much you are like Mr. A, Mr. B., and Mr. C. If you are a full-time student, imagine how you will experience your most likely full-time employment after completing school.

Mr. A works primarily to earn enough money to support his life outside his job. If he were financially secure, he would not continue with his current line of work but would do something else instead. Mr. A's job is basically a necessity of life, a lot like breathing or sleeping. He often wishes the time would pass more quickly at work. He greatly anticipates weekends and vacations. If Mr. A lived his life over again, he probably would not go into the same line of work. He would not encourage his friends and children to enter his line of work. Mr. A is very eager to retire.

Mr. B basically enjoys his work but does not expect to be in his current job five years from now. Instead, he plans to move on to a better, higher-level job. He has several goals for his future pertaining to the positions he would eventually like to hold. Sometimes his work seems like a waste of time, but he knows that he must do sufficiently well in his current position to move on. Mr. B can't wait to get a promotion. For him, a promotion means recognition of his good work and a sign of his success in competition with his coworkers.

Mr. C's work is one of the most important parts of his life. He is very pleased that he is in this line of work. Because what he does for a living is a vital part of who he is, it is one of the first things he tells people about himself. He tends to take his work home with him and on vacations, too. The majority of his friends are from his place of employment, and he belongs to several organizations and clubs relating to his work. Mr. C feels good about his work because he loves it and because he thinks it makes the world a better place. He would encourage his friends and children to enter his line of work. Mr. C would be pretty upset if he were forced to stop working, and he is not particularly looking forward to retirement.

How much are you like Mr. A, Mr. B, and Mr. C?

3 = Very much   2 = Somewhat   1 = A little   0 = Not at all

____   Mr. A?

____   Mr. B?

____   Mr. C?

Source: Wrzesniewski, McCauley, Rozin, & Schwartz, 1997, p. 24.

Amy Wrzesniewski and her colleagues (1997) found that most adults tend to experience their work as a *job* (Mr. A), a *career* (Mr. B), or a *vocation* (Mr. C). In fact, they report that people found it relatively easy to make a choice, with roughly one-third falling into each category. Do you see your own employment (present or future) as a job, a career, or a vocation?

Work as a Vocation

How you view your work makes a difference because it can shape your well-being (Caza & Wrzesniewski, 2013). When work becomes a vocation, obligation merges with enthusiasm. Those who regard their work as a vocation report both higher work satisfaction and greater life satisfaction than those who see their work as a job or as a career. Not surprisingly, people who feel a vocation or "calling" (Wrzesniewski, 2012) devote more time to their work, compensated or not. Such work provides meaning (Berg, Dutton, & Wrzesniewski, 2013). Interestingly, they also report that work brings more satisfaction than does leisure. In contrast, those with "jobs" and "careers" rate the satisfaction they receive from leisure higher than the satisfaction they get from work. For people with a vocation, work becomes life's passion; for people with a job or career, the deepest satisfactions come from hobbies and relationships outside the workplace (Wrzesniewski et al., 2003).

So is it the worker or the workplace that makes work a vocation? Is it personality traits or job characteristics that make our primary occupation fulfilling? The person and the situation are both important.

Worker engagement is linked to a variety of situational variables (Harter et al., 2003). For example, people are more likely to be committed when managers communicate clear expectations, provide the materials and equipment for them to do their work, praise good performance, encourage development, and care about them as people. Furthermore, when employees feel their opinions count, believe that they have the opportunity to do their best every day, and know that their associates are also committed to doing quality work, they feel more satisfaction in their work and, as one might predict, are more productive.

At the same time, it is clear that the person shapes the work experience. We play an active role by shaping the meaning of our own work (Wrzesniewski, Dutton, & Debebe, 2003). Wrzesniewski and her colleagues (2003) report all three work orientations—job, career, and vocation—among administrative assistants, and evidence of both job and vocation orientations among hospital cleaners. They speculate that traits such as optimism and conscientiousness may be linked to a sense of vocation. Indeed, a person's attitudes toward work are highly stable over time and across different kinds of occupations (Staw, Bell, & Clausen, 1986). Perhaps, conclude Wrzesniewski and her colleagues, "a calling orientation is a portable benefit of those who tend to have a more positive outlook on life in general."

Perhaps what's most important to commitment is the match of the person to the situation. When people identify with the purpose of their role and the mission of their organization, they become deeply committed to their work. "Employees who know their own guiding values or purposes," suggests Daniel Goleman (1998), "will have a clear, even vivid sense about whether there is a 'fit' with an organization. When they feel a match, their commitment is spontaneous and strong" (p. 120). Clearly, self-awareness is one building block of commitment. The other is for companies and organizations to have a well-formulated mission—one that clearly defines how its efforts make the world a better place. People are likely to show little allegiance to organizations whose vision statements are merely public relations ploys. More ideal places to work are those that positive psychologists refer to as "positive institutions." *Positive institutions* are work settings and organizations that intentionally seek to cultivate civic virtues, the sorts of values that help people act as good citizens while also promoting what we might call the collective good (Huang & Blumenthal, 2009; Luthans & Youssef, 2009). Think about the places you have worked already—do they qualify as positive institutions? What would your ideal work setting be like in terms of the values it might promote? Discovering the right match, of course, is not automatic. Sometimes it takes time to find one's calling and the setting where it can flourish.

⇒ IN REVIEW

Often our strivings are neither joyful nor exciting. Commitment enables us to persevere in meeting our needs for competence, relatedness, and autonomy. Obligations merge with enthusiasm when our goals have lasting meaning or value. We may view our work as a job, a career, or a vocation. When our work is a vocation, we feel the highest levels of commitment and the most satisfaction in work and life.

Fostering Commitment

How do we nurture lasting commitment in ourselves and in our children? Psychological research suggests specific directions, including the following nine:

1. **Look for meaning.** People become vitally engaged in activities that they find have long-term importance. Mere enjoyment is not enough. Even teenagers who find the arts absorbing are likely to withdraw if they do not find that their involvement serves some larger purpose (Csikszentmihalyi et al., 1993). Similarly, people persist even in a boring laboratory task if they are provided a meaningful rationale. Edward Deci and his colleagues (1994) asked introductory psychology students in their laboratory to press a bar whenever a light appeared on a screen. If told that this was a task air controllers used to enhance their signal detection ability, the students continued the task in a free activity period following the laboratory assignment. When asked, they reported that they found the task both meaningful and enjoyable.

   Parents strengthen their children's commitment to an otherwise onerous task by providing a meaningful rationale. Children are more likely to clean their room if they have a credible reason—"so your toys won't get lost or stepped on." We fulfill an obligation if we grasp its meaning and find that it is consistent with other goals and values.

2. **Transform a "should" to a "want."** Some people perceive value in social obligations more easily than others. For example, some teenagers see a visit to relatives as an unpleasant but necessary obligation, while others see the potential for good conversation and positive feelings. Some students regard going to class as merely a requirement, while others see it as a unique opportunity to learn. And some parents find that driving their children to activities is a monotonous task that simply erodes precious time, whereas other experience it as an opportunity to enjoy their children's company.

   When challenged to find value in social obligation, most research participants in one study could do so (Berg, Janoff-Bullman, & Carter, 2001). People listed obligatory tasks such as studying for a test, visiting a sick friend, going to work, and cleaning a room. After being asked to identify reasons why these tasks might be regarded as "wants" rather than "shoulds," almost two-thirds of the participants produced at least one reason. Research findings further indicated that transforming a "should" to a "should + a want" increased not only the likelihood of attaining the goal but also raised the person's level of life satisfaction.

3. **Choose commitments.** Centuries ago, Samuel Butler observed, "He who agrees against his will, is of the same opinion still." We prize a sense of freedom. People lose interest in even intrinsically satisfying activities if they feel pressured to engage in them. How many promising student-athletes, for

example, lose interest in a sport because the joy of play is lost in the demand to win no matter what? Parents and teachers can learn an important lesson from Jonathan Freedman's (1965) experiment with elementary school children. He found that either a severe threat or a mild threat could keep kids from playing with an attractive toy—a battery-controlled robot—but only temporarily. Some weeks later, when the children were given another opportunity to play with the toy, the children who had been severely threatened succumbed to temptation and played freely with the robot. The children given the mild deterrent did not. Feeling that they had freely chosen not to play with the toy, they internalized their decision.

In the laboratory task in which students were instructed to press a bar whenever a light came on, Deci's research team (1994) found that conveying choice as well as a meaningful rationale fostered commitment. A simple change in instruction from "You should start the activity by pressing the space bar" to "If you are willing to continue, all you need to do is start pressing the space bar" promoted internalization. Acknowledging the conflicting feelings that subjects might experience also strengthened commitment. Stating, "I know that doing this is not much fun; in fact many subjects have told me that it's pretty boring. So I can perfectly understand and accept that you may not find it very interesting" conveyed respect for the person's inclinations and right to choose.

Wise parents strengthen their children's commitment to moral values, such as honesty, by providing them with just enough reason to do the right thing. As Robert Cialdini (2001) observes, a powerful threat like "It's bad to lie, honey, so if I catch you at it, I'll cut your tongue out" will be effective as long as you are present. A subtler approach that provides only enough reason for the child to tell the truth—"Things go more smoothly when people are honest"—is more likely to strengthen conscience. In addition, teachers and parents who communicate empathy by saying "I know that it's not fun for you to spend time picking up your room" convey that the children's feelings are legitimate and not necessarily inconsistent with doing the activity.

4. **Enact commitments.** Sometimes we need to "just do it." We strengthen our commitments not only by changing our thoughts but also by altering our actions (Myers, 2002). Psychologists have long recognized that not only does belief shape behavior, but behavior shapes belief (Wilson, 2011). Sometimes actions even precede commitments. Consider the following:

- Doing a favor for another person, including tutoring a student, increases liking of that person (Blanchard & Cook, 1976).

- When asked, voters almost always indicate they will vote. Compared with voters who are not asked, voters who express their intentions are significantly more likely to vote (Greenwald et al., 1987).

- Older children who teach a moral norm to younger children subsequently follow the moral code better themselves (Parke, 1974).
- People who agreed (everyone asked did) to wear a lapel pin publicizing a Cancer Society drive were later twice as likely to donate (Pliner et al., 1974).

As Sir Thomas More suggested in *A Man For All Seasons*, we come to know ourselves through our own actions. "I write," said the famous author Flannery O'Connor, "because I don't know what I think until I read what I say" (cited by Cytowic, 1993, p. 213).

5. **Go public.** If we make our commitments public, we are more likely to keep them. We want to appear consistent not only to ourselves but to others. Society rightly values integrity. When Charles DeGaulle was asked why his announcement to quit his heavy smoking obliged him to quit forever, he proudly proclaimed, "DeGaulle cannot go back on his word." It is no wonder that many weight-reduction clinics require their clients to write down their weight-loss goal and show it to as many friends, relatives, and neighbors as possible. This simple strategy sometimes works when all else has failed (Cialdini, 2001).

6. **Set priorities.** Our specific strivings and commitments sometimes conflict with one another. If so, we need to set priorities. If we are committed to too many things, we end up being committed to none. Lewis Smedes (1987) notes that some people "are committed to commitment, or to their run at praise for being highly committed people."

When Mark Starr (2003) asked premier figure skater Michelle Kwan about her commitment to her sport, she wisely responded: "Skating can take control of your life. I've learned that you have to take control—to try to balance having a boyfriend, going to school, friends, and family. Skating is a huge part of my life, but the rest is just as important. Skating is not going to keep you company. It's not going to make you laugh. The ice doesn't talk to you."

7. **Review commitments.** Commitments serve us well by giving our lives direction. We are more efficient when we don't have to revisit the merits of every action. But periodically we do need to review our prior decisions and actions. If we don't do so, we can end up pursing activities that no longer interest or challenge us—in other words, if we take no real pleasure in them any longer, why dedicate ourselves and our time and energy to them? At the end of his life, Nazi Albert Speer, architect of the Third Reich asked, "How could I have given my life to this monstrous evil?" He provided his own answer: "I committed myself early on and never allowed myself to examine or criticize my commitment" (Smedes, 1987, p. 51). Sometimes commitments should be broken. Imagine how many people choose a job or career because someone told them it would "make a lot of money" or "carry prestige" or "provide security," only

to discover their work provides no challenge, no meaning, and no real sense of purpose?

Robert Cialdini (2009) shows how professionals who use compliance techniques sometimes manipulate us by securing a commitment from us that serves their own ends, not our own. A good example is the low-ball technique. Car dealers may get a customer to commit to buying a new car because of its low price. In completing the sales forms, the salesperson removes the price advantage by charging for options the buyer thought were included, or by checking with the sales manager, who disallows the deal: "We would be losing money." Because of their initial commitment, customers accept a higher price than they would have agreed to at the outset. Cialdini recommends that we always ask ourselves, "Knowing what I now know about the real price, if I go back in time, would I make the same choice again?"

8. **Maintain hope.** We are most likely to persevere when a striving is meaningful and we believe that the objective is attainable. Hope enables us to endure temporary setbacks. Our interpretation of negative events plays a crucial role in continued commitment to our strivings. Hope reflects willpower—the motivation to keep moving toward our goals—and waypower—the perceived ability to generate routes to achieve them. Hope nourishes commitment, and commitment fosters hope.

Many thought Michelle Kwan's second failure to win a gold medal in the 2002 Olympics would end one of America's greatest skating careers. Younger and talented rivals were positioned to replace her as the grande dame of the ice. But Kwan remained hopeful. When asked, "Do the two Olympic losses weigh heavily?" she responded, "I don't think so. I've had so many great years of skating, it doesn't all ride on two Olympic competitions." She went on to whip her younger rivals for her seventh national championship and her fifth world title in 2003.

9. **Use structured, voluntary activities.** Reed Larson (2000) suggests that we need to provide adolescents with more opportunities to learn *initiative*. The devotion of cumulative effort over time to achieve a goal, Larson argues, is a key component of creativity, leadership, altruism, and civic engagement. Neither traditional schoolwork nor unstructured leisure provide the ideal conditions for learning commitment.

In doing schoolwork, adolescents report low levels of intrinsic motivation. Adults typically control the structure of academic work. Although adolescents may report strong intrinsic motivation during unstructured leisure, often it is not associated with high concentration or challenge. For example, watching TV, being online, and interacting with friends consume a huge proportion of the average adolescent's waking hours. So the context best suited for the development of commitment, suggests Larson (2000), is structured voluntary activities such as sports and the arts. These activities occur within a structure of constraints, rules, and specific goals. Students are likely to learn and practice commitment where they value the activity and where they must invest time and effort in achieving some skill. Participation in school extracurricular activities is associated with higher self-esteem, feelings of control over one's life, lower rates of delinquency, and higher educational aspirations.

The Road to Resilience

Commitment involves dedication and goal pursuit. But what happens when people are confronted by a challenging or even traumatic life event, such as a serious accident, a natural disaster, or some form of loss? Some people display a trait known as resilience in the face of such challenges. *Resilience* refers to an individual's capacity to recover and even flourish following some tumultuous life event. People who are resilient cope well with threats and manage to hold on to, mend, and even heighten their mental and physical health (Ryff & Singer, 2003). Resilient responses have been examined as people deal with divorce, alcoholism, mental illness, war, and the death of relatives and close others (e.g., Bonanno, 2004, 2009). Outside observers might conclude that the threatening events were so severe that anyone would be expected to collapse emotionally or physically under the pressure—yet some people press on through the calamities and emerge much stronger than before.

Table 6.1 Ten Actions for Cultivating Resilience

1. Always keep a hopeful outlook for the future.

2. Think of yourself in positive ways.

3. Put problems and challenges in proper perspective—don't let them overwhelm you.

4. Be vigilant for situations that allow you to engage in self-discovery.

5. As much as possible, be decisive and try to solve problems by using task-focused coping.

6. Promote positive connections between yourself and family members, friends, and community members.

7. Don't catastrophize when facing a daunting challenge or an unexpected problem—most threats can be overcome.

8. Accept the fact that change is an inevitable part of life.

9. Always move forward so as to achieve your goals.

10. Engage in positive self-care by paying close attention to what you need and how you feel.

Source: American Psychological Association

If resilience is a trait, does that mean that some people are born with it and others lack it? Not necessarily. Psychologists believe that although resilience is trait-like, people can learn to cultivate it. Table 6.1 lists 10 things people can do to try develop resilience so that when an unexpected challenge comes along, they will be prepared to deal with it. Take a look at the list shown in Table 6.1. How many of these behaviors do you already routinely perform? Which others can you cultivate from this point forward?

⇒ IN REVIEW

Finding meaning in our strivings and transforming our "shoulds" to "wants" strengthens commitment. Lasting commitments are chosen, enacted, and made public. Periodically, we need to review our commitments and set priorities. Hope strengthens commitment, and adolescents may best learn initiative through structured voluntary activities. Resilience, too, can be learned if we are willing to take steps to develop it.

Happiness

Assessing Happiness

Satisfying Life Experiences

Pursuing Happiness

Happiness is the meaning and the purpose of life, the whole aim and end of human existence. —ARISTOTLE (384–322 B.C.)

Happiness is not something ready made. It comes from your own actions. —DALAI LAMA, 1998

Everything we do, suggested Aristotle, is motivated by our drive to experience happiness. In fact, he argued, it is the supreme good. We pursue health, fame, and wealth because we think they will make us happy. But the Dalai Lama also reminds us of another compelling quality of happiness. Being happy can very much depend on our actions, on what we do in our daily lives, especially when it comes to doing things for other people. Both quotes suggest that we seek happiness as an end in itself.

Test the idea with this mental challenge: Imagine someone could grant you fame and fortune or happiness. You could have the world's respect and own everything you could dream of but be without happiness. Or you could live each day joyfully, having only your basic needs met. Which would you pick (Fordyce, 1977)?

For virtually everyone, it's no contest: Happiness wins hands down. No wonder that college students report thinking of happiness often, rating it 6.58 on a scale of 1 to 7, where 1 is "of no importance" and 7 is "extraordinarily important and valuable" (Diener, 2000). College students from 47 diverse nations rated happiness as the most important and valued domain, one that surpassed love, health, and wealth—it was even rated higher than "getting into heaven" (Diener, 2000). In almost every culture that researchers have examined, happiness ranks as one of life's most cherished goals (Diener, 2012; Lyubomirsky, 2001).

What about for you? Where does happiness rank in your life?

Assessing Happiness

The following scale was designed to gather data on people's general satisfaction with life (Diener et al., 1985a). Try it yourself.

Satisfaction with Life Scale

There are five statements with which you may agree or disagree. Using the scale provided, indicate your agreement with each item by placing the appropriate number on the line preceding that item. Please be open and honest in your responses.

7 = Strongly agree   6 = Agree   5 = Slightly agree   4 = Neither agree nor disagree
3 = Slightly disagree   2 = Disagree   1 = Strongly disagree

_____ **1.** In most ways my life is close to my ideal.

_____ **2.** The conditions of my life are excellent.

_____ **3.** I am satisfied with my life.

_____ **4.** So far I have gotten the important things I want in life.

_____ **5.** If I could live my life over, I would change almost nothing.

Source: Diener et al., 1985a.

Add up your answers to the five items to obtain your total score. Scores can range from 5 to 35. Scores above the midpoint of 20 suggest satisfaction with life. As we will see in the next section, most folks are pretty satisfied!

In daily life, most of us use the word "happiness" to refer to our individual, positive, subjective states of being, and most of us assume that "being happy" is truly an individual experience, though it is one we can talk about with others. Psychologists and other social scientists prefer a somewhat more technical term to characterize these experiences—that term is "subjective well-being." *Subjective well-being*, a person's current status in the social world, is based on combining positive affect (that is, the person is not experiencing negative affect) with general life satisfaction (appreciating life's benefits and rewards) (Diener, 2000; Diener, Oishi, & Lucas, 2009). When researchers write about subjective well-being, they are essentially referring to people's happiness.

Are Most People Happy?

Is life a tragedy? Sophocles thought so. "Not to be born surpasses thought and speech (1962, p. 1225)," he observed. "The second best is to have seen the light and then to go back quickly whence we came." Centuries later, Rousseau agreed: "...our pains greatly exceed our pleasures: so that, all things considered, human life is not at all a valuable gift (1754, p. 119)." Similarly, in his classic work *Civilization and Its Discontents*, Sigmund Freud observed that "Life, as we find it, is too hard for us, it brings us too many pains, disappointments and impossible tasks (1930/1961, p. 23)." Sentiments like these invite many questions about the nature and sustainability of happiness.

So, how happy are people? Below are some faces expressing various feelings (Andrews & Withey, 1976). Which face comes closest to expressing how you feel about your life as a whole?

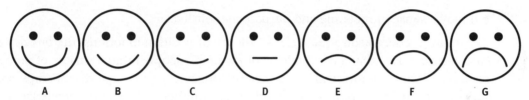

Springer, Plenum. Social indicators of well-being: Americans' perception of life quality, Appendix A, 1976, p.13, Frank M. Andrews, Stephen B. Withey, With permission of Springer Science + Business Media.

Which face do most respondents select? Contrary to the idea that most people are unhappy, a whopping 92 percent of respondents in the United States picked a happy face (Myers, 2000). Nearly two-thirds picked A or B.

And how do people score on the Satisfaction with Life Scale? Most Americans score in the 21 to 25 range. In other words, you would need a score above 25 to be more satisfied than most Americans. A Harris poll (Reilly & Simmons, 2003) reported that 57 percent of Americans indicated that they were "very satisfied" with life, and 34 percent said they were "fairly satisfied." A relatively small 6 percent were "not very satisfied," and a miniscule 2 percent were "not at all satisfied."

Americans are not uniquely happy. Research from around the world suggests that most people are happy. Although cultural differences exist—the Swiss are happier than Bulgarians, and Danes seem happier than South Koreans—people of most nations average above the midpoint on happiness scales (Diener, 2000).

Still the idea that *others* are probably not happy persists. For example, more than two-thirds of respondents in Minnesota rated their capacity for happiness to be in the upper 35 percent of people their own age and sex (Lykken, 1999). Despite the pessimistic views of Sophocles, Rousseau, and Freud, most people see themselves as even happier than the popular, powerful, and wise!

Why Be Happy?

The benefits of happiness extend beyond the enjoyment of good feelings. In fact, research indicates that joy pays major physical and psychological dividends.

Compared with their dour counterparts, happy people (Diener & Scollon, 2014; Seligman, 2002):

- Are healthier and live longer
- Are more productive at work and have higher incomes
- Are more tolerant and creative and make decisions more easily
- Select more challenging goals, persist longer, and perform better in a variety of laboratory tasks
- Demonstrate greater empathy, have more close friends, and enjoy better marriages
- Have strong immune functioning and healthy cardiovascular systems
- Enjoy a sense of meaning and purpose to their lives

Barbara Frederickson's (2001, 2007) theory of positive emotions, the *broaden and build theory*, states that a certain level of joy helps people build a variety of personal resources. Some are physical (skills, health, longevity) and social (friendships, social support networks) resources, while others are intellectual (expert knowledge, intellectual complexity) and psychological (resilience, optimism, creativity). Her theory emphasizes that positive emotions strengthen resources that are drawn on throughout life to improve coping and our odds of survival.

Happiness, then, can have potentially long-term consequences for well-being. Harker and Keltner (2001) wondered if happiness assessed at one point in time could predict life satisfaction later on—much later on. The intriguing aspect of their study is that they examined women's smiles, analyzing 114 photographs from the 1958 and 1960 yearbooks of Mills College, a private school for women in Oakland, California. The women from these classes are part of a longitudinal study on the effect of important life events on psychosocial adjustment. Although almost all the women were smiling in their photos, some of their smiles were genuine or authentic smiles (which psychologists refer to as "Duchenne smiles") while the others were inauthentic, posed, or forced smiles ("non-Duchenne smiles"). You probably can recognize the difference between a real, warm smile you receive from someone as compared with a false smile, and Harker and Keltner trained a group of coders to discern one from the other. Compared with the non-Duchenne group, women with genuine smiles in their early 20s displayed lower negative emotionality, higher competence, and more affiliation with others when they were ages 27, 43, and 52. Those with genuine smiles also demonstrated consistently higher levels of personal well-being and satisfaction with their lives, as well as lower levels of psychological and physical problems than their false-smile counterparts.

Now, correlation does not imply causation—no variables were manipulated here nor was there any random assignment to group—but these results are interesting because they suggest that positive emotionality, as assessed through facial expressions, can have long-term consequences, including stronger social and psychological resources for coping with life's challenges. A little thing like a smile may not seem like much—most of us give and receive them every day, many times a day—thus, we may overlook their connection to happiness.

Perhaps we need to recognize the little things like smiling that promote happiness. Robert Louis Stevenson was likely right when he said, "There is no duty we so much underrate as the duty of being happy. By being happy, we sow anonymous benefits upon the world (Stevenson & Phelps, 2008, p. 40)." The "feel-good do-good effect" is in fact now a well-established psychological principle. Genuine smiles may indeed indicate the presence of personal well-being. People who are in a good mood not only display more empathy, they are also more helpful. Happy people are less self-focused, like others more, and try to spread their good cheer.

Who Is Happy?

Helen Keller said, "Your success and happiness lie in you. External conditions are the accidents of life, its outer trappings (1920, p. 110)." Was she right? What do you think? Are there are also important demographic predictors of well-being?

CRITICAL THINKING

Happiness

Complete the following true-or-false quiz.

T F **1.** Men have a greater sense of well-being than do women.

T F **2.** The teen and elderly years are the least happy times of life.

T F **3.** More years of formal education are linked with a more joyful life.

T F **4.** White people are happier than members of minority race groups.

T F **5.** By and large, the single life is happier than the married life.

T F **6.** Compared with religiously active people, the nonreligious tend to enjoy a greater sense of well-being.

T F **7.** In North America and Europe, those with higher annual incomes, and especially the very rich, live happier lives.

Researchers have addressed all of these issues, and all of the above statements are false!

Gender provides little clue to happiness levels. Although women may be more susceptible to depression and anxiety, and men more are more apt to have antisocial disorders or become alcoholic, numerous studies indicate that the genders are equally likely to report being "very happy" and "satisfied" with their lives.

Like gender, age tells little about a person's level of happiness. Contrary to the conventional wisdom that adolescent stress or physical decline in old age makes a person miserable, repeated surveys show that people of all ages report similar feelings of well-being. Unhappiness does not surge in women during menopause or when children leave home. (The "empty nest" for most parents is actually a happy place.) Nor do most people go through a midlife crisis. One study of nearly 10,000 men and women found "not the slightest evidence" that distress peaks in the early forties (McCrae & Costa, 1990).

Years of formal education, IQ, and race are not significant predictors of happiness either. "People who go to work in their overalls and on the bus," concludes David Lykken (1999, p. 17), "are just as happy, on the average, as those in suits who drive to work in their own Mercedes." Studies in both North America and Europe show that education and race account for very little of the person-to-person variation in happiness. For example, in spite of decades of disadvantage, African-Americans report about the same sense of well-being as do white Americans.

Surveys of both Americans and Europeans report that married people who are heterosexual feel happier and have more life satisfaction than do those who are single or widowed, especially compared with those who are divorced or separated. For example, among the thousands of Americans surveyed by the National Opinion Research Center over the past 30 years, 40 percent of married adults declared themselves very happy, almost double the 24 percent of never-married adults who said the same (Seligman, 2002). Data from national surveys in 19 countries confirm this marriage–happiness link. The idea that the marriage–happiness link is gender specific—strongly predictive of men's but not women's happiness—is also a myth. Throughout the Western world, both heterosexual men and women report more life satisfaction than those never married, or those who are divorced or separated. (However, there is also evidence that single people are not less happy than married people, which means we should be cautious in presuming the link between marriage and happiness is absolute; see DePaulo, 2006; DePaulo & Morris, 2005).

Active religious practices are also linked with happier and healthier lives. In reviewing the research on faith and well-being, David Myers (2000) notes how active religiosity is associated with several mental health criteria. Actively religious North Americans are much less likely than the nonreligious to become delinquent, to abuse drugs and alcohol, to divorce, or to commit suicide. The religiously devout also seem to cope with stress more effectively. Compared with religiously inactive widows, recently widowed women who attend worship services regularly report more life satisfaction. People of faith also tend to retain or regain greater happiness after going through a divorce, unemployment, or a serious illness. For the elderly, the two best predictors of life satisfaction seem to be health and religiousness.

Basic needs must be met for us to be happy. However, once we have life's necessities, income makes little difference. For example, in those nations whose gross national product is more than $8000 per person, there is little relationship between wealth and well-being. Moreover, within wealthier countries such as the United

States and Canada, the correlation between income and personal happiness, reports Ronald Inglehart (1990, p. 242), "is surprisingly weak (indeed virtually negligible)." A survey of the *Forbes* 400 list of the wealthiest Americans found the very rich to be only slightly happier than the average American (Diener et al., 1985b). In fact, 37 percent were less happy.

What other factors fail to predict happiness (e.g., Dunn & Brody, 2008)? Physical attractiveness—how good-looking you are—too, has no impact on happiness. Having children is presumed to make life complete but children's presence is not associated with more happiness. Even living in an ideal climate or a lovely part of the world does not ensure happiness.

Given that age, gender, race, educational level, intelligence, income, appearance, parental status, and climate play little role in our happiness, might we gain better clues from knowing people's personality traits?

CRITICAL THINKING

Personality and Happiness

Think of a person you know well who seems especially happy. Identify at least three of that person's distinguishing traits:

_____

_____

_____

_____

_____

When asked to name one condition for happiness, psychologist Ed Diener (Elias, 2002) responded, "The happiest people all seem to have good friends." When Diener and Martin Seligman (2002) studied very happy people—those who scored about 30 on the Satisfaction with Life Scale at the start of this chapter—they found that they were highly social. In contrast to those who were only moderately happy or very unhappy, the happiest people spent the least amount of time alone and the most time socializing. Outside observers rated the happiest people highest in interpersonal relationships. So, having close, enjoyable social relationships contributes a great deal to people's happiness (Diener & Biswas-Diener, 2008). This should probably not come as a surprise, given that people are such social animals.

Indeed, *extroverts* are generally happier than *introverts*. They are sociable, outgoing people. Extroverts are more successful in meeting the fundamental need to belong.

Happy people have both the desire and the ability to foster strong social relationships. This motivation and competence seems linked to their basic *trust* in others. They assume the best, seeing others as fundamentally honest and trustworthy. In contrast, those who are skeptical, cynical, and assume that others may be dishonest or dangerous tend to be unhappy. Extroverts' greater sensitivity to positive information also seems to foster their sense of well-being. Told that they have done well on a test or to imagine they have won a lottery, they are happier than introverts given the same news. Interestingly, extroverts' and introverts' reactions to negative news (hearing about a poor test performance or imagining being expelled from school) are the same (Larsen & Ketelaar, 1991).

Happy people are also *conscientious.* One study of the happy personality found that the trait of conscientiousness was the strongest positive correlate of life satisfaction (DeNeve & Cooper, 1998). The researchers suggest that engaging in goal-directed activity—exerting control over ourselves and our environment—enhances quality of life. Conscientious people set higher goals for themselves and tend to achieve more in work settings. When they are very challenged and have the skills to meet the challenge, they are especially likely to report *flow*, an optimal experience we will focus on later in this chapter.

Linked closely to conscientiousness is a sense of *personal control*. In reviewing the University of Michigan's nationwide surveys, Angus Campbell (1981, p. 218) concluded that "having a strong sense of controlling one's life is a more dependable predictor of positive feelings of well-being than any of the objective conditions of life we have considered." Those with a strong desire for control are assertive, decisive, and are more likely to attain their personal goals. They take credit for their successes but also accept responsibility for their failures.

Happy people also enjoy high *self-esteem* (Schimmack & Diener, 2002). They like themselves. People who feel good about themselves are less susceptible to insomnia and ulcers, are more persistent after failure, and are less likely to conform. The University of Michigan surveys (Campbell, 1981) have shown that satisfaction with self is a more powerful predictor of well-being in America than is satisfaction with family life, friendships, or income. Self-esteem is, however, a stronger predictor of well-being in countries that value personal autonomy, such as the United States and Europe, than in collectivist cultures such as China, Korea, and India, where people think more about how their families are doing.

Have you noticed the common thread that runs through these personality characteristics? Happy people tend to make optimistic interpretations in everyday life. They see the best in others, in their work, and in themselves. Optimists don't deny their setbacks but rather seem to interpret them differently. Because they are convinced that effort and self-discipline make a difference, they believe the future is bright. They are hardy individuals who use more effective coping strategies in managing stress. Ironically, those who deny threatening life events and the existence of negative emotions are among the unhappiest (DeNeve, 1999).

⇒ I N   R E V I E W

> Happiness is one of life's most important goals. Happy people live longer, are more productive, and enjoy better interpersonal relations. Most people report relatively high levels of life satisfaction. Gender, age, race, formal education, and income level seem to make little difference in people's level of happiness. On the other hand, those who are married, actively religious, extroverted, conscientious, and self-confident express more life satisfaction.

Satisfying Life Experiences

Some psychologists have attempted to understand happiness by studying specific life experiences or events that promote our subjective well-being.

 **SELF-ASSESSMENT**

Satisfying Life Event

Consider the past month of your life. Think back to the important occurrences of this period of time. Bring to mind the single most personally satisfying event that you experienced. Use your own definition of "satisfying." That is, think of "satisfying" in whatever way makes sense to you. Take a couple of minutes to come up with a very impactful experience and then describe it (Sheldon et al., 2001).

1. _____
2. _____
3. _____
4. _____

What do people find most satisfying? Ken Sheldon and his colleagues (2001) report that American students most commonly recount experiences in which they felt a strong sense of self-respect, successfully completed a difficult task, experienced emotional intimacy with other people, or had been free to do things their own way. They were less likely to report their most satisfying experiences as having involved buying the things they wanted, physical pleasure, or exercising strong influence over others' beliefs and behaviors. When people reflect on their most satisfying experiences, they think primarily of times when they felt worthy, competent, related to others, or free of external pressure. Our experiences of position, pleasure, or power are less important.

This pattern seems to hold across time and place. Sheldon found that this same order emerged when he asked people to reflect on a shorter period of time ("Think of the most satisfying experience in the past week") as well as a much longer period ("Think of the most satisfying experience in the entire semester"). South Koreans offered similar reflections. Compared with their American counterparts, however, South Koreans were somewhat more likely to report that feelings of relatedness were a crucial aspect of their most satisfying life events and somewhat less likely to identify self-esteem as being important.

Tim Kasser and Richard Ryan (1993, 1996) wondered if prominent elements of the American dream—striving to become rich, famous, and attractive—really foster happiness. In a series of studies, they examined how different aspirations were related to well-being. Adults, including college students, rated the relative importance and likelihood of attaining seven different goals. They also ranked the goals in terms of how much each one was a "guiding principle" in their lives. Results indicated that strivings for financial success, social recognition, and an appealing appearance were associated with lower vitality, less self-actualization (fulfillment of one's potential), and more physical distress. In contrast, the pursuit of self-acceptance, affiliation, community feeling (helpfulness), and physical fitness were linked with greater psychological and physical well-being. Kasser and Ryan concluded: There may well be a "dark side to the American dream" (see also Kasser, 2002). Ed Diener agrees: "Materialism is toxic for happiness" (Elias, 2002).

We know this and yet we don't. Most of us agree—you can't buy happiness. Still, we are not so sure. In a University of Michigan survey, people were asked what would improve the quality of their life. The first and most frequent answer was "more money" (Campbell, 1981). Early in the twenty-first century, to fulfill their dreams, Americans claimed they needed an annual income of $102,000 (Myers, 2000). (Inflation may well have increased the dollar amount people report now, but the desire for more money, not the figure per se, is the issue.) Moreover, nearly three-quarters of college freshman consider being "very well-off financially" to be a "very important" or "essential" goal. Among 19 possible objectives, they ranked it highest, well ahead of "developing a meaningful philosophy of life," "raising a family," or "becoming an authority in my field."

CRITICAL THINKING

Identifying Opportunities for Prosocial Spending

Money and materialism do not bring us happiness—we know that—but is there any way we can use our material wealth to promote our well-being? Recent evidence suggests that we can put money to work in ways that will make us a bit happier. Dunn, Gilbert, and Wilson (2011) suggest that choosing to spend money in three ways can lead to increased happiness. First, buying experiences (remember those satisfying life events, especially when others are present), such as attending plays, movies, concerts, festivals, and so on, provide more benefits than does purchasing material goods (e.g., clothes, trinkets, gadgets). Spending money on smaller pleasures—tea with a friend, a rich dessert—is more satisfying than going after big-ticket items, such as a new car, an expensive bicycle, or even a new tablet or smartphone. More stuff is just that—more stuff. Third, using our funds to somehow benefit others rather than ourselves—treating a friend to dinner or a show, donating money to a charity, giving a thoughtful or needed gift to a loved one—can heighten our happiness (Dunn, Aknin, & Norton, 2008).

This third option is rife with possibility, as it clearly operates as a means to promote those close relationships we all enjoy with others. One set of studies found that people who spent money on others (whether it was $5 or $20) ended up being much happier than those who were directed to spend the money on themselves (Dunn, Aknin, & Norton, 2008). The investigators also found that people who give a larger part of their income to charities turn out to be much happier than those who spend their capital on themselves (see also Aknin et al., 2010).

What is the underlying power of this prosocial spending? Why does it lead to more happiness for the spenders? When we give to or do things for others, our actions on their behalf make us feel like caring, responsible, and giving people (Dunn & Norton, 2013); we become what we do behaviorally. Further, what we do—spending our money on others—creates stronger bonds with them, which again highlights the favorable affective impact of strong social connections with others. Quite simply, we end up feeling good about ourselves (Anik et al., 2011) while others feel good about our actions toward them.

Can you generate a list of prosocial spending opportunities for yourself? Write them on the lines below and resolve to carry at least one of them out in the next week or so. Once you do, reflect on how you feel about the experience: Does spending on behalf of others enhance your happiness?

_____

_____

_____

_____

Flow in Work and Leisure

Have you ever "lost" yourself in an engaging or interesting activity? Mihaly Csikszentmihalyi (1990; Ullén et al., 2012) claims that what makes experiences genuinely satisfying is a state of consciousness called *flow*, in which our concentration is so focused that it amounts to absolute absorption in an activity. "This is happiness," said American novelist Willa Cather, "to be dissolved into something completely great." Consider your own experience with flow in the following activity.

Flow

Do you ever get involved in something so deeply that nothing else seems to matter and you lose track of time?

Often _____   Sometimes _____   Rarely _____   Never or don't know _____

If you have had such an experience, briefly describe it.

_____

_____

_____

_____

_____

Now think about how you felt while engaged in the experience and answer the questions below. Using the following scale, select the number that best describes your experience.

1 = Strongly disagree   2 = Disagree   3 = Neither agree nor disagree
4 = Agree   5 = Strongly agree

_____ **1.** My attention was focused entirely on what I was doing.

_____ **2.** I felt in total control of what I was doing.

_____ **3.** Time seemed to alter (either slowed down or speeded up).

Source: Jackson & Marsh, 1996, items 5, 6, and 8, p. 34.

These are sample items from a longer scale that measures the degree to which individuals experience flow. These three items are representative of the kinds of things people say they feel and do when engaged and absorbed in an activity. If you took the longer scale, the more items that you agreed with, the closer you would come to experiencing flow.

As an "optimal experience," flow is intrinsically rewarding. When they enter the flow state, most people report becoming less self-aware and that they lose all track of time while their energies and attention are focused on some engaging task.

Csikzentmihalyi formulated the flow concept after studying artists who worked with enormous concentration. Immersed in a project, they would work as if nothing else mattered and then would promptly forget about it once it was finished. The work was so engrossing and enjoyable that it was worth doing for its own sake, even though it may have had no consequence outside itself.

Do only highly skilled and creative people experience flow? No, ordinary folks fully absorbed and engaged in a favorite activity report the flow experience. When a representative sample of Americans was asked what you were just asked ("Do you ever get involved in something so deeply that nothing else seems to matter, and you lose track of time?"), about one in five said that this happens to them often, as much as several times a day. Only 15 percent said that this never happens (Csikszentmihalyi, 1997). Cross-cultural comparisons suggest these frequencies are quite stable and universal.

Flow comes in playing touch football, repairing a broken appliance, preparing a good meal, conversing with friends, dealing with customers, and even driving a car. One college student even seemed to find it in taking a final exam. He transformed his answer to an essay question into a rap (Frantz, 2003)!

Clearly, flow is not achieved by passively accepting whatever comes our way, or in leisure that's merely relaxing or enjoyable. For example, people rarely report flow when watching TV or while "just sitting relaxing." They do not experience flow if the task they are performing is dull, monotonous, or repetitive, or is one that can be mastered quickly and easily. Similarly, the flow state doesn't occur when a task proves to be uniquely difficult, requiring strenuous concentration. Thus, the flow experience comes with mindful challenge rather than mindless passivity, and whatever the activity entails, it needs to match the person's level of skill.

There are other qualities that describe the flow experience—nine of them are listed below. Look back at the flow experience you wrote about above, at the start of the critical thinking exercise. Which of the following characteristics best describe your experience?

____ **1.** *Challenge–skill balance*. The situational demands match skill level. (Challenges that are too high lead to anxiety. Challenges that are too low lead to boredom.)

____ **2.** *Action–awareness merging*. Engagement in the activity becomes so strong that it becomes spontaneous or automatic.

____ **3.** *Clear goals*. Goals may be set in advance or evolve while engaged in the action.

____ **4.** *Unambiguous feedback*. Immediate and clear feedback provides information about progress.

5. *Concentration.* There is a total focus on the task at hand.

6. *Sense of control.* There is a sense of being in control without actively trying to exert control.

7. *Loss of self-consciousness.* Concern for the self disappears. One is "unself-consciously" involved.

8. *Transformation of time.* Time alters perceptibly, either slowing down or speeding up. Alternatively, time may be out of awareness.

9. *Autotelic experience.* An activity is "autotelic" if it is done for its own sake, with no expectation of reward. In other words, the experience is intrinsically motivating.

For the most part, people are happy not because of what they do, but because of how they do it (Csikszentmihalyi, 1999). Happy people tend to immerse themselves in their daily activities—generally doing things for their own sake rather than to achieve some external reward. Fully absorbed in the current of life, they actively attend to what is happening around them. People seek out flow when they can because it feels good, serves as a motivational source, blocks negative affect, and encourages both commitment to goals and achievement (Nakamura & Csikszentmihalyi, 2009). Feeling flow helps us to notice more and to relish the experience.

The first step in achieving flow is to have a clear goal. Without a goal, it is difficult to concentrate and avoid distraction. The second step is practicing the habit of doing what needs to be done with concentrated focus—with skill rather than inertia. Even routine tasks like washing windows, vacuuming, and driving to work become rewarding when done with focus.

Interpreting Life Events

Abraham Lincoln once observed, "Most people are about as happy as they make up their minds to be (in Crane, 1914)." Was he right? Is it our life experiences or how we interpret them that make the difference? Our earlier examination of personality traits and happiness suggested that our interpretations can be important.

We all know people who just seem upbeat. They see the world through rose-tinted glasses, discover the silver lining in the worst of times, and find happiness in everyday occurrences. Others seem chronically unhappy. Nothing is ever right, they always feel the thorns in the roses, and each day seems to bring disaster (Lyubomirsky, 2001). What is the real difference between these two types of people? We'll address that question by considering how people differ in their levels of maximizing, regret, savoring, and gratitude.

Maximization and Regret

In considering life's many choices—from selecting toothpaste to choosing a college— are you more likely to ask, "Is this alternative acceptable?" or "Is this the best?" Are you a *satisficer* or a *maximizer*? The following scale assesses these two contrasting orientations to goals.

Maximization

What about you? Are you a maximizer when it comes to making decisions? Do you sweat every decision, whether it's great or small? Take the below short-form of the Maximization Scale and find out.

Indicate how much you agree with each of the following statements by using the following scale to respond. Write the appropriate number next to each item. Please try not to skip any items.

1	2	3	4	5	6	7
Completely agree						Completely disagree

_____ **1.** No matter how satisfied I am with my job, it's only right for me to be on the lookout for better opportunities.

_____ **2.** When I am in the car listening to the radio, I often check other stations to see if something better is playing, even if I am relatively satisfied with what I'm listening to.

_____ **3.** I often find it difficult to shop for a gift for a friend.

_____ **4.** Renting videos is really difficult. I'm always struggling to pick the best one.

_____ **5.** I never settle for second best.

_____ **6.** No matter what I do, I have the highest standards for myself.

Source: Nenkov et al. (2008).

No items are reverse scored. To obtain a total score, add up the numbers in front of the six statements. Scores can range from 6 to 42. People who score above the median on the scale are typically classified as maximizers; those who score below the median are typically labeled satisficers.

What difference do these contrasting orientations make? In some cases, maximizing is the better strategy for making decisions. For example, in responding to a serious health threat, seeking and settling for only the best treatment increases your chances of survival. Maximizers plan more carefully in solving problems, and their high standards may spur them on to higher achievement, but maximization can come at a significant cost to well-being. The following scale assesses feelings of regret.

Regret

Use the following scale to respond to each statement:

1 = Completely disagree   2 = Disagree   3 = Disagree somewhat   4 = Neither disagree nor agree   5 = Agree somewhat   6 = Agree   7 = Completely agree

_____ **1.** Whenever I make a choice, I'm curious about what would have happened if I had chosen differently.

_____ **2.** Whenever I make a choice, I try to get information about how the other alternatives turned out.

_____ **3.** If I make a choice and it turns out well, I still feel like something of a failure if I find out that another choice would have turned out better.

_____ **4.** When I think about how I'm doing in life, I often assess opportunities I have passed up.

_____ **5.** Once I make a decision, I don't look back.

Source: Schwartz et al., 2002, p. 1182.

Reverse the number you gave to item 5 (i.e., 1 = 7, 2 = 6, 3 = 5, 4 = 4, 5 = 3, 6 = 2, 7 = 1), then add up the numbers you gave in response to all five items. Scores range from 5 to 35, with those above the midpoint of 20 reflecting a tendency to experience some regret about your life choices.

Schwartz and his team (2002) found that the tendency to want to maximize outcomes is highly correlated with potential regret. In several samples of adults, the researchers also found that maximization was negatively related to happiness, life satisfaction, optimism, and self-esteem. Maximizers seem especially susceptible to two common psychological processes—social comparison and adaptation—that sometimes drain joy from life. And maximizers tend to keep their options open, which can lower life satisfaction.

To some degree, we all compare our life's outcomes with those of others. The gap between what we have and what our friends and neighbors possess can foster feelings of relative deprivation. An important reason why money fails to boost life satisfaction is our strong tendency to compare ourselves with those who have more. Especially as we climb the ladder of success, we tend to compare ourselves with those one rung higher rather than those a rung lower and we often become dissatisfied.

Maximizers, in their eagerness to decide whether they have attained the "best" life outcomes, need some standard for making that judgment. Often, an objective criterion is not available, so they compare themselves with others. Research confirms that, relative to satisficers, maximizers do engage in more social comparison and experience stronger feelings of relative deprivation.

Our remarkable capacity to adapt also short-circuits happiness. Good experiences—a promotion, a new car, gaining entrance to a prestigious school—boost our spirits only briefly. Similarly, bad experiences—a car accident, a rejected job application, a low score on an entrance exam—deflate us, but only temporarily.

Although we may understand the adaptation principle, we underestimate its power. We adapt more quickly than we think. Researchers at the University of Illinois asked people to report on every significant positive or negative experience in the preceding year. If the good or bad events occurred only 3 months back, their effects on present mood were nearly impossible to distinguish. After 6 months, there was no difference between mood prior to the good or bad event and current mood (Suh, Diener, & Fujita, 1996). In a survey of 128 accident victims who had become permanently paralyzed in all four limbs a year or so earlier, researchers found that most described their quality of life as good or excellent. Although many admitted having considered suicide shortly after their injury, only 10 percent now considered their quality of life to be poor (Myers, 2001).

Because they have higher standards of acceptability than do satisficers, maximizers find adaptation more distressing. Given the huge investment they have made in weighing alternatives before making a choice, maximizers feel that they deserve a higher rate of return. Expecting more from every situation, maximizers more often become disappointed.

Finally, maximizers strive to keep their options open. For this they may pay an unanticipated price. Dan Gilbert and Jane Ebert (2002) conducted an intriguing series of studies in which participants made a reversible or an irreversible choice. Participants strongly preferred keeping their options open to having their choice made final. Surprisingly, however, the researchers found that participants were less satisfied with the outcomes of reversible decisions than with those that were irreversible. Why? Perhaps when we make a final decision, we work to convince ourselves that we have made the right choice. In keeping our options open, as maximizers tend to do, we remain ambivalent.

Savoring and Gratitude

Now that you've considered how you may be affected by the way you plan when setting goals, and your levels of regret as a result, examine your style of reflecting on past life events. Consider your levels of savoring and gratitude.

Savoring

Assess each question by selecting the number that best describes your response. To what degree do you savor the present moment?

_____ **1.** When good things have happened in your life, how much do you feel you have typically been able to appreciate or enjoy them?

   1 = Not at all   2 = A little bit   3 = Some   4 = A lot   5 = A great deal

_____ **2.** Compared to most other people you know, how much pleasure have you typically gotten from good things that have happened to you?

   1 = None   2 = A little bit   3 = Some   4 = A lot   5 = A great deal

_____ **3.** When something good happens to you, compared to most other people you know, how long does it usually affect the way you feel? Provide a number ranging from 1 (not for very long) to 7 (for a very long time): _____

_____ **4.** When good things have happened to you, have there ever been times when you felt like everything was really going your way; that is, when you felt on top of the world, or felt a great deal of joy in life, or found it hard to contain your positive feelings? How often would you say you felt like that?

   1 = Many times   2 = Sometimes   3 = Once in a while   4 = Never

_____ **5.** How often would you say that you feel like jumping for joy?

   1 = Never   2 = Rarely   3 = Sometimes   4 = Often

Source: Bryant, 1989, p. 782.

Reverse the number you gave to question 4 (i.e., 1 = 4, 2 = 3, 3 = 2, 4 = 1) and then total your numbers for the five items. Scores can range from 5 to 25, with higher scores reflecting greater savoring of positive outcomes. Undergraduates in an introductory psychology course scored a mean of 18.76.

Most of us describe ourselves as very busy and we are often overcommitted, pulled in different directions by both our responsibilities and our desires. How often do you have the chance to slow down in order to really reflect on what you are doing, feeling, and thinking? In other words, why don't we bother to savor more of our daily experiences?

Savoring refers to a person's ability to focus on, value, and enhance the pleasure associated with almost any experience, no matter how major or minor it might be (Bryant & Veroff, 2007). When we savor, we reflect on the moment or moments linked to some event—we focus on the stages that lead us somewhere and not necessarily on the proverbial destination. This "process, not product" approach allows people to savor a sunrise or sunset, a bracing cup of good coffee, a pleasurable lunch with a pal, a stroll on the beach or through a lovely garden, or a piece of familiar music that reminds us of joyous times in our past.

Let's be clear: Savoring goes beyond simple enjoyment of an activity—there must be reflection involved. Bryant and Veroff (2007) identify several qualities that influence the intensity of savored experiences, including:

- *Duration.* Setting aside dedicated time increases the likelihood that we can savor an experience.

- *Complexity.* Complex experiences—looking at a complex painting, reading an absorbing novel—can deepen our savoring experiences.

- *Stress reduction.* Savoring is more likely to occur if we can distract ourselves from pressing, yet nonetheless stressful, concerns of daily life (e.g., homework, chores to be done).

- *Social connection.* Savoring seems like it should be a solitary activity but often it's best when shared with others. Looking at a rainbow is much more satisfying when there is another person or people there to share the experience.

- *Balanced self-monitoring.* Trying too hard or thinking too much can derail the ease with which we savor an experience. Savoring should be natural, not forced.

By adding clarity and vividness to experience, savoring contributes directly to well-being and happiness (Brown & Ryan, 2003). Making a modest effort to savor has decided psychological benefits. Engaging in savoring can turn us into more relaxed and happier individuals (Jose, Lim, & Bryant, 2012) while also diminishing negative emotions and depressive symptoms (Hurley & Kwon, 2012). We all have the opportunity to savor at one time or another, but are we wise enough to catch the moment?

Without attention and awareness, fleeting but important moments pass us by. In reflecting from the Columbia shuttle a few days before its scheduled landing, mission specialist Laurel Clark described her delight at the simple, unexpected wonder of a sunset in space: "There's a flash; the whole payload bay turns this rosy pink," she observed. "It only lasts about 15 seconds and then it's gone. It's very ethereal and extremely beautiful."

Can you recall having such a moment—a perfect surprise? Oprah Winfrey shared about having experienced such a beautiful moment. And what was it? A walk down a Santa Barbara lane, a hummingbird, and the smell of orange blossoms. It was one of those rare times, she related, when she could say she was truly happy. A mere 10 seconds, suggests Craig Wilson (2003), can stretch a smile for a lifetime.

Noticing and appreciating even small benefits relates to another important attribute of happy people assessed by the following questionnaire.

Gratitude

Use the following scale to respond to each question:

1 = Strongly disagree 2 = Disagree 3 = Slightly disagree 4 = Neutral
5 = Slightly agree 6 = Agree 7 = Strongly agree

_____ **1.** I have so much in life to be thankful for.

_____ **2.** If I had to list everything that I felt grateful for, it would be a very long list.

_____ **3.** When I look at the world, I don't see much to be grateful for.

_____ **4.** I am grateful to a wide variety of people.

_____ **5.** As I get older I find myself more able to appreciate the people, events, and situations that have been part of my life history.

_____ **6.** Long amounts of time can go by before I feel grateful to something or someone.

Source: McCullough et al., 2002.

Reverse the numbers you gave in response to items 3 and 6 (i.e., 1 = 7, 2 = 6, 3 = 5, 4 = 4, 5 = 3, 6 = 2, and 7 = 1), then add up the numbers for all six statements. Scores range from 6 to 42, with higher scores suggesting a more grateful disposition. A sample of 156 undergraduate psychology students obtained a mean score of about 35.

Gratitude is considered to be a virtue. It involves recognizing the good things in daily living and being thankful (often demonstrably so) for them. Gratitude is rooted in the experience of positive outcomes and in seeing oneself as the recipient of another's generosity. In contrast, ingratitude—the act of being ungrateful or failing to be gracious to others—is treated as a personal vice (Bono, Emmons, & McCullough, 2004). The easiest way to feel gratitude is to express a simple but sincere "thank you" to someone, whether a friend, family member, or a complete stranger, in response to a kindness committed on your behalf. The key is genuine sincerity—being and feeling thankful for someone's kindness (Emmons, 2005).

Stretching our attributions for success to include the wide range of people who contribute to our well-being leads us to feel affirmed, esteemed, and valued (McCullough et al., 2002). Such an interpretation boosts our self-esteem and our feelings of social support. Highly grateful people may possess a worldview in which everything they have, indeed life itself, is a gift. Such appreciation helps people to avoid taking benefits for granted. They may be less likely to adapt to positive life circumstances and thus may sustain happiness and well-being over time. Experiencing feelings of gratitude triggers happiness, even joy, and can also provide people with a sense of contentment (Wood, Froh, & Geraghty, 2010).

Research with the gratitude questionnaire identifies several important correlates of a grateful disposition. In addition to experiencing more life satisfaction, grateful people are less prone to negative emotions such as depression, anxiety, and envy. Furthermore, they are more empathic, forgiving, and helpful. Grateful people seem less focused on materialistic goals.

Do these correlations reflect a causal relationship? Does a grateful outlook actually contribute to health and happiness? In one Gallup (1998) survey, American teens and adults certainly thought so. Over 90 percent of the respondents indicated that expressing gratitude helped them to feel happy.

A series of studies asked different groups of volunteers to remember "things in your life you are grateful for," hassles, life events, or "ways in which you are better off than others" (Emmons & McCullough, 2003). Both undergraduate students without disabilities and people with neuromuscular disease participated in the research and kept records of their moods, life satisfaction, physical symptoms, and coping behaviors. Relative to other groups, those with a grateful mindset, regardless of their physical disabilities, exhibited heightened well-being, especially on the measures of positive affect.

The good news is that gratitude is relatively easy to experience in daily life: Just look for opportunities to thank those who are gracious to you and also be vigilant for chances to be kind to others so that they, in turn, can express gratitude. If you are interested in trying your hand at a more structured way to express gratitude, think of someone (e.g., a grandparent, teacher, coach, professor, boss, friend) who did something above and beyond the call of duty to be helpful in your life, perhaps when you were in a rough spot. You may have said "thank you" but perhaps felt it was somehow insufficient. Peterson (2006) recommended writing a *personal gratitude letter* (handwritten, please, not typed—and no emailing or texting) that contains depth and detail aimed at acknowledging your patron's kindness and the depth of your appreciation. Ideally, you should read your letter to the person *in person.* If that's not possible, then mail it. If the person is no longer living, the writing exercise can still be beneficial for you because you are acknowledging a kindness that can never be repaid.

If you prefer a more private approach to developing gratitude, try keeping a gratitude journal for 2 or more weeks (Tsang, Rowatt, & Buechsel, 2008). Take 5 or so minutes in the evening to write about the things you were thankful for during each day. When you can, describe those situations or events that motivated you to feel gratitude and be sure to indicate any specific individuals to whom you felt grateful.

Either of these simple and personal activities can enhance your gratitude. And don't forget why such feelings are important: Grateful people are much happier than those who do not express gratitude (Park, Peterson, & Seligman, 2004).

People report their most satisfying experiences to be the times when they felt worthy, competent, related to others, and free of external pressure. Aspirations of fame, fortune, and image are linked with a lowered sense of well-being. A state of consciousness called flow occurs when our concentration is so focused that we are completely absorbed in an activity. It is most likely to happen when we have clear goals, when the challenge matches our level of skill, and when we receive immediate feedback.

People's perceptions of their lives are more important to their well-being than are objective circumstances. The desire to maximize all of our outcomes decreases our life satisfaction and is often associated with feelings of regret. Savoring life's best moments fosters joy. Those who have a grateful outlook on life and see themselves as the recipients of others' generosity report greater positive feelings.

Pursuing Happiness

Back in Chapter 1 of this book, we learned that psychologist Sonja Lyubomirsky (2008) found that a person's happiness is determined by three factors (recall the "happiness pie"): An individual happiness set point that remains stable across time (some of us are naturally happier than others, some less so), which accounts for 50% of our happiness; another 10% is due to our life circumstances (whether we are attractive or not, rich or poor, married or divorced, well or unhealthy, and so on); and the last 40% is attributable to intentional activities or the things we do that can increase (or decrease) happiness. In effect, 60% of our happiness is more or less beyond our control—but 40% is subject to change, that is, we can do things to make ourselves (and often those close to us) happier. But we have to be intentional and exert effort in the process. Here are some research-based recommendations for intentional acts that you can undertake in order to increase your happiness:

1. *Don't confuse well-being with being well-off.* Don't equate stuff with success. Remember: A growing income, along with all it can purchase, is associated with little in the way of increased well-being. We quickly adapt to our changing circumstances, including income increases, and only notice momentary variations from it. Rather, acknowledge the joy of nonmaterial experiences. "When you're outside at night with your kids," counsels Jane Hammerslough, "say 'I love it when the stars are out and the snow looks so beautiful.' Put emphasis on things that aren't stuff—on the nonpurchasable" (cited in Hamilton, 2001).

2. *Make wise comparisons.* Research suggests that as we climb the ladder of success we tend to compare ourselves with those a rung or two above. Choose not

to. Instead, compare yourself with those who have less. Psychologist Abraham Maslow (1972, p. 108) suggested, "All you have to do is to go to a hospital and hear all the simple blessings that people never before realized were blessings—being able to urinate, to sleep on your side, to be able to swallow, to scratch an itch, etc. Could exercises in deprivation educate us faster about all our blessings?" Even imagining others' misfortune produces renewed life satisfaction (Dermer, 1979). College women who merely viewed vivid depictions of how grim life was in 1900 or who imagined and then wrote about various personal tragedies such as being burned or disfigured expressed more life satisfaction.

3. *Keep a gratitude journal.* Savor the present moment and say thank you often. When you say thank you, argues Hammerslough, "you're reminding yourself that something good has come to you" (Hamilton, 2001). In her book *Simple Abundance*, Sarah Ban Breathnach (1995) suggests that each night you write down five things that happened that day for which you are thankful. These need not be major surprises or achievements but simple gifts such as finding a good parking space, enjoying a sunny day, meeting a work deadline, tasting a delicious dessert, or watching a child laugh. Robert Emmons found that those who did this in daily or even weekly journals were not only more joyful they were healthier, less stressed, more optimistic, and more likely to help others (Morris, 2001).

4. *Discover your flow.* Keep a diary of the high points and low points of each day. Notice patterns. We all experience life differently. An important step in improving the quality of our lives is to pay close attention to what we do every day and to notice how we feel doing different things, in different places, at different times, and with different people (Csikszentmihalyi, 1997). It may be helpful to experiment with one's surroundings, activities, and companions. There may be surprises. It may be that you really like being alone, that you like work more than you thought, that grocery shopping is really not so bad, that reading makes you feel better than watching television, that socializing with friends is actually more satisfying than going to the movies. When it becomes clear which activities produce the high points for you, increase their frequency.

5. *Finish what you start and wholly experience it along the way.* Be conscientious and accomplish something every day. Strive for excellence, not necessarily perfection. Heed Father Laurence's sage advice (Monks of New Skete, 1999, p. 311):

Being happy means entering wholeheartedly into everything—no matter what kind of challenge it presents, no matter what the possible difficulties involved—entering into it body, soul, mind, and spirit. We have to enter into it in such a way that we're no longer separate from what we're doing. We forget ourselves at the same time that we give ourselves completely. And when we do enter into life totally and completely, then, if we stop and reflect for just a moment, we'll notice that somehow we're beginning to experience happiness. This is what we're made for.

David Niven (2001) relates how a Chicago Transit Authority motorman has made his work a true expression of himself. Victor loves his job. "Thank you for riding with me this evening on Electric Avenue. Don't lean against the doors, I don't want to lose you," he tells his passengers as the train departs. He points out all the interesting sites and identifies the connecting buses in the street below. "Our equipment may be junky," the veteran motorman admits, "but for a dollar-fifty, I want to give a Lincoln Town Car ride." Victor's commitment has deep roots: "My father is a retired motorman, and one day he took me to work with him and I was so impressed looking out that window. Ever since I was 5 years old, I knew I wanted to run the trains" (p. 98).

6. *Find a hobby.* Turn off the TV. It fosters our hunger for possessions while reducing our personal contentment (Wu, 1988). Most important, television steals time from engagement in more mindful leisure challenges. Researchers of flow found that only 3 percent of those watching TV reported flow, while 39 percent felt apathetic. In contrast, of those engaged in arts and hobbies, 47 percent reported flow and 4 percent felt apathetic. The less expensive and more involving a leisure activity, the happier people tend to be while pursuing it. Most people are happier gardening than power boating, conversing than watching TV (Myers, 1992). By extension, you might also turn off other devices, too. Try taking a break from your computer or from playing video games or listening to your music player. Disengage from TV and these other devices in order to be more engaged with life.

7. *Cultivate family ties.* Remember your roots. "The sun looks down on nothing half as good," observed C.S. Lewis (1949, p. 32), "as a household laughing together over a meal." As we grow older and typically more distant from our origins, this is easy to forget. We do better when bonds are maintained. "Call your mother," is the final word of advice from "Life's Little Instructions."

8. *Know your neighbors.* Join a group. Build friendships. Aristotle labeled us the "social animal." Research concurs: We have a fundamental need to belong. Relative to more communal societies, those in individualist societies who learn independence at an early age often end up contending with more loneliness, alienation, and stess-related diseases. Those who enjoy close relationships cope better with life's challenges.

9. *Volunteer.* Do something that turns attention from yourself. As we have seen, researchers of altruism have uncovered a "feel-good, do-good effect"; that is, happy people are helpful people. However, the link goes both ways. Kind acts lead one to think more kindly about oneself. Service to others contributes to well-being by decreasing boredom and increasing a sense of meaning in life.

10. *Practice spirituality.* "Don't let your religious beliefs fade," suggests author David Niven (2001). "Take care of the soul," advises psychologist David Myers (1992).

A wealth of research has found that religious people are happier. They cope better with life's challenges. For many, faith provides a supportive community, a sense of meaning, the experience of acceptance, and a focus beyond self.

11. *Capitalize on other's good fortune.* How we share and react to good news can have beneficial effects for ourselves and others (Gable et al., 2004). Telling another about our good fortune—a high test score, a career success, a happy day—can lead to *capitalization*, where the listener responds with real interest and enthusiasm. A positive response to a story or event creates positive emotions in the sharer, leading to mutual respect, delight, and a more positive relationship. The trick, of course, is that we, in turn, have to capitalize on the things others share with us—we need to listen carefully and then respond with warmth and enthusiasm, not disinterest or boredom. Sometimes doing so can be a challenge, especially if we have had a long and tiring day. Still, if we want to our small triumphs to be celebrated then we must be certain to celebrate others' modest achievements.

12. *Recognize unhappiness and do something about it.* We've spent this chapter discussing the dynamics of happiness but we should also note what it means when happiness is absent, that is, when we are unhappy. Unhappiness is a negative state marked by sadness, gloom, and even despair. When we are unhappy, we are not pleased with a situation or with ourselves. Feeling sad often points to some threat or imbalance in our lives. Unhappiness calls for action. This chapter (and indeed, much of this book) provides various assessment tools and suggested activities to promote well-being. If you find that these exercises are not working—that you continue to be unhappy for long periods of time or, worse, that you are possibly depressed—then you should seek professional help. Do so as soon as possible: Taking action is the first step to recovering your sense of well-being

⇒ IN REVIEW

To foster life satisfaction, research suggests that we not confuse well-being with being well-off. Comparing ourselves with those who have less rather than more is likely to foster gratitude and happiness. Monitoring the daily activities that bring us the most satisfaction may enable us to increase life's flow. Clearly, the mindful challenge of a hobby is preferable to the mindless passivity of watching television. Strengthening family ties, fostering friendships, and volunteering our service are all likely to increase well-being. Practicing spirituality can infuse life with meaning and provide a focus beyond self, as can celebrating the good things that happen to others with them.

Self-Respect and Humility

8

Self-Concept

Self-Esteem

Humility

Practicing Self-Forgetfulness

*To free us from the expectations of others, to give us back to ourselves—
there lies the great singular power of self-respect.* —JOAN DIDION, 1968

*No man, deep down in the privacy of his heart, has any considerable
respect for himself.* —MARK TWAIN, 1897

People are inherently interesting to us. We watch them, speculate about them, and develop beliefs about them. We can't help ourselves. We find ourselves to be even more fascinating than others. Perhaps it should come as no surprise that the self is one of the most researched topics in psychology (Baumeister, 1999, 2010).

Self-Concept

Start by taking a moment to reflect on your own self-concept.

 **SELF-ASSESSMENT**

Who Am I?

*Begin by writing 20 different statements in response to the simple question "Who am I?"
Begin each statement with "I am…". Respond as if you are giving answers to yourself, not
to someone else. Write your answers in the order that they occur to you. Do not worry
about importance or logic. Go fairly fast.*

1. I am _____.

2. I am _____.

3. I am _____.

4. I am _____.

5. I am _____.

6. I am _____.

7. I am _____.

8. I am _____.

9. I am _____.

10. I am _____.

11. I am _____.

12. I am _____.

13. I am _____.

14. I am _____.

15. I am _____.

16. I am _____.

17. I am _____.

18. I am _____.

19. I am _____.

20. I am _____.

Taken as a whole, your answers to the question "Who am I?" define your self-concept. We'll return to your answers in a moment, but first consider the idea of a self-concept more generally. Our sense of self organizes our thoughts, feelings, and actions. Our self-concept affects our memories, our present perceptions, and our future goals (Myers, 2002; Oyserman, Elmore, & Smith, 2012).

Consider the self-reference effect. When we think about something in relation to ourselves, we remember it better. For example, if asked whether a specific word, such as "thoughtful," characterizes us, we subsequently remember the word better than if we are asked whether it describes someone else. Memories form around our primary interest, namely, ourselves. I hope the self-assessment exercises throughout this book will help you remember research on the human strengths!

Our self-perceptions also affect what we notice and how we process social information. We seek information that helps us appraise our abilities, opinions, and traits. We especially notice and welcome feedback that is consistent with our self-concept. Moreover, our self-concept affects what we attend to in others. If musical skill is a central component of our self-concept, we are more likely to notice others' musical gifts and limitations.

Finally, our self-concepts include not only our current characteristics but also what we might become—our possible selves (Erikson, 2007). They include visions of what we hope for—the wealthy self, the educated self, the famous self—as well as images of what we fear becoming—the unloved self, the unhealthy self, the unemployed self. Such future aspirations and fears shape our everyday actions and directions.

Impact of Culture

Self-concepts differ across cultures (e.g., Adams, 2012). Consider the following responses college students made to the request "Describe yourself briefly."

> I like to live life with a lot of positive energy. I feel like there is so much to do and see and experience. However, I also know the value of relaxation. I love the obscure. I play ultimate Frisbee, juggle, unicycle, and dabble on the recorder and concertina. I have a taste for the unique. I am very friendly and in most situations very self-confident. I'm almost always happy, and when I am down, it is usually because of stress (Markus & Kitayama, 1998, p. 63).
>
> I cannot decide quickly what I should do, and I am often swayed by other people's opinions, and I cannot oppose the opinions of people who are supposed to be respected because of age or status. Even if I have displeasure, I compromise myself to the people around me without getting rid of the displeasure. When I cannot make a decision, I often do it according to other people's opinions. Also, I am concerned about how other people think about me and often decide based on that consideration. I try to have a harmless life. I calm down by being the same as others (Markus & Kitayama, 1998, p. 64).

An American student gave the first self-description; a Japanese student provided the second. They reflect very different themes. To an American observer, the first student shows self-reliance, energy, and optimism. The second student is tentative, passive, and even insecure. A Japanese reader would see the accounts quite differently. The first student seems self-serving, inflated, and too confident. The second student shows proper modesty, deference, and solidarity.

Individualist societies such as the United States promote an *independent self* that emphasizes being unique and expressing the self. Its members are likely to complete "I am…" statements with personal traits: "I am ambitious," "I am creative," "I am open-minded." Collectivist societies such as those of East Asia encourage an *interdependent self* that emphasizes social connectedness. Its members are more likely to complete "I am…" statements with their social identities: "I am Jee-Seon's friend," and "I am the second son in my family."

Look back at your responses to the "Who am I?" exercise that opened this chapter. Examine each answer and score it with an *S* if it implies a social response (for example, I am a son = family; I am a Catholic = religious group; I am a member of the XYZ Athletic Club = club). Respondents who have more than four S scores tend to be *collectivists*—social membership is part of their identity. Those with four or fewer S scores lean more toward being *individualists*—they define themselves in terms of their personal attributes rather than their social groups. The most common total S score on this exercise for a group of University of Illinois undergraduates was zero (Triandis, 1994).

People with an independent self are concerned with personal success, achievement, and self-fulfillment. They shun conformity and affirm that "the squeaky wheel gets the grease." In contrast, those with an interdependent self are focused on group goals, developing solidarity, and fulfilling social responsibilities. They disapprove of egotism. Their motto might be "The nail that stands out gets pounded down."

As you might imagine, individualists and collectivists differ in their tendencies to attribute positive versus negative traits to themselves. In comparison with Americans, Japanese people make far fewer spontaneous positive statements about themselves (Herzog et al., 1995). Japanese people are also more likely to express their positive traits in the form of negations: "I'm not lazy." Americans are more likely to say: "I'm a hard worker."

Evaluating the Self

In addition to the knowledge component of self, there is an even more thoroughly studied evaluative component. Not only do we ask, "Who am I?" but we also ask, "How do I feel about who I am?" (Campbell & Lavellee, 1993). Do your answers to "Who am I?" suggest anything about your level of self-regard? One study found that American adults gave four times as many positive attributes as negative (Herzog et al., 1995). In this section you will have three opportunities to evaluate your self-concept more closely.

The Rosenberg Self-Esteem Scale is the most frequently used assessment of *global self-esteem*—a person's overall evaluation of self or sense of self-worth. Try it for yourself.

 **SELF-ASSESSMENT**

Rosenberg Self-Esteem Scale

Indicate your agreement or disagreement with each statement using the following scale:

1 = Strongly disagree   2 = Disagree   3 = Agree   4 = Strongly agree

_____ **1.** I feel that I am a person of worth, at least on an equal basis with others.

_____ **2.** I feel that I have a number of good qualities.

_____ **3.** All in all, I am inclined to feel that I am a failure.

_____ **4.** I am able to do things as well as most other people.

_____ **5.** I feel I do not have much to be proud of.

_____ **6.** I take a positive attitude toward myself.

_____ **7.** On the whole, I am satisfied with myself.

_____ **8.** I wish I could have more respect for myself.

_____ **9.** I certainly feel useless at times.

_____ **10.** At times I think I am no good at all.

Source: "Rosenberg Self-Esteem Scale" from *Society and the Adolescent Self-Image* by Morris Rosenberg © 1989 published by Wesleyan University Press. Used by permission.

This scale was designed to assess the degree to which people are generally satisfied with their lives and consider themselves worthy people. In scoring it, you should first reverse the numbers you placed in front of items 3, 5, 8, 9, and 10 (4 = 1, 3 = 2, 2 = 3, 1 = 4). Leave the numbers in front of the remaining five items the same. Then add the numbers in front of all 10 items to obtain a total score. Scores can range from 10 to 40, with scores above the midpoint of 25 reflecting a stronger sense of self-worth.

Now, how do you see yourself in comparison with others? Try the following exercise.

SELF-ASSESSMENT

Social Comparisons

When you think of yourself relative to others of the same age, education, and sex as you, how do you think you compare? Specifically, how would you rate yourself on the following characteristics? Use the scale in making your response.

1 = Well below average   2 = Below average   3 = Average   4 = Above average
5 = Well above average

_____ **1.** Leadership ability

_____ **2.** Ability to get along with others

_____ **3.** Energy level

_____ **4.** Helpfulness

_____ **5.** Responsibility

_____ **6.** Patience

_____ **7.** Trustworthiness

_____ **8.** Sincerity

_____ **9.** Thoughtfulness

_____ **10.** Cooperativeness

Add up the numbers you placed in front of the 10 traits and divide by 10 to find your mean. A mean below 3 suggests that, in comparison with your peers, you see yourself as below average. Scores above 3 indicate that you see yourself as better than average.

Finally, consider your strengths and weaknesses and your attitudes toward your strengths and weaknesses by completing the following scale.

Strengths versus Weaknesses

Try to respond to the following questions as honestly as you can. Answer each question using the following scale:

1	2	3	4	5	6	7
Not at all						Very much

_____ **1.** How athletic are you?

_____ **2.** How much do you care about whether you are athletic?

_____ **3.** How musically talented are you?

_____ **4.** How much do you care about whether you have musical talent?

_____ **5.** How physically attractive are you?

_____ **6.** How much do you care about whether you are physically attractive?

_____ **7.** How creative are you?

_____ **8.** How much do you care about whether you are creative?

_____ **9.** How mechanically skilled are you?

_____ **10.** How much do you care about whether you are mechanically skilled?

We tend to value our strengths but see our weaknesses as much less important. Research (for example, Hill, Smith, & Lewicki, 1989) suggests that people care much more about their strengths than about their weaknesses. Do your scores match this pattern?

How highly do most people regard themselves? Do they more commonly have inflated or deflated self-images? Was psychologist Carl Rogers right when he argued, "The central core of difficulty in people…is that in the great majority of cases they despise themselves, regard themselves as worthless and unlovable" (1956, pp. 13–14)? Or was Henry Ward Beecher closer to the truth in claiming, "Conceit is the most incurable disease that is known to the human soul" (1875, p. 351)?

One review (Baumeister, Tice, & Hutton, 1989) of Rosenberg Esteem Scale responses found that very few respondents scored at the low end. Not many people view themselves negatively. Total scores typically run from the midpoint of 25 to the high end of the scale, with a mean of 31. Males score somewhat higher than females.

When people are asked to compare themselves with others on a list of socially desirable traits, as in the Social Comparisons Scale, the overwhelming majority see themselves as "better than average." For example, the U.S. College Board invited the million students who take their achievement test yearly to indicate "how you feel you compare with other people your own age in certain areas of ability" (cited by Myers, 2002, p. 62). In "leadership ability," 70 percent rated themselves above average, 2 percent as below average. Sixty percent of the respondents thought themselves better than average in "athletic ability," and only 6 percent as below average. And in their "ability to get along with others," 0 percent of the students rated themselves below average while 25 percent saw themselves in the top 1 percent! A recent and comprehensive survey of entering freshmen in the United States indicates these self-serving positivity biases have not changed (Eagan et al., 2013). For example, more than 72% of first-year students rated their academic ability as in the "highest 10%" or "above average." Seventy-eight percent felt the same about their "drive to achieve," and 63% claimed they had superior "leadership ability." As David Myers (2002, p. 61) concluded, "Every community seems like Garrison Keillor's fictional Lake Wobegon, where 'all the women are strong, all the men are good-looking, and all the children are above average." It is clear that people are not very skilled at self-assessment on any number of important dimensions (Dunning, Heath, & Suls, 2004).

Is such bias universal? Respondents from cultures that value modesty and self-restraint, such as those of China and Japan, do tend to express less self-serving bias. Nonetheless, most people from around the world seem privately self-enhancing. For example, researchers have observed the self-serving bias among Dutch college students, Belgian basketball players, Australian workers, Hong Kong sportswriters, Singaporean schoolchildren, and French people of all ages (Myers, 2002).

The Strengths versus Weaknesses exercise reveals that in case we actually do have any perceived weaknesses, we conveniently protect our self-esteem by caring less about our weaknesses than about our strengths!

Clearly, research findings challenge the popular notion that most people suffer from a negative self-image. A very positive view of self seems more common than an inferiority complex.

⇒ IN REVIEW

Our responses to the question "Who am I?" define our self-concept. Our self-understandings organize our thoughts and actions and affect our memories, perceptions, and future goals. Some cultures encourage the development of an independent self in which people define themselves in terms of their personal traits. Other cultures promote an interdependent self in which people see their identity in terms of their social connections. Globally, most people tend to have a very positive self-image.

Self-Esteem

Perhaps the fact that most people enjoy high self-esteem is good news. Research seems to suggest that people who feel good about themselves are less susceptible to insomnia, are not as conforming, and are less shy, lonely, and depressed. They are also confident, generally not discouraged by failure, relatively immune to negative criticism (Heimpel et al., 2002), and quite certain of who they are—and are not (Campbell, 1990). People with high self-esteem are also happier. Low self-esteem, on the other hand, seems to be linked to failure in school, substance abuse, eating disorders, teenage pregnancy, and marital discord (Crocker & Wolfe, 2001). Some psychologists argue that people with low self-esteem are not necessarily more negative on evaluative dimensions than those with higher self-esteem; rather, those with low self-esteem are more confused, uncertain, and tentative about their self-views and identities (Campbell & Lavallee, 1993). Their self-concepts are less solid, more subject to change or fluctuation.

Many public officials, teachers, and helping professionals have hoped that fostering self-esteem would solve a variety of personal and social problems. For example, the California Task Force to Promote Self-Esteem and Personal and Social Responsibility asserted that self-esteem "is the likeliest candidate for a social vaccine" to inoculate individuals and society "against the lures of crime, violence, substance abuse, teen pregnancy, child abuse, chronic welfare dependency, and educational failure." The task force's final report asserted that "the lack of self-esteem is central to most personal and social ills plaguing our state and nation" (1990, p. 4).

Benefits and Dangers of High Self-Esteem

Self-esteem studies have been mostly correlational and thus raise questions about cause and effect. Does low self-esteem destine us to screw-ups and misery? Or does life's misery and our failure cause low self-esteem? Maybe liking oneself follows rather than produces success. Perhaps high self-esteem is the fruit rather than the root of surmounting difficulty.

The presumed links between self-esteem and a variety of positive human characteristics are often based on self-reports that may not be entirely accurate. People who make favorable statements about themselves on self-esteem scales tend also to provide positive self-reports of their other characteristics, including interpersonal skills, attractiveness, and performance at school and work. When researchers use more objective measures of these characteristics, they find that people aren't as wonderful as they think they are (Baumeister et al., 2003)! Thus, high self-esteem might not be a desirable commodity when the self-beliefs underlying it are bloated and unrealistic (Crocker & Park, 2004).

Consider physical appearance, for example. Research finds a strong positive relationship between self-esteem and self-reported attractiveness. Those with high self-esteem love what they see in the mirror. But are they gorgeous to others? Hardly. In fact, when observers' assessments of looks are used as the measure of attractiveness, the correlation between self-esteem and appearance doesn't merely shrink. It evaporates. There's no relationship.

In his review of the literature, Roy Baumeister (1996) concludes: "The enthusiastic claims of the self-esteem movement mostly range from fantasy to hogwash. The effects of self-esteem are small, limited, and not all good." Although he acknowledges that high self-esteem has a small number of practical benefits, including making people happier and strengthening their persistence in the face of failure, most social and personal problems are not caused by a lack of self-esteem. Thus, raising self-esteem is unlikely to solve them (Baumeister et al., 2003).

One important point: High self-esteem is distinct from *narcissism*, the tendency to regard oneself in grandiose terms that highlight a preoccupied sense of self-importance. Unlike true narcissists, however, people with high self-esteem are able to control and even moderate their desire to act in self-enhancing ways in front of others (Horvath & Morf, 2010). A bigger problem is that narcissists sometimes respond aggressively when their self-views are challenged by others (Bushman & Baumeister, 1998), something that people with a secure sense of themselves or who are not provoked do not do (see also, Twenge & Campbell, 2003).

Still, Baumeister and his colleagues do find that high self-esteem has a dark side (Baumeister, Smart, & Boden, 1996). People who think too highly of themselves are more likely to be obnoxious, to interrupt, and to talk *at* other people rather than *with* them. They lash out at others who fail to agree with their grandiose self-views, which also serves as a strategy for avoiding the need to revise downward their sense of self-worth. "People who believe themselves to be among the top 10 percent on any dimension may be insulted and threatened whenever anyone asserts that they are in the 80th or 50th or 25th percentile," observes Baumeister (cited by Slater, 2003). "In contrast, someone with lower self-esteem who regards himself or herself as being merely in the top 60 percent would only be threatened by the feedback that puts him or her at the 25th percentile.... In short, the more favorable one's view of oneself, the greater the range of external feedback that will be perceived as unacceptably low." Overall, Baumeister (1996) concludes, "Forget about self-esteem, and concentrate on self-control" (p. 43). Thinking well of ourselves has some merits, but being able to regulate our thoughts, feelings, and actions is probably more beneficial in the long run.

Sources of Self-Worth

We can better understand the paradoxical links between self-esteem and behavior, suggest Jennifer Crocker and Connie Wolfe (2001), by examining possible sources of self-esteem. "Contingencies" of self-worth are the areas of life in which people believe that success means they are worthwhile and failure means they are worthless (see also Crocker & Knight, 2005; Crocker & Park, 2012). Crocker and Wolfe's research has identified seven possible domains in which people may invest their self-esteem.

✔ SELF-ASSESSMENT

Contingencies of Self-Worth Scale

The following sample items assess domains that may or may not be relevant to your sense of self-worth. Please respond to each of the following statements by using the scale.

1 = Strongly disagree   2 = Disagree   3 = Disagree somewhat   4 = Neutral
5 = Agree somewhat   6 = Agree   7 = Strongly agree

_____ **1.** When my family members are proud of me, my sense of self-worth increases.

_____ **2.** My self-worth is affected by how well I do when I am competing with others.

_____ **3.** When I think I look attractive, I feel good about myself.

_____ **4.** My self-worth is based on God's love.

_____ **5.** Doing well in school gives me a sense of self-respect.

_____ **6.** Whenever I follow my moral principles, my sense of self-respect gets a boost.

_____ **7.** My self-esteem depends on the opinions others hold of me.

Source: Copyright © 2003 by the American Psychological Association. Adapted with permission. Table 2 (adapted) Crocker, J., Luhtanen, R. K., Cooper, M. L., & Bouvrette, A. (2003). Contingencies of Self-Worth in College Students: Theory and Measurement, *Journal of Personality and Social Psychology, 85(5)*, 894–908. No further reproduction or distribution is permitted without written permission from the American Psychological Association.

The full Contingencies of Self-Worth Scale uses five items, not one, to assess the importance of each domain to one's sense of self-worth. Still, you can make some initial comparisons with Crocker, Luhtanen, & Bouvrette's (2001) sample of 1300 college students. Compare your number for each statement with the following mean scores (also on a scale from 1 to 7) that their sample obtained.

Family support = 5.3
Competition = 5.0
Appearance = 4.9
God's love = 4.2
Academic competence = 5.3
Virtue = 5.5
Others' approval = 4.6

Crocker and Wolfe (2001) do not claim that this is an exhaustive list of the areas in which people find their self-worth or that one contingency is necessarily preferable to another. The list merely reflects some of the more common domains that respondents identify as important to their self-esteem. Can you think of other domains that might be important?

Contingencies of Self-Worth and Behavior

The source of our self-esteem provides a powerful guide for our behavior. If our self-worth is rooted in being virtuous, we will act quite differently from someone whose self-esteem is based on appearance.

In a study of 600 college freshmen (Crocker, Luhtanen, & Bouvrette, 2001), self-esteem based on appearance was linked to spending more hours per week grooming, shopping, and partying. Self-esteem rooted in God's love was linked to spending more hours in religious activities, such as praying and going to church or synagogue, and to fewer hours partying. Self-esteem based on academic competence was associated with more success in gaining admission to graduate school.

Crocker and Wolfe (2001) argue that major problems such as depression, drug abuse, and aggression may be linked not so much to our general level of self-esteem as to the source of our self-esteem. For example, research indicates that basing one's self-esteem on physical appearance increases one's susceptibility to eating disorders. Similarly, people who have high but fragile self-esteem that is based on social approval seem especially prone to anger and hostility when others challenge them.

People who are unable to secure self-respect on one basis may shift to another source. Frustrated in their pursuit of self-esteem, they may even reject goals that are important to a successful life. For example the high dropout rate among African-American college students may be the result of disconnecting self-worth from academic performance after numerous frustrating attempts to succeed in an environment that assumes they are academically inferior (Steele, 1997, 2010). Others who don't have the means to garner a positive image on the basis of good grades in school or strong relations with peers may organize their self-esteem around strength, power, or physical superiority (Staub, 1999). Several factors foster this unfortunate tendency. Having been abused, having readily available models of aggression, and living in a culture that prizes male physical power and superiority can all increase the likelihood of aggression and antisocial behavior.

The shifting of sources of self-worth also explains why overall level of self-esteem does not decline as we grow older. As people age, note Crocker and Wolfe, contingencies of self-worth typically change from competition and appearance to a more internal and intrinsic basis such as virtue or family.

Contingencies of Self-Worth: Assets or Liabilities?

Are contingencies of self-worth beneficial or limiting?

Some psychologists have argued that high-functioning people have a self-concept that is sensitive to what others in their environment think of them. Others recommend that children be encouraged to base their self-esteem on their objective accomplishments, skills, and abilities. Roy Baumeister and his colleagues (2003) suggest that we try to boost self-esteem as a reward for worthy achievements and ethical behavior. To avoid social comparisons that lead people to boost themselves at the expense of others, they recommend emphasizing *improvement* so that people learn to compare themselves with themselves rather than with their peers.

Some research hints that having multiple contingencies of self-worth is best. People with several independent sources of self-worth may react less extremely to negative life events. Bumps and bruises in one area of life shift one's attention to other important areas where things are going well (Linville, 1985, 1987).

Can self-esteem be "noncontingent"? "I like you for just being you," television's Fred Rogers fondly told the young visitors to his friendly neighborhood. Because contingent self-esteem is so often associated with anxiety, hostility, defensiveness, and the risk of depression, perhaps what people need most is the awareness that they have inherent value. Edward Deci and Richard Ryan (1995) distinguished between contingent and "true" self-esteem, which is more stable and securely based in a solid sense of self. True self-esteem develops, argue Deci and Ryan, when one acts autonomously, experiences a sense of competence, and is loved for who one is rather than for matching some external standard. It follows that environments that satisfy the three fundamental needs for autonomy, competence, and relatedness foster true self-esteem. People with such "noncontingent" self-esteem are pleased when they succeed and disappointed when they fail, but their sense of self-worth is not at risk in the process.

Carl Rogers (1951) emphasized the importance of parents providing their children with unconditional positive regard. Such children mature into adults who never feel that their self-worth is on the line. However, we've since learned that simply telling people with low self-esteem "you can do it" does not truly strengthen their self-confidence. Better to help them understand: "It's all right if you can't do it; it doesn't mean you are a bad person" (Brown, 1998).

Those whose self-worth is not continually put to the test spend less time analyzing themselves. They may even be self-forgetful, which, as we will see next, is one very important ingredient of humility.

⇒ IN REVIEW

Psychologists debate the benefits of high self-esteem. Although a positive self-concept seems to promote happiness and perseverance, most personal and social problems are not caused by low self-esteem. In fact, those with an inflated self-concept may be more prone to interpersonal violence. Examining specific sources of self-esteem helps us to understand the links between self-concept and behavior. Those who have several independent sources of self-esteem may have a more stable sense of self-worth. Those with noncontingent self-esteem have an awareness of their inherent value and do not question their self-worth.

Humility

Given the general public's preoccupation with the merits of positive self-views, how do people view *humility*, the willingness to be humble or modest? Should we agree with the Shakers that "'Tis a gift to be simple"? Is humility a strength or weakness? Consider your own perceptions of humility by answering the following questions.

Reflections on Humility

1. When you think of the word humility, what words, images, or associations come to your mind?

_____

_____

_____

_____

_____

_____

2. Is humility a strength or a weakness? Do your immediate associations with the word tend to be negative or positive (select a number)?

-5	-4	-3	-2	-1	0	1	2	3	4	5
Negative										Positive

3. Think of a person whom you see as being very humble (either someone famous or someone you know). Who is the person? _____

Please give a brief description of the person. What makes you see this person as humble?

_____

_____

_____

_____

4. To what extent do you see humility as being similar to low self-esteem?

0	1	2	3	4	5	6	7	8	9	10
Not at all										Extremely

5. Recall a real-life situation in which you felt humble. Give a brief description of the situation. Why did you feel humble in this situation?

_____

_____

_____

_____

6. What did you learn from this experience, if anything? What emotions did you experience when you recalled this situation?

_____

_____

_____

_____

7. To what extent is this memory pleasant or unpleasant to recall?

	Not at all									Extremely	
Pleasant to recall	0	1	2	3	4	5	6	7	8	9	10
Unpleasant to recall	0	1	2	3	4	5	6	7	8	9	10

8. If you wanted to put yourself in a humble frame of mind right now, what kinds of things would you think about?

_____

_____

_____

9. To what extent do you:

	Not at all										Extremely
View yourself as a humble person?	0	1	2	3	4	5	6	7	8	9	10
Believe that people who know you well view you as a humble person?	0	1	2	3	4	5	6	7	8	9	10
Think that it would be good if you were less humble?	0	1	2	3	4	5	6	7	8	9	10
Think that it would be good if you were more humble?	0	1	2	3	4	5	6	7	8	9	10

Source: Copyright © 2004 from "Perceptions of humility: A preliminary study," _Self And Identity, 3(2)_, 95–114, by Exline, J., & Geyer, A. L.. Reproduced by permission of Taylor & Francis LLC (http://www.tandfonline.com).

Results with undergraduates (Exline & Geyer, 2004) on the humility self-evaluation indicated that students' overall views of humility were positive. For example, on the

10-point scale (from −5 to +5), they gave "humility" an average rating of 2.4. Moreover, humility was not seen as reflecting low self-esteem (mean = 2.3 on a scale from 0 to 10). Open-ended definitions of humility suggested substantial overlap with modesty, including "not bragging" and "not taking full credit for success." Humility was associated with a variety of positive attributes including unselfishness and generosity. Rather than viewing humility as a preoccupation with shortcomings, respondents saw humility as reflecting an unassuming attitude toward one's positive qualities.

When asked to recall a real-life situation in which they felt humble, undergraduates reported much higher levels of pleasant than unpleasant feelings. Interestingly, the majority of participants recalled experiences that involved success or accomplishment, that is, doing something good, receiving praise, winning, or getting more credit than they deserved. A minority of students reported situations that involved humiliation, for example, a loss, a failure, or feeling threatened by someone who was more successful.

Asked to identify a humble person, participants picked friends, classmates, roommates, relatives, celebrities, saints, and religious leaders. When asked to indicate why the person was seen as humble, the research participants identified positive characteristics such as kindness or caring toward others, self-sacrifice, competence, and intelligence. Only a small minority suggested that a humble person was timid, quiet, or unassertive. Thus, research participants generally perceived humility as a human strength. They indicated that they themselves wanted to become more humble.

How do your results compare?

These surprising findings contrast sharply with dictionary definitions of humility that link the trait to self-abasement or low self-esteem. At the same time, they are consistent with ancient wisdom that presents humility as a virtue. "It was pride that changed angels into devils," observed St. Augustine (cited in Kurtz & Ketcham, 2009, p. 188); "it is humility that makes men into angels." Confucius agreed. "Humility," he noted, "is the solid foundation of all the virtues" (cited in Urban, 2006, p. 12). As a character strength, humility may well help people engage in self-regulation, thereby avoiding making bad decisions, taking undue risk, or maximizing outcomes at any cost (Weiss & Knight, 1980). In fact, some argue that humble people make the best leaders of all (Prime & Salib, 2014).

Humility is a trait we obviously respect. Apparently people especially like to see the attribute in attorneys. A survey in the *National Law Journal* ("Jurors Prefer Lawyers," 1993) found that humility was the characteristic jurors most admired in lawyers! Similarly, few traits are more grating to us than arrogance—humility's opposite. We relish puncturing the pride of those who know it all and who seem in love with themselves. Most of us take special delight in Javad Hashtroudian's (2003) retelling of the Mullah Nasrudin story, simply entitled "The Boatman."

The Mullah earned his living by running a ferry across a lake, and one afternoon he took a pompous scholar to the other side. When the learned academic asked if he had read Plato's *Republic*, the Mullah replied, "Sir, I am a simple boatman. What would I do with Plato?" The scholar scoffed, "In that case, half of your life's been wasted." Some time passed before the Mullah inquired, "Sir, do you know how to swim?" "Of course not," replied the professor, "I am a scholar. What would I do with swimming?" The Mullah replied, "In that case, all of your life's been wasted. We're sinking."

More than an admired personal quality, humility is an important human strength. Consider the following research findings:

- In attempting to understand what transforms a good company into a great one, researchers studied companies that increased their value eight times faster than the stock market (Collins, 2001). They concluded that all great companies share one common factor: They have leaders who blend personal humility with professional willpower. Compellingly modest and never boastful, these leaders shun public adulation. They take personal responsibility for failure and attribute the company's success to others. Most important, they are not self-seeking but show an unwavering, single-minded commitment to the long-term interests of everyone.

- In attempting to answer why some people devote themselves to good deeds, Kathleen Brehony (1999) interviewed dozens of men and women of all ages, ethnicities, and lifestyles who have quietly committed themselves to helping others. In her book *Ordinary Grace*, she highlights how grace is all around us—in both profoundly moving experiences and in small, hardly noticed acts. People who demonstrate social concern, she suggests, share a number of common qualities. Most important, their strong social connections are marked by an abiding faith in others, personal humility, and the belief that helping others is not service but a privilege and blessing.

- In an effort to understand Abraham Maslow's concept of self-actualization more fully, researchers undertook an exhaustive case study of Eleanor Roosevelt (Piechowski & Tyska, 1982). They analyzed biographical accounts of Roosevelt's "years on her own" for the presence of traits that contributed to self-actualization. Among their important conclusions was that Maslow may have overlooked two crucial traits of the self-actualizing person. One was equitableness—the capacity to advocate for what is in the best interests of all concerned. The other was humility.

Characteristics of Humility

What are the essential features of humility? June Tangney (2009) identified the following:

- Accurate, realistic estimate of abilities and achievements
- Ability to acknowledge one's mistakes, imperfections, gaps in knowledge, and limitations

- Openness to new ideas, contradictory information, and advice
- Keeping one's abilities and accomplishments in perspective
- Relatively low self-focus or an ability to "forget the self"
- Appreciation of the value of all people and their unique contributions

Recent research also reveals that those high in humility are also apt to be generous to others, whether through actual charitable donations or through just sheer kindness (Exline & Hill, 2012).

If asked to complete the Rosenberg Self-Esteem Scale, "humble" people, says Tangney, would endorse statements such as "I feel that I am a person of worth, at least on an equal plane with others," and "I feel I have a number of good qualities."

It seems that, in the final analysis, humility reflects a sense of security in which feelings of personal worth are based on stable, reliable sources (such as feeling unconditionally loved or having a belief in the value of all life) rather than on more transient, external sources (such as achievement, appearance, or social approval) (Peterson & Seligman, 2004).

Practicing Self-Forgetfulness

Given what is often a pervasive drive toward self-enhancement in our cultures, coupled with our limited abilities to engage in reasonably accurate self-assessment, how do we begin to cultivate humility? One way is through self-forgetfulness; that is, by behaving unselfishly or without self-interest. In cultures that emphasize the relative worth of people based on their achievements, appearance, athleticism, celebrity, and material worth, is it possible to practice intentional self-forgetfulness?

Of all the human strengths, humility may be the most elusive. Benjamin Franklin certainly thought so. After he publicly displayed a list of virtues he intended to pursue, a friend suggested that he had overlooked one. Franklin, he bravely noted, was often guilty of pride. So the patriot dutifully added "humility" to his list. Later, Franklin observed that he had never come close: "There is perhaps no one of our natural passions so hard to subdue as pride; disguise it, struggle with it, beat it down, stifle it, mortify it as much as one pleases, it is still alive and will every now and then peep out and show itself" (cited by Isaacson, 2003, p. 47).

Tongue in cheek, media mogul Ted Turner agrees. "If only I had a little humility," he laments, "I would be perfect." It's not easy to become one of the humble. As soon as you think you belong, you have excluded yourself. Franklin captured the irony: "Even if I could conceive that I had completely overcome pride, I would probably be proud of my humility."

Nonetheless, the extensive research on the development of self-esteem as well as early work on humility hints at how this human strength unfolds.

1. **Demonstrate balance.** Fostering humility, notes Julie Exline (Exline & Geyer, 2004; see also Peterson & Seligman, 2004), can be risky. Probably more caution needs to be exercised in attempting to induce humility than in the development of the other strengths. Strategies backfire if they cause a person to feel helpless, ashamed, or insignificant. People often defend against ego threat through self-enhancement or even by behaving aggressively. Reducing our self-focus needs to occur without feeling we have been diminished or threatened, or that some part of ourselves has been damaged. Remember, humility does not mean that you lack worth or that your desires don't matter. Rather, humility leads people to consider the needs and feelings of others as well as themselves.

2. **Admit bias.** Our self-perceptions may not reflect reality. For the minority of us who may suffer from an unrealistically poor self-concept, it helps to examine its roots. What negative messages might you have received about yourself early in life? Was there any evidence to support them? Begin to challenge your present negative self-talk and replace it with the truth.

   For most of us, however, overcoming bias is a matter of admitting our pride. "If anyone would like to acquire humility, I can, I think, tell him the first step," observes C. S. Lewis (1960, p. 101). "The first step is to realize that one is proud. And a biggish step, too." Research points to a pervasive self-serving bias—a powerful tendency to see oneself favorably. We saw evidence of it earlier in this chapter in our tendencies to see ourselves as better than average and to value our strengths but downplay our weaknesses. As Lewis suggests, it's tough to admit vulnerability. In fact, when most students learn of the self-serving bias, they congratulate themselves on being better than average at not thinking of themselves as better than average (Friedrich, 1996)! Sometimes our expressed modesty barely conceals underlying pride in our better-than-average humility. When students were invited to write about an important success experience, those who anticipated that they would be reading their story to others readily acknowledged the help and emotional support they had received from others (Baumeister & Ilko, 1995). Those who wrote anonymously portrayed themselves as having achieved success on their own.

3. **Seek accurate feedback.** Some forms of the self-serving bias are controllable through clear and accurate feedback. Deliberately seeking honest feedback from others—friends, relatives, roommates, instructors, managers, or supervisors—gives us one important strategy for assessing both our strengths and weaknesses. It is encouraging to know that when people receive feedback about themselves from others (dating partners and roommates) they prefer

accurate feedback even when this information is relatively negative (Katz & Joiner, 2002).

4. **Learn to laugh at ourselves.** Arrogant people have no sense of humor, especially about themselves. Conscientious people may also take their work and themselves too seriously. Certainly we have important tasks to do and others depend on us. To be productive and happy we must believe our actions make a difference. However, the world won't end if we stumble. And others are not noting our every miscue. Cultivate the capacity to laugh at yourself—to admit your weaknesses and not take yourself too seriously. Try to be a little self-deprecating. People like those who have some flaws more than those who appear (however falsely) to be perfect (Aronson, Willerman, & Floyd, 1966).

5. **Learn from other cultures.** Humble people recognize that they are part of a large whole. As we have seen, people in collectivist cultures are keenly aware of their interdependence. They also value modesty. There is little evidence of self-enhancement among the Japanese, for example (Heine et al., 1999). Instead, a self-critical posture is the norm. This effort at self-improvement, suggest the researchers, is indicative of a strong sense of belonging.

   Secure social connections enable us to admit our uncertainty and frailty. One researcher conducted two experiments in which he temporarily led Yale University students to feel accepted or rejected by their peers (Dittes, 1959). He then gave them a fabricated parable and asked them to interpret it. Although the parable was incoherent, students who had been rejected proudly declared its meaning. Those who felt accepted and supported were more likely to humbly admit they did not know what the parable meant.

6. **Cultivate the other strengths.** Humility is a natural by-product of pursuing the other human strengths. For example, the practice of gratitude increases life satisfaction and fosters a mindset of humility. The word *gratitude* is the derivative of the Latin word for "grace"—getting something for nothing. In keeping a gratitude journal, people acknowledge receiving the undeserved benevolence of another.

   Similarly, in developing empathy (recall Chapter 3), we recognize our "oneness" or equality with others. A belief in the value of all life enables us to have both compassion for others and "self-compassion" (Neff, 2003). Perceiving our common humanity enables us to be kind and understanding toward others and ourselves, particularly in times of failure. Like everyone else, we are limited and imperfect human beings. However, cautions Neff, self-compassion does not mean that we allow our failings to go unnoticed or unchanged. Rather, by showing compassion to ourselves as well as others, we provide the emotional safety needed for self-examination. We are motivated to grow and to change.

7. **Assume a cosmic perspective.** Albert Einstein taught us an important lesson in humility by showing us that we are mere specks in an unfathomably large universe. "A spirit is manifest in the laws of the universe," he once observed, "in the face of which we with our modest powers must feel humble" (cited in Isaacson, 2007, p. 388)." With humility, we can recognize we are among several billion people inhabiting this planet, that the historical moments of our lives—mere blips on the screen of the cosmos—represent a surprisingly short span in a human history covering millions of years. Add to that the fact that we each occupy but a few cubic feet in a vast and continuously expanding universe.

8. **Experience awe.** Awe-inspiring experiences that connect us to the world's beauty and excellence foster a recognition that we are a small part of a much larger whole (Keltner & Haidt, 2003; Peterson & Seligman, 2004). Most important, the experience of awe fosters self-forgetfulness. A wide range of physical and social stimuli can elicit the experience—a grand cathedral, a marvelous symphony, a beautiful poem, a wondrous landscape, an elegant theory. Famous, exceptionally skilled, or morally admirable people also elicit awe. All of these encounters are characterized by *vastness*—the recognition of something larger than ourselves—and by a need for *accommodation* because the experience does not fit into our existing mental structures. Besides a sense of wonder, awe slows the experience of time, influences decisions, and promotes a sense of satisfaction with life (Rudd, Vohs, & Aaker, 2012). Unfortunately, some people go about their daily lives wearing blinders. Others have minds and hearts tuned to what is moving and beautiful around them. It's a sensitivity worth cultivating.

9. **Focus beyond self.** Healthy self-respect makes it easier to forget about ourselves. Proving our worth is no longer a driving concern. At the same time, trying not to think about ourselves is somewhat like trying not to think about pink elephants. The harder we try, the more memorable they become. Only when we shift our attention from ourselves to something more interesting do we master humility. When we become genuinely invested in others or in a task larger than ourselves we also forget about ourselves.

10. **Promote secure attachment.** Factors that facilitate secure attachment in infants also lay the groundwork for humility (Peterson & Seligman, 2004). Parents who are responsive to their infants' needs encourage them to approach life with an attitude of trust rather than fear. This basic sense of security enables the older child to tolerate both positive and negative feedback, which is fundamental to accurate self-appraisal.

11. **Practice authoritative parenting.** Several researchers report that children with the highest self-esteem have had warm, concerned, authoritative parents. Such parents set rules and enforce them in an atmosphere of nurturance and genuine respect for the child as a person. They validate the child's intrinsic

worth by avoiding perfectionistic performance standards as well as extreme emphasis on appearance, popularity, or competitive comparisons with siblings and peers. Moreover, parental approval of commendable behavior can be communicated in a way that encourages the child to internalize standards of conduct rather than remain dependent on external feedback. Telling him or her, "You must be very pleased with yourself for what you did" will encourage internalization and not just convey personal pleasure that the child did what you wanted (Harter, 2002). Most important, parents who communicate to their children that they have intrinsic merit and thus need not establish their worth enable a healthy sense of self-forgetfulness.

12. **Model humility.** Observational learning is as important to the development of humility as it is to fostering the other strengths. Important models of humility come from adults who are keenly sensitive to the beauty and excellence around them and who clearly communicate that they see themselves as part of a larger whole. Parents who demonstrate healthy self-appraisal are able to admit their weaknesses and accept both positive and negative feedback about themselves without overreacting to either. Teachers who convey the intrinsic worth of all people lay the foundation for students' understanding that they are neither inferior nor superior to their peers.

⇒ IN REVIEW

Humble people view their strengths and weaknesses realistically. They are able to "forget themselves" because they possess stable, reliable sources of self-worth. We cultivate humility by admitting our pride, by seeking accurate feedback, by learning to laugh at ourselves, and by taking a cosmic perspective. Parents who promote secure attachment, practice authoritative parenting, and model humility help their children to understand their intrinsic worth and to recognize that they are neither inferior nor superior to their peers.

Hope

Optimism

Exploring Hope

Fostering Hope

Hope is a good thing, maybe the best of things. And no good thing ever dies. —Andy Dufresne in The Shawshank Redemption (Marvin & Darabont, 1994)

If you have watched the film *The Shawshank Redemption*, then you know that Andy Dufresne has no reason to hope. In fact, he should be depressed. Once a successful banker, he has been wrongly convicted of his wife's murder and sentenced to life in Shawshank prison. It's hardly a place to call home. Taunted by veteran prisoners, beaten by hardened guards, Shawshank's new recruits see no light at the end of the tunnel.

Still, neither maggots in his oatmeal nor gang rape by fellow inmates dims Andy's optimism. After 2 weeks in solitary, he returns to the prison yard still gushing hope: "We need it so we don't forget...that there are places in the world that aren't made out of stone, that there's, there's somethin' inside that they can't get to, that they can't touch. It's yours." Andy's friend, Red, a prisoner more firmly anchored in reality, counters: "Let me tell you something...hope is a dangerous thing. Hope can drive a man insane. It's got no use on the inside" (Marvin & Darabont, 1994).

Andy and Red echo the centuries-old debate over the merits of hope. Do you agree with Karl Menninger that hope is a "life instinct" (Menninger, Mayman, & Pruyser, 1963, p. 357), or are you more sympathetic with Benjamin Franklin, who once said, "He who lives upon hope will die fasting" (cited in Bennett, 2013, p. 125)? Was Martin Luther right when he said, "Everything that is done in the world is done by hope" (cited in Markway & Markway, 2003, p. 1)? Or was Friedrich Nietzsche closer to the truth: "Hope is the worst of all evils because it prolongs the torments of man" (cited in Lloyd & Mitchinson, 2009, p.145)?

Contemporary psychology provides fascinating new insights into this continuing controversy over the power and peril of positive thinking. In this chapter, we will examine optimism—the general belief that a bright future awaits us—and its links to psychological and physical well-being. Next, we will reflect on closely related investigations of hope. We will see how a positive orientation to specific life goals relates to achievement. Finally, we will consider some important strategies for fostering hope in ourselves and in others.

Optimism

Do you believe that good things or bad things will generally occur in your life?

To assess your optimism, take the following Revised Life Orientation Test (LOT-R) by Michael Scheier, Charles Carver, and Michael Bridges (1994).

SELF-ASSESSMENT

Revised Life Orientation Test (LOT-R): How Optimistic Are You?

Respond to each statement using the following scale:

0 = Strongly disagree   1 = Disagree 2 = Neutral 3 = Agree 4 = Strongly agree

_____ **1.** In uncertain times, I usually expect the best.

_____ **2.** It's easy for me to relax.

_____ **3.** If something can go wrong for me, it will.

_____ **4.** I'm always optimistic about my future.

_____ **5.** I enjoy my friends a lot.

_____ **6.** It's important for me to keep busy.

_____ **7.** I hardly ever expect things to go my way.

_____ **8.** I don't get upset too easily.

_____ **9.** I rarely count on good things happening to me.

_____ **10.** Overall, I expect more good things to happen to me than bad.

Source: Scheier, M. F., Carver, C. S., & Bridges, M. W. (1994).

To obtain your score, first reverse the numbers you placed in answer to statements 3, 7, and 9 (i.e., 0 = 4, 1 = 3, 2 = 2, 3 = 1, and 4 = 0). Sum items 1, 3, 4, 7, 9, and 10 to obtain an overall score. Items 2, 5, 6, and 8 are filler items only. They are not scores as part of the revised scale. Scores range from 0 to 24, with higher scores reflecting more optimism. The average (mean) score is between 14 and 15.

Optimism and Psychological Well-Being

Optimism is the tendency to look on the favorable side of events and to expect positive outcomes in the future. Given this predisposition, do optimists fare better than pessimists? Past prophets of positive thinking would be pleased with the findings of recent research. In general, optimism is linked with a positive mood and higher morale. Indeed, numerous studies find that optimism is associated with diverse measures of good psychological health. For example, LOT scores are positively related to both a sense of self-mastery and self-esteem and negatively linked to depression and anxiety (Carver et al., 2009; Scheier & Carver, 2007; Scheier, Carver, & Bridges, 1994).

Even more important, optimism confers resistance to distress. A bright outlook fosters well-being. Optimists cope with stressful events, from dealing with unfamiliar environments to major health concerns, more effectively than pessimists. Consider the following:

- Students who entered college with an optimistic outlook handled the new challenges more successfully (Aspinwall & Taylor, 1992). Those with higher LOT scores at the start of college had lower levels of emotional distress at the end of the semester. Optimists seem to experience less stress, depression, and loneliness than pessimists.

- Optimism seems to confer resistance to the development of postpartum depression. Expectant mothers anticipating the birth of their first child completed the LOT and a depression scale during the last weeks of their pregnancy. They took the depression measure a second time 3 weeks after giving birth. Those who were optimistic before giving birth were less likely than those who were pessimistic to show any increase in depression after the birth (Carver & Gaines, 1987).

- Optimism makes the experience of major surgery less stressful (Shelby et al., 2008). Optimistic patients who have heart bypass surgery experience less presurgical distress than pessimistic patients. Further, controlling for presurgical life satisfaction, optimism was associated with better psychological well-being after surgery. Independent of disease severity, a general sense of optimism seemed to funnel into specific confidence regarding the surgery, and from there to more life satisfaction (Fitzgerald et al., 1993). Patients undergoing surgery for breast cancer showed similar effects. LOT scores assessed at the time of diagnosis were used to predict levels of distress. Optimism predicted not only lower initial distress, but resilience to distress during the year following surgery (Carver et al., 1993).

- Optimism positively affects caregivers' well-being (Given et al., 1993). Higher levels of optimism in people caring for cancer patients was linked with lower depression, better physical health, and fewer detrimental effects on caregivers' daily schedules. Optimism in the caregiver spouses of Alzheimer's patients conferred similar benefits.

Optimism and Physical Well-Being

Optimism proves to be good medicine. Numerous case studies hint that hopefulness extends life and hopelessness takes it.

When Bruno Bettelheim (1960) observed concentration camp inmates in Nazi Germany, he learned that some measure of hopefulness was necessary for survival:

> Prisoners who came to believe the repeated statements of the guards—that there was no hope for them, that they would never leave the camp except as a corpse—these prisoners were in a literal sense walking corpses.... They were people so totally exhausted, both physically and emotionally, that they had given the environment total power over them.... Shortly after the beginning of captivity, these men stopped eating, sat mute and motionless in corners, and finally died (pp. 151–152).

Careful research confirms that people with a positive outlook not only feel better, they also enjoy better physical health than those with a negative outlook. Optimists are bothered by fewer physical illnesses and live longer. When compared with pessimists, optimists make fewer visits to the doctor, receive better ratings of general health from their physicians, have stronger immune system functioning, and show faster rehabilitation from major surgery. Here are some specific examples:

- Optimistic college students reported better physical health at both the start and end of the final month of the semester (Scheier & Carver, 1985). Most important, optimism at the start of the month predicted fewer physical symptoms at the end of the month. The positive link between optimism and good health was not the result of fewer symptoms producing a brighter outlook. Rather, optimism was an independent predictor of good health.

- Optimists were less likely to suffer a heart attack during bypass surgery, and they achieved behavioral milestones more quickly afterward (sitting up in bed, walking around the room, and so on) (Scheier et al., 1989). A 6-month follow-up found that optimists were more likely to have resumed vigorous physical exercise and to have returned to work full time. All the "optimism" advantages were independent of the patient's medical status at the outset of the study. That is, optimists didn't do better simply because they were less sick at the time of the surgery.

- Optimism was associated with a lower risk of death in 839 Mayo Clinic patients observed over a 30-year period (Maruta et al., 2000). In fact, optimists lived significantly longer than their more pessimistic counterparts. Additionally, optimistic content in the handwritten early-life autobiographies of Catholic nuns was highly predictive of their longevity (Danner & Snowdon, 2001). More than half of those who wrote with joy and optimism in early adulthood were still alive at 94. In contrast, only 11 percent of those who had expressed little positive emotion in their diaries survived to that age.

- For 660 older adults, attitudes toward aging, measured up to 23 years earlier, were strongly predictive of survival (Levy et al., 2002). People with positive perceptions ("I have as much pep as I did last year," "As I get older, things are better than I thought they would be") lived 7.5 years longer than people with less positive perceptions of aging ("As you get older, you are less useful").

Why does optimism provide so many apparent health benefits? Psychological research highlights a consistent fact: Optimists cope with stress more constructively than do pessimists (Carver, Scheier, & Segerstrom, 2010). In contrast to pessimists, optimists are problem-focused and they take action to cope with whatever challenges they face. Optimists also tap into available social support, seeking solace and input from family and friends when facing upsetting events. Pessimists do not cope nearly as well, as most rely on counterproductive strategies when they encounter stress—they try to avoid it altogether, don't think about it, or even deny (in the psychological sense) that it exists. Quite a few simply give up when stress comes to call. Interestingly, pessimists seem particularly more vulnerable than optimists to accidental or violent death (Peterson et al., 1998). The finding recalls the sage advice given the victim lamenting, "I broke my nose in two places." "Well," responded his sympathetic listener, "I'd stay out of those two places if I were you" (Peterson & Bossio, 2001, p. 139). Male pessimists, especially, seem to have a habit of being in the wrong place at the wrong time.

Realistic Optimism

Clearly, optimism is beneficial, but there is another important angle to take in assessing this strength. Try the Future Life Events scale.

 **SELF-ASSESSMENT**

Future Life Events

Compared with other students of your sex at your school, what do you think are the chances that the events listed will happen to you? Use the following scale in making your responses:

1 = 100% less (no chance)   2 = 80% less   3 = 60% less   4 = 40% less
5 = 20% less   6 = 10% less   7 = Average (my chances are equal to the average)
8 = 10% more   9 = 20% more   10 = 40% more   11 = 60% more
12 = 80% more   13 = 100% more   14 = 3 times average   15 = 5 times average

Note: Do NOT respond to events in terms of how likely they are. Instead, be sure to evaluate the likelihood of events for you compared with other students at your school. In other words, for each item think "Compared with other students, I am _____% more (or less) likely to _____."

_____ **1.** Have a drinking problem

_____ **2.** Like my post-college job

_____ **3.** Own my own home

_____ **4.** Attempt suicide

_____ **5.** Have a heart attack before age 40

_____ **6.** Be fired from a job

_____ **7.** Have a starting salary of more than $40,000 per year

_____ **8.** Travel to Europe

_____ **9.** Graduate in the top third of my college class

_____ **10.** Get lung cancer

_____ **11.** Trip and break a bone

_____ **12.** Live past 80

_____ **13.** Control my weight for at least 10 years

_____ **14.** Get divorced a few years after my marriage

Source: Weinstein (1980).

To score your responses, find your average (mean) response to items 1, 4, 5, 6, 10, 11, and 14—sum the numbers you gave in response to those items and divide by 7. Also find your average (mean) response to items 2, 3, 7, 8, 9, 12, and 13—total and divide by 7. The first list represents negative life events and the second list contains positive life events. Most respondents to this exercise have a mean below 7.0 for the first list and a mean above 7.0 for the second list. That is, they think that, compared with their peers, they are less likely to experience negative events and more likely to experience positive events.

Many of us, suggests Neil Weinstein (1980, 1982, 2003), are unrealistically optimistic about future life events. The result? In underestimating our risk, we may be less likely to take preventive action. By discounting their personal susceptibility to the risks of smoking, cigarette smokers avoid trying to quit (Gibbons, Eggleston, & Benthin, 1997; Weinstein, Slovic, & Gibson, 2004). Seeing themselves as less vulnerable to unwanted pregnancy than other women of childbearing age, sexually active heterosexual college women don't consistently use contraceptives (Burger & Burns, 1988). Clearly, optimism has its limits.

So "Don't get your hopes up" is sometimes good advice. At Shawshank prison, Red warns Andy that optimism can disappoint: "There's no escape. We are destined to die here and hoping will drive you insane" (Marvin & Darabont, 1994). "Blessed is he who expects nothing," wrote poet Alexander Pope, "for he shall never be disappointed" (cited in Bent, 1887, p. 628).

In contrast to unrealistic optimism, "flexible" or "realistic" optimism (Seligman, 1990; Schneider, 2001) characterizes hope-filled people who keep their eyes open. In viewing the past, they give themselves and others the benefit of the doubt; they see current obstacles as challenges; and they look expectantly to the future. At the same time, they know that wishful thinking by itself does not improve things, nor is everything under personal control. And optimists show acceptance in uncontrollable situations, while pessimists are more likely to engage in active denial (Carver & Scheier, 1999). So, optimism—especially flexible optimism—is beneficial. But why? How exactly does optimism work to provide its advantages?

How Optimism Works

First, realistic optimism motivates. We are more likely to invest effort if we believe that the desirable is attainable. People who make favorable appraisals of their future are more likely to initiate action. When they encounter obstacles (and everyone does) and their progress is temporarily impeded, optimists are also more likely to persist. Why? The key is how people interpret setbacks. Optimists and pessimists, Martin Seligman (1990) explains, provide different explanations for life's disappointments.

✔ SELF-ASSESSMENT

Explanatory Styles

Imagine for a moment your bank has just informed you that your checking account is overdrawn. After reflecting a bit on the possible reasons for this notice, write down in a sentence or two what you believe to be the single most important cause.

_____

_____

_____

_____

In thinking about what you have just written, answer the following questions:

1. Is the cause something that is permanent or is it temporary; that is, will the cause be present in the future?

_____

2. Is the cause something that influences other areas of your life or only your checking account balance?

_____

3. Does the cause you describe reflect more about you or about other people and circumstances?

_____

Seligman reports that pessimists tend to explain troubles in terms that are *stable* ("It's going to last forever"), *global* ("It's going to affect everything I do"), and *internal* ("It's all my fault"). Such explanations leave them feeling helpless. Since life is not controllable, they ask, "Why put forth the effort?" Pessimism paralyzes.

Contrast this style of explaining life's problems with that of the optimistic Andy Dufresne at Shawshank. "Sure, I'm in prison," Andy admits, "but my loss of freedom is temporary. Moreover, imprisonment need not undermine everything I do. My efforts still make a difference. Look," he says to himself, "I write letters, read books, teach students, even continue financial accounting. And what brought me to Shawshank is really not my fault." Clearly, his optimistic outlook energizes him.

As Andy illustrates, optimists are more likely to explain negative events in terms that are *temporary* ("This is only momentary"), specific ("This is only one small aspect of life"), and *external* ("This is really not my fault") (Peterson & Steen, 2009). Such explanations are more likely to invigorate while also providing some psychological protection (Wise & Rosqvist, 2006). Clearly, the troubling event can be surmounted.

It's no wonder that this motivating way of explaining things is associated with higher levels of achievement and the ability to bounce back from failure. Seligman and Schulman (1986) evaluated the success of new life-insurance salespeople whose outlooks were more or less optimistic. Those who saw their initial setbacks as flukes or as suggesting the need for a new approach sold more policies and were half as likely to quit.

Still, it is more than sheer persistence that gives optimists their advantage. They also tend to cope well with problems.

 **SELF-ASSESSMENT**

Coping Strategies

Take a few minutes to identify the most important problem you faced during the last year. Then, using the scale, indicate how often you used each of the following strategies to deal with it.

0 = Not at all   1 = A little   2 = Occasionally   3 = Fairly often

_____ **1.** Took things one day at a time

_____ **2.** Tried to find out more about the situation

_____ **3.** Tried to reduce tension by drinking more

_____ **4.** Talked with a professional person (doctor, lawyer, cleric)

_____ **5.** Took it out on other people when I felt angry or depressed

_____ **6.** Prayed for guidance and/or strength

_____ **7.** Talked with a friend about the problem

_____ **8.** Tried to reduce tension by taking more tranquilizing drugs

_____ **9.** Told myself things that helped me feel better

_____ **10.** Kept my feelings to myself

_____ **11.** Bargained or compromised to get something positive from the situation

_____ **12.** Tried to reduce tension by exercising more

_____ **13.** Tried to reduce tension by smoking more

_____ **14.** Tried to see the positive side of the situation

_____ **15.** Considered several alternatives for handling the problem

_____ **16.** Made a plan of action and followed it

_____ **17.** Went over the situation in my mind to try to understand it

_____ **18.** Tried to reduce tension by eating more

_____ **19.** Got busy with other things to keep my mind off the problem

_____ **20.** Drew on my past experiences

_____ **21.** Avoided being with people in general

_____ **22.** I knew what had to be done and tried harder to make things work

_____ **23.** Tried to step back from the situation and be more objective

_____ **24.** Refused to believe that it happened

This questionnaire, abbreviated from one designed by Charles Holahan and Rudolph Moos (1987), assesses three different kinds of strategies for coping with problems. The authors believe that active-cognitive _strategies (assessed by items 1, 6, 9, 14, 15, 17, 20, and 23) represent active efforts to construct thoughts to help cope with the problem._ Active-behavioral _strategies (assessed by items 2, 4, 7, 11, 12, 16, 19, and 22) constitute active efforts to change the situation, and_ avoidance _strategies (assessed by items 3, 5, 8, 10, 13, 18, 21, and 24) reflect efforts to keep the problem out of awareness. To determine which strategy you tend to use more, find your mean score for each subscale. That is, add up the numbers you gave in response to the items on each of the three subscales and, for each subscale, divide by 8. Which mean is highest and which is lowest for you?_

As noted earlier, research suggests that optimists cope with stress in more adaptive ways; that is, they tend to use active-cognitive and active-behavioral rather than avoidance strategies. They not only take action but are more focused and more inclined to plan when faced with challenges. Intent on making the best of negative situations, they try to grow personally from adversity.

Consider optimistic college freshmen, who seem to have an easier time adjusting to college life than do pessimistic students. In studying their coping strategies, Aspinwall and Taylor (1992) found that the optimists were more likely to deal with the stress of attending new classes, forming new relationships, and living in a strange environment by trying to do something about these challenges directly. They faced the challenge of an upcoming exam through direct problem solving, such as preparing for the test and talking with other students. Pessimists were more likely to pretend the problems did not exist or to disengage by wishful thinking and social withdrawal.

Pessimism, particularly when it is based in feelings of helplessness, suppresses the immune system and thus leaves people more vulnerable to physical illness (Rodin, 1986). The positive link between optimism and physical well-being also has its basis in attitudes and actions that contribute to good health. Optimists pay more attention to health-related information than do pessimists (Aspinwall & Brunhart, 1996) and are less prone to self-destructive habits such as substance abuse (Carvajal et al., 1998). They are more successful in limiting saturated fat in their diet, reducing body fat, and increasing their aerobic capacity (Shepperd, Maroto, & Pbert, 1996). And when diagnosed with a serious illness such as cancer, optimists are more likely not only to accept its reality but to take active steps to meet the unexpected challenge (Carver et al., 1993). In short, optimism benefits us by energizing us and fostering more effective problem solving.

⇒ I N   R E V I E W

Philosophers, theologians, and psychologists have long debated the merits of hope. The Revised Life Orientation Test (LOT-R) of Scheier, Carver, and Bridges (1994) assesses optimism—the extent to which we believe that good as opposed to bad things will generally occur in our lives. Research has linked optimism to both psychological and physical well-being. Optimists seem to cope better with stressful life events and actually live longer than pessimists. Although unrealistic optimism can disappoint and even endanger a person, flexible optimism energizes and fosters effective problem solving.

Exploring Hope

Andy Dufresne: Dynamo with an Agenda

Andy dreams of freedom. Most prisoners at Shawshank do, at least when they first enter. However, an experienced resident like Red knows better. For him and all other veterans, hope is bubble-headed optimism. He warns Andy, "It would take a man

600 years to tunnel through the wall." Most inmates eventually became "institution-alized." "These walls are funny," Red continues, "first, you hate 'em, then you get used to 'em. Enough time passes, it gets so you depend on 'em." Hope withers in a wretched environment.

But not for Andy. His will seeks a way. And some early prison success only fuels his optimism. Six years of weekly request letters to the State Senate secure a $200 check along with boxes of books for a new inmate library. Andy's smart legal advice saves Captain Hadley's inheritance and earns Andy and his coworkers a break with three cold beers each on a hot summer day. Finally, Tommy Williams, a new arrival serving a 2-year sentence for breaking and entering, seems to provide the route out. Imprisoned elsewhere, Tommy heard a fellow inmate confess to the murder of Andy's wife.

But hope is short-circuited. Warden Norton, the real criminal in the story, kills Tommy before he can testify and prove Andy's innocence. The road to freedom dead-ends. The lesson? Strong wills do not guarantee fruitful ways.

Nineteen years pass. Then, amazingly, Shawshank's early morning headcount finds Andy's bunk empty. Rushing to the vacant cell, a dumbfounded warden stumbles onto the escape route. Behind a wall-sized poster of Raquel Welch, Andy had meticulously chiseled a passageway to freedom. Patiently over the years, he had toted his wall out to the exercise yard, pocketfuls at a time. His tool of redemption? A small rock hammer carefully concealed in a hollowed-out Bible, the warden's gift to every new Shawshank inmate. Andy's driving hope was realized. Its ingredients? A clearly defined objective, back-breaking determination, and a carefully planned route.

Psychology of Hope

Close your eyes for a moment and think of your future. Write down the first image that comes to mind.

_____

_____

_____

_____

How long does it take to see that something? If you are like most people, suggests C. R. Snyder (1994), it takes only a few seconds to imagine something you want to happen. We are intrinsically goal directed. Goals are the target of hopeful thinking, from the immediate short term ("I hope to complete today's reading assignment") to the more significant long term ("I hope to earn a college degree"). But goals are only one ingredient of hope, said Snyder. To appreciate its other elements, complete his Hope Scale (Snyder et al., 1991; see also, Snyder, 1994).

Hope Scale

Read each of the following items carefully. Using the scale, enter the number that best describes you in the blank provided.

1 = Definitely false   2 = Mostly false   3 = Mostly true   4 = Definitely true

_____ **1.** I energetically pursue my goals.

_____ **2.** I can think of many ways to get out of a jam.

_____ **3.** My past experiences have prepared me well for my future.

_____ **4.** There are lots of ways around any problem.

_____ **5.** I've been pretty successful in life.

_____ **6.** I can think of many ways to get the things done in life that are most important to me.

_____ **7.** I meet the goals that I set for myself.

_____ **8.** Even when others get discouraged, I know I can find a way to solve the problem.

Hope, suggests Snyder, reflects one's willpower and "waypower" in reaching future goals. Agency is the willpower, or energy needed to keep moving toward your goals. Pathways is the waypower, or perceived ability to generate routes to achieve those goals.

Derive your agency subscale by adding the numbers you placed in front of items 1, 3, 5, and 7. Determine your pathways subscale by adding items 2, 4, 6, and 8. Add the four agency and four pathways items to obtain a total "hope" score. Mean or average scores on each subscale are 12, making the average total hope score 24. Higher scores reflect more hope, lower scores reflect less hope.

Can a score on the Hope Scale predict how will feel or behave? The late C. R. Snyder, a social, clinical, and positive psychologist, was once interviewed about hope on the TV show *Good Morning America* (Lopez, 2006a, b). Prior to his appearance on the program, Snyder had three of the show's cast (the host, the medical reporter, and the weatherman) complete the same Hope Scale you did. Later, when the show was live, Snyder had the three cast members each take a turn at the "cold pressor task," a traditional research tool from experimental psychology. The task is simple: Each person plunges his or her right fist into an ice bath of freezing water and holds it there until it becomes too painful (if this sounds easy and not at all painful, try it—you may be surprised by the experience). During the demonstration, Snyder outlined hope theory for the audience and explained how higher levels of hope are linked to a higher tolerance for pain. (Do you see where this is going?) As Snyder anticipated, the scores each of the cast members received earlier on the Hope Scale predicted how long they endured the frigid water and the pain and numbness it created. Simply put, higher levels of hope were associated with the ability to withstand discomfort for longer periods of time (see also Snyder et al., 2005).

How else can hope help people face obstacles and challenges?

Goals of Hopeful People

High-hope people seem to set more objectives for themselves than low-hope people (Snyder et al., 1991). They set several goals, not just one, for each of their life roles, including their careers, their relationships, and their recreation. Hopeful people also set more difficult goals for themselves (Snyder et al., 1991). The objectives of hopeful people tend to be concrete and vivid (Snyder, 1995). They are fully describable to themselves and to others.

Hopeful Connections to Others

When does hopeful thinking or a hopeful outlook start? Hope's origins probably lie in childhood, emerging as a result of positive interactions between children and their adult caregivers, mentors, and role models. Hopeful people are adept at taking the perspective of others (Rieger, 1993), which means they are socially competent (Snyder et al., 1997) and are likely to be less lonely than those low in hope (Sympson, 1999). Higher levels of hope are positively associated with having close personal connections with others. People with hope are as interested in advancing the goals of others as they are in promoting their own (Snyder et al., 1997).

Willpower of Hopeful People

High-hope people are routinely optimistic and believe they control their own destiny (Snyder, 1994). Difficult goals are viewed as invigorating challenges rather than as insurmountable obstacles. Hopeful people experience disappointments like everyone else, but they tend to think about them differently. With self-talk like "I'll make it," "I can do it," and "I won't give up," hopeful people endure. Rather than ruminating over setbacks, they focus on what still needs to be done (Snyder et al., 1998).

Waypower of Hopeful People

In comparison with less hopeful people, those with high hope are more skilled at finding alternative routes to their goals. For example, researchers asked college students what they would do if they were taking a course for which they had set a grade goal of a B but then received a D on their first examination. Hopeful students generated a variety of adaptive strategies, such as going to talk to the instructor, outlining their notes and readings, scheduling specific times each day to study, and hiring a tutor (Yoshinobu, 1989).

In times of stress, hopeful people seem to have a larger arsenal of coping strategies to draw from. They have a bigger support network to use in both good and bad times. They are more likely to use humor to cope with life's trials and to engage in prayer or meditation to renew their mental energy. Recognizing the importance of their health, they are more likely to exercise as well.

Hope and Achievement

Those who score high on the Hope Scale do not have higher IQs than low scorers, but they are more successful. They are more likely to persevere and to reach their goals. For example, in one study (Snyder et al., 1991), introductory psychology students took the Hope Scale at the beginning of the semester. A few weeks later they were asked to predict the final grade they would receive for the course. Hope Scale scores were positively correlated with both expected and obtained grades.

⇒ **I N   R E V I E W**

> Goals are the targets of hopeful thinking. Willpower is the motivation to keep moving toward goals. Waypower is the perceived ability to generate routes to achieve those goals. These ingredients of hope are interconnected. For example, identifying clear goals energizes a person's search for appropriate routes.
>
> Hopeful people set more challenging goals for themselves. Moreover, they have objectives that are concrete and vivid. They are routinely optimistic and view obstacles as invigorating challenges rather than as insurmountable obstacles. They are skilled at finding alternative routes to their goals and thus enjoy higher levels of achievement.

Fostering Hope

Hopeful people can tell you what they hope for. Periodically, we all need to take inventory of our hopes and why we hope for the things we do, suggest Diane McDermott and C. R. Snyder (1999).

Identifying Goals

One effective strategy for setting goals is to identify the major areas of your life—perhaps relationships, family, work, health, leisure—and list important goals under each. Doing this even for the first time doesn't take long. Once you formulate the list, put it away for a week and then take it back out. Add or delete goals as you see fit. Try to increase the number of goals in each area. Hopeful people tend to have many objectives across the various arenas of life.

As you identify goals, keep in mind that hopeful people have goals that are vivid and concrete. Vague goals such as "to be successful" are of little use in terms of motivation. Remember also that manageable goals induce hope. It's fine to have inspiring, long-range goals, but try to break them down into step-by-step subgoals. The journey is always more satisfying when you can measure progress along the way.

After you have identified multiple goals in each area, prioritize. Sort the goals from the most to the least important. Give A's to the extremely important things, to the quite important, C's to the somewhat important, and D's to the slightly important. Until you do this, you will probably be pulled in too many directions. Following Snyder's guidelines, it should not be too difficult to generate your own inventory.

Rank	Relationships	Family	Work	Health	Leisure
A	Express more appreciation	Help daughter select high school classes	Finish faculty guide for video series	Purchase new glasses	Purchase season tickets for film series
A	Take computer class together	Visit elderly mother weekly	Write letters of recommendation	Exercise 30 minutes daily	Schedule weekly golf game
B	Finish home repair projects	Help daughter learn to drive	Prepare chapter on empathy	Lose 8 pounds	Read book on aquarium care
B	Remember anniversary	Plan family reunion	Prepare course syllabi for new semester	Eat more balanced diet	Plan summer garden/ purchase seeds
B	Attend concert series with friends	Write aunts and uncle	Prepare for department seminar	Schedule annual physical	Find 4 hours weekly to read recommended novels
C	Plan vacation	Build college fund	Prepare schedule of committee meetings	Get more sleep	Take evening class in woodworking

 ✔ SELF-ASSESSMENT

Now try identifying and ranking your own goals.

Rank	Relationships	Family	Work	Health	Leisure

Strengthening Willpower and Waypower

Having identified their goals, hopeful people take responsibility for moving toward reaching those goals. Their sense of agency and pathways are primarily rooted in the ways they think about themselves and their worlds.

As we noted earlier, hopeful people tend to view their goals as challenges and in so doing, focus on success rather than failure. Instead of appraising them as difficult, they think of them as opportunities. "Taking this class on the Korean language offers the chance to stretch myself"; "It's satisfying to help these intellectually disabled kids master a vocational skill they can use." And when obstacles do come, hopeful people continue the positive internal dialogue with "I can," "I'll make it," and "I won't give up."

To assess the content of your internal dialogue, you might keep a diary of your goal-related thoughts for one week. How many of your thoughts are put-downs in which you repeatedly tell yourself that you cannot do something or that bad things are going to happen to you? Such thought patterns undermine willpower. Don't feel deflated. Rather, recognize that this awareness is the first step toward change.

Visualizing Success (and Enacting It)

"Hold the image of yourself succeeding," recommended positive-thinking advocate Norman Vincent Peale (1982, p. 15). "Visualize it so vividly that when the desired outcome comes, it seems to be merely echoing a reality that has already existed in your mind." Good advice? Sports psychologists now include mental simulation as a standard part of training to improve performance. Many athletes report that they actually experience the muscle twinges associated with their performance as they imagine themselves diving, serving in tennis, or jumping in skating.

In some cases, such mental simulation fosters willpower. More important, however, mental simulation seems to work by fostering waypower. Rehearsing the *process* needed to reach a desired goal pays better dividends than simply imagining the *destination*.

About a week before their midterm exam in psychology, students received training in mental simulation (Pham & Taylor, 1997). Some were told to imagine themselves earning an A. Other students were told to visualize themselves studying for the exam in a way that would lead them to obtain an A. They were told to visualize themselves at their desks, on their beds, or at the library studying the chapters, going over the lecture notes, eliminating distractions such as the television or stereo, and declining a friend's invitation to go out.

Each group practiced this simulation for 5 minutes each day until the exam. Those who simply thought about the outcome showed little improvement, adding only two points to exam scores. However, those who reflected on the process began to study sooner, spent more time on it, and improved performance by eight points. Rehearsing the process needed to reach a goal, suggested the researchers, helps one to identify the steps necessary to get there by creating a plan. Once a plan is established, you have only to begin to enact it.

Learning Optimism

Recalling our previous successful pursuits of goals, particularly as we face difficulties in the present, fosters perseverance. Not only do they remind us that if we did it once, we can do it again, but they often provide insight into specific strategies that once worked and just might work again.

Although we sometimes think that obstacles to goals necessarily have negative consequences, psychologist Albert Ellis (1989) taught otherwise. People are predisposed to analyze the causes of disappointment, he argued, and the specific answers they give are a key element in understanding why two people respond so differently to the same event.

For example, Jake's failure to make the soccer team leads him to believe, "I'm a terrible athlete," and he never tries out for another sports team. Ricardo's failure to make the cut leads him to the conclusion, "I didn't try hard enough," and he is inspired to try harder for track. In short, Jake's failure is paralyzing, while Ricardo's is energizing. As we saw earlier, pessimists tend to explain adversity in terms of causes that are internal ("I'm not good at athletics"), permanent ("I have poor eye-hand coordination"), and pervasive ("I'm such a loser"). Optimists favor causes that are external ("The coach doesn't like sophomores"), temporary ("I didn't get enough sleep"), and specific ("I'm not good at soccer").

In learning optimism, Martin Seligman (1990) suggests that we first understand its underlying ABCs. When we experience **a**dversity, we react by attempting to understand it. That understanding congeals into **b**eliefs that have real **c**onsequences for our feelings and actions.

✓ SELF-ASSESSMENT

Learning Optimism

To see how the ABCs of optimism work, try the following. In each case the adversity is identified along with either the belief or the consequence. You fill in the missing component. Note that some of these examples reflect an optimistic outlook and others do not.

1. A. Someone breaks into line ahead of you to buy concert tickets.
   B. You think _____
   _____.

   C. You get angry and shout at the other customer.
2. A. An acquaintance you made at a coffee shop hasn't returned your phone calls.
   B. You think _____
   _____.

   C. You are not perturbed by it and go about your day's work.

3. A. You lose the key to your apartment.

    B. You think, "I never do anything right."

    C. You feel (or do) _____

    _____.

4. A. Your employer complains that you arrived for work five minutes late.

    B. You think, "He must really be having a bad day."

    C. You feel (or do) _____

    _____.

As part of your week's diary of goal-related thoughts, you might record several ABCs from your own life. Try to analyze the connection you draw between adversity, no matter how small, and your consequent feelings and actions. For example, adversity might be discovering that you overslept, missed the bus, or forgot to pay the telephone bill. Your beliefs are how you interpret the adversity: "I can't do anything right." For consequences, record your feelings and what you did. Were you depressed, angry, or sad? Did you lose energy, perhaps even waste the day?

People can learn to change their pessimistic explanatory styles to a more optimistic style (Seligman et al., 1999). If successfully challenged, our pessimistic beliefs are unlikely to recur when the same adversity repeats itself. Learning to counterargue, to offer alternative causes for the disappointment, to recognize that we are overreacting, and even to show that the belief is factually incorrect undermine the pessimistic explanation and enable us to cope with setbacks more effectively.

Communal Hope

Hope flourishes best in community, where individuals connect with others, exchanging social support. Research confirms that high-hope people have a social support network that they rely on in both good and bad times (Snyder, 1994). The corollary also happens to be true. The less hopeful are characterized by loneliness. They seem unable to initiate and sustain relationships.

Thus, a social environment that undermines the need to belong not only feeds loneliness, it may also fuel hopelessness. In analyzing the epidemic depression rate among Westerners, Seligman (1990) concludes that our society's message that we are masters of our own fate and thus should do our own thing comes with a cost. Such individualism has led to a decline of commitment to family, religious groups, and community. Thus, when disappointment comes, Westerners weather it alone. The self-focused individual assumes personal responsibility for problems and has no one to turn to for support. In more collectivist societies, where close-knit relationships and cooperation are the norm, depression is less common and less linked to self-blame over personal failure.

But Seligman's analysis penetrates more deeply. He raises fundamental questions about the very targets of our hope. Our best dreams will always include hopes for health, hopes for success at work and play, and even hopes for qualities of character and of what we can become. Our most fundamental hope is probably for our own well-being and happiness. But do our hopes also reach beyond ourselves? Do we have hope that others will experience the best that life offers? To what extent are we global hopers? Do we keep hope alive for our physical environment, for hungry and lonely people, for those suffering oppression and injustice?

Optimism is just a tool, suggests Seligman, to help people achieve the goals they have set for themselves. It is in the selection of goals that meaning or emptiness resides, and finding meaning requires a commitment to something larger than yourself. "When learned optimism is coupled with a renewed commitment to the commons," concludes Seligman, "our epidemic of depression and meaninglessness may end" (1990, p. 291).

Snyder agreed. Hope is ultimately counterproductive, he argued, to the extent that individuals pursue their goals to the detriment of others. What is needed are environments in which people living and working together can interact to support one another so that both individual and collective goals can be met (Snyder & Feldman, 2000). Hope is for the many, not just the few.

Interestingly, research with the Hope Scale you completed earlier reports that hopeful people can and do think about communal or shared goals (Snyder, 1994). They have learned that while people gain satisfaction from individual goals, they gain even more meaning in joining with others in pursuing goals aimed at a greater good. Those who have realized their own dreams want to make the hopes of others real as well.

So it is finally with Andy Dufresne. As much a giver as a receiver of help, he repeatedly renews despondent spirits at Shawshank. From his unorthodox winning of three beers apiece for his roofing coworkers to dissolving prison walls with an unauthorized broadcast of an Italian opera over the PA system, Andy instills hope in others. Most of all, he convinces his best friend Red that he, too, "can make it on the outside." By story's end, Red has internalized Andy's words: "One must either get busy living or get busy dying."

⇒ IN REVIEW

> Fostering hope begins with identifying and prioritizing goals. Positive self-talk from the outset strengthens motivation and the search for appropriate pathways. Rehearsing the process, not simply the destination, promotes goal attainment. And interpreting disappointments in terms of causes that are external, temporary, and specific serves to maintain willpower.
>
> Hope survives best in community. Hopeful people have a strong support network and join with others in the pursuit of collective well-being.

Friendship and Social Support

Functions of Friendship

Features of Friendship

Forming and Maintaining Friendships

Without friendship, life is not worth living. —CICERO, 106–43 B.C.

How we live shapes how we feel when we die. In their final years, observed psychologist Erik Erikson (1963), the elderly ask whether their lives have had purpose or have been a failure. Answers lead to either integrity—the feeling that one's life has been meaningful and lived with purpose and fulfillment—or despair—the conclusion that the time has been wasted and that the approaching end is more bitter than bittersweet. To set life's priorities, we might anticipate Erikson's end-of-life question (Suzuki, 2000). The deathbed test helps us identify the human strengths and what is really worth pursuing in life (Peterson & Seligman, 2004). Try it for yourself.

The Deathbed Test

Imagine that you have lived a rich, meaningful life and now are on your deathbed. As you reflect back, what memories fill you with happiness, pride, and satisfaction? Verbalize at least one before reading on.

Your answer is probably not designer clothing, an expensive house, a sport utility vehicle, or a yacht. It may not be your greatest educational or career achievement. Most people say that the best things in life have been close, satisfying relationships, especially bonds with family and friends (Reis & Gable, 2003; Maisel & Gable, 2009; Suzuki, 2000). In late-life reminiscences, even those who have enjoyed exceptional career success attach more meaning to their close relationships than to their stellar accomplishments (Sears, 1977).

Functions of Friendship

How does friendship foster human flourishing? What specific needs do friends meet? Our close relationships are those ties with others that are significant, mutually supporting, and long lasting. People in these sorts of relationships work to maintain their close connections with the people who matter to them. Let's begin by considering what friends do for each other as well as what it means to be rejected.

Life Satisfaction

Social connections predict life satisfaction across time and place. From childhood through old age, those with friends experience greater psychological well-being than those without friends (Hartup & Stevens, 1997). An extensive cross-cultural review found only one common predictor of happiness across all countries studied: social relationships (Diener, 2001).

Time spent with friends seems to be particularly satisfying (Larson & Bradney, 1988). In one study, adults and teens were paged every 2 hours and asked what they were doing; who, if anyone, was with them; and how they felt. About 65 percent of the time the volunteers were in the presence of others. The most striking result was that participants of all ages reported higher levels of enjoyment and excitement when they were with friends than when they were alone or with casual acquaintances, coworkers, or family. Even married adults were happier with friends than when they were alone with their spouses. These adults' happiest times, however, were when they and their spouses were together with friends. Summarizing their results, the investigators concluded:

> With friends our attention becomes focused, distractions lessen, awareness of time disappears: We emerge into a world in which the intimacy and joy shared with others is the fundamental reality, and for a time the world becomes a different place (Larson & Bradney, 1988, p. 124).

Social Support

Friends do much more than make for a fun-filled life. "My friends have made the story of my life," observed Helen Keller. "In a thousand ways they have turned my limitations into beautiful privileges, and enabled me to walk serene and happy in the shadow cast by my deprivation" (2009, p. 179). Three-time cancer survivor Kathlyn Conway agrees. Friends provided an anchor during her most difficult times (Steiner, 2001, pp. 69–70). They gave *emotional support*—a listening ear for confiding painful feelings. "I had friends I could talk to at any time," she reports. "If I was upset, it was easy for me to call someone and expect them to listen no matter what."

At other times, they provided *instrumental assistance*—tangible goods and services. "One friend went to the hospital after my mastectomy and helped me wash my hair. Later, another friend left her very busy job in the middle of the week to go shopping with me for a wig." Friends also offered *informational support*—expert counsel and advice: "Another, who had had breast cancer herself, visited and stealthily, humorously, kindly opened her blouse to show me her implanted breast in order to reassure me."

The social support that is the basis of high-quality friendships, then, is linked to happiness, in large part because good friends satisfy people's basic psychological needs (Demir & Ozdemir, 2010). Among college students, those with solid friendships are not only optimistic, they also cope with stressful life events more readily than peers with less stable friendships (Brissette, Scheier, & Carver, 2002). Having good friends usually means having good and reliable social support.

How strong is your social support? Complete the following scale to find out.

 **SELF-ASSESSMENT**

Your Social Support

Decide whether each of the following statements is true or false for you.

T   F   **1.** If I needed an emergency loan of $100, there is someone I could get it from.

T   F   **2.** There is someone who takes pride in my accomplishments.

T   F   **3.** I often meet or talk with family or friends.

T   F   **4.** Most people I know think highly of me.

T   F   **5.** If I needed an early-morning ride to the airport, there's no one I would feel comfortable asking to take me.

T   F   **6.** I feel there is no one with whom I can share my most private worries and fears.

T   F   **7.** Most of my friends are more successful making changes in their lives than I am.

T   F   **8.** I would have a hard time finding someone to go with me on a day trip to the beach or country.

From Insel, P. M., & Roth, W. T., *Core Concepts in Health* (9th ed.). New York: McGraw-Hill (2002); Adapted from Japenga, A., A family of friends. *Health*, November/December (1995). Reprinted by permission of McGraw Hill Education and Ann Japenga.

Add up the number of true answers to questions 1–4 together with the number of false answers to questions 5–8. If your score is 4 or more, your support network may be adequate. If your score is 3 or less, you should probably work on strengthening your social ties (Insel & Roth, 2002).

Why develop social ties? Having a social network with a variety of relationships predicts overall wellness—physical as well as psychological. Good friends are good for your health. A social network decreases the likelihood of contracting an illness and improves the course of recovery from an illness. People who enjoy strong support consistently are shown to have a lower risk of early death (see Straub, 2002, for a review). Here are some examples:

- A survey of 7000 adults in Alameda County, California, revealed that having a large number of social contacts enabled women to live an average of 2.8 years longer and men an average of 2.3 years longer. This greater longevity remained even when rates of smoking, alcohol use, physical activity, and obesity were taken into account.

- A 7-year study of 50-year-old men in Sweden found that social support was inversely related to mortality. Those with the highest levels of support had the lowest mortality rates. Low levels of social support had an impact on mortality equivalent to that of cigarette smoking.

- Over a 17-year period, cancer patients with the fewest daily social contacts were more than twice as likely to die than those with more social support. And over a 9-year period, heart disease patients with low social support had a 50 percent survival rate compared with an 82 percent rate for those with a strong social network.

- Both men and women with strong social ties are less likely to suffer heart attacks or even to contract colds. Social support has been linked with either better adjustment to, or faster recovery from, coronary artery surgery, rheumatoid arthritis, childhood leukemia, and stroke.

How does social support convey its health benefits? Some researchers suggest that it provides a buffer against the effects of stress. By providing important resources, our social network helps us cope more effectively. Friends may see that we receive medical attention more quickly. In addition to providing tangible support, they help us to evaluate and overcome the stressful events, perhaps by giving us reassurance or by bolstering our self-esteem. Psychologists suggest that social support is always beneficial, whether we are experiencing stress or not. For example, those who support us may help us eat, smoke, and drink less.

Social support comes from a variety of sources, including family, neighbors, coworkers, and social, community, and religious organizations. Perhaps most significantly, though, it comes from friends. For example, in studying senior citizens' social networks, psychologist Laura Christensen reports that "it is the quality of their relationships that matters—not the quantity. In our work we find that three is the critical friend number. If you have three people in your life that you can really count on, then you are doing as well as someone who has ten friends. Or twenty, for that matter. If you have fewer than three friends, then you could be a little precarious" (Steiner, 2001, pp. 67–71).

So take out a piece of paper and begin listing your friends. Do you have three people you really get excited about seeing and are certain you can trust? If you have fewer than three good friends, try to make an effort to deepen your friendship with a casual acquaintance. You will be glad you did.

Lessons of Social Rejection

We've learned plenty about the functions of social bonds by studying social rejection. Cut off from family and friends, we suffer. At one time or another, each of us has been through the discomfort of being unwelcome or left out. Some of us may even have been bullied by others. We feel deviant, defective, or just "different."

At times, individuals and groups deliberately exclude or ignore others. As Kipling Williams and Lisa Zadro (2001) observe, ostracism ranges from complete removal of an individual or group from the community (solitary confinement, exile, banishment) to giving another the "silent treatment" (see also DeWall, 2013; Nezlek et al., 2012). By adulthood everyone has been both a victim and a perpetrator of some form of ostracism. Consider those feelings more closely in the following exercise.

 **SELF-ASSESSMENT**

Feeling Excluded

Reflect on a time when you felt excluded or ignored. Perhaps it was a time when you were the target of the "silent treatment." What led to your being excluded or ignored? What feelings did the ostracism elicit and how did you attempt to deal with them?

_____

_____

_____

_____

_____

_____

_____

_____

A full 67 percent of a representative U.S. sample admitted using the silent treatment (deliberately not speaking to a person in their presence) on a loved one, and 75 percent indicated that they had been a target of the silent treatment (Williams & Zadro, 2001).

Structured interviews reveal the pain of being ignored. Consider the following:

In high school, the other students thought me weird and never spoke to me. I tell you in all honesty that at one stage they refused to speak to me for 153 days, not one word at all. That was a very low point for me in my life and on the 153rd day I swallowed 29 Valium pills. My brother found me and called an ambulance. When I returned to school, the kids had heard the whole story and for a few days they were falling over themselves to be my friend. Sadly, it didn't last. They stopped talking to me again and I was devastated. I stopped talking myself. I figured that it was useless to have a voice if no one listened (Williams & Zadro, 2001, pp. 41–42).

Another interviewee explained a familial tendency to use the silent treatment:

At the present time, my sister, aged 58, in the U.S. won't talk to either my father or myself—for supposedly differing reasons. My father's sister has not spoken to him for over 30 years. My mother's brother once refused to talk to his wife for 6 months. My mother regularly refused to talk to me or my sister for days at a time. It seems like ostracism is a congenital condition in my family (Williams & Zadro, 2001, p. 42).

One source of ostracism described not only the devastating consequences of ostracism but how, once started, it is difficult to stop:

After two weeks, I woke up one morning with a blinding flash of insight: "What are you doing to your relationship with your son?" In that short period of time my son had already become intimidated by this treatment—he did exactly what his mother said at all times and whenever he spoke, it was in a quiet whisper. I am ashamed to say that I was sort of pleased with the effects of my ostracism but, as I say, one day I realized that it was making him weak and submissive and that it was eroding the future quality of our relationship.

To terminate the ostracism, however, was an extremely difficult process. I could only begin with grudging monosyllabic responses to his indirect overtures. I was only able to expand on these responses with the passing of time and it is only now, about six weeks since the ostracism ceased, that our relationship appears to be getting back to pre-row normality.…if it had lasted much longer, I might not have been able to stop and not only would our relationship have been destroyed but also my son himself might have been permanently emotionally and psychologically disfigured. Further…it may have led to illness and perhaps, ultimately, to his premature death…ostracism can be like a whirlpool or quicksand. If you, the user, don't extract yourself from it as soon as possible, it is likely to become impossible to terminate regardless of any subsequent will to do so (Williams & Zadro, 2001, p. 43).

From their interviews, Williams and Zadro conclude that ostracism undermines our need for belonging ("You didn't belong. You thought, 'I'm a mistake, I shouldn't be here, I'm not wanted here'"), our need for self-esteem ("I'm just no good at anything...failure, failure, failure"), our need for control ("I felt helpless in so many areas of my life"), and our need for meaning ("[The silent treatment] made me question 'What's it all for? Why am I still here?' whereas before I never questioned that. I knew why I was there and I knew what it was all for").

Social rejection also affects behavior. Not surprisingly, perhaps, it can undermine self-regulation. Roy Baumeister explains:

> A great deal of psychological functioning is predicated on belonging to the group and enjoying the benefits, both direct and indirect, of that belongingness. Social exclusion undermines the basis for these sacrifices—it ceases to be worth it. The whole purpose of controlling yourself, behaving appropriately and making sacrifices is defeated. And so behavior may become impulsive, chaotic, selfish, disorganized and even destructive (2002).

In one laboratory study, Baumeister (2002a) asked research participants in small groups to privately name one fellow participant with whom they would like to continue working. Some participants were then told that all the other participants had chosen them; others were told that no one had chosen them. In another manipulation, participants took a personality test and then were informed that people with their profiles tended to be surrounded by friends as they grew older. Others were told that people with their profile tended to become increasingly isolated.

Results of the studies indicated that being excluded increases antisocial and self-defeating behaviors. Compared with their well-liked counterparts, people who felt excluded were more aggressive, more likely to cheat, less likely to help others, more likely to procrastinate, less likely to choose healthy behaviors, and less able to delay self-gratification. Indeed, ostracism seems to increase dishonest behavior because it triggers a sense of entitlement in the rejected person (Poon, Chen, & DeWall, 2013). In short, ostracized people exercise less self-control.

Are there any consequences for ostracizers— those, who for whatever reason, agree to socially isolate or reject another? Apparently, yes. One set of studies found that there are clear psychological costs to intentionally and actively rejecting another person. Perhaps this should come as no surprise, as ignoring others or giving them the silent treatment requires both vigilance and energy. Still, the intriguing finding here is that causing another the social pain of rejection leads to discomfort (bad mood) among those doing the rejecting (Legate et al., 2013).

The study of social rejection suggests that communities provide a lot more than a sense of belonging. Social connections, especially our friends, reassure us of our worth (Duck, 1983). They do this not only directly by admiring and supporting us but also by listening to us, seeking our advice, and by generally indicating that they value our perspective. By giving us the chance to help them, friends also foster our sense of personal control and responsibility. They meet our need for meaning by providing necessary anchor points for opinions, beliefs, and emotional responses. They suggest how we should react, and they guide our actions in subtle ways. Friends help us to see where we are right and where we are wrong.

Of course, social influence is not always beneficial. Friends, suggested author Alexander Lockhart, are like the buttons on an elevator—they can take you up or take you down (cited in Kleiser, 2005, p. 174). For example, peer influence is among the most powerful predictors of drug use. If an adolescent's friends use drugs, chances are good that he or she will too. If friends do not, the opportunity to use drugs may never present itself. Recognizing that social influence can work both ways, Cicero aptly noted, "Friendship was given by nature to be an assistant to virtue, not a companion to vice" (cited in Shubnell, 2000, p. 68). The lesson? Select your friends carefully and wisely and hold on to those who are genuine.

⇒ IN REVIEW

> Many people recall bonds with family and friends as life's greatest satisfaction. Research indicates that social support predicts both psychological and physical well-being. Ostracism not only undermines our need to belong, but also weakens our sense of self-esteem, personal control, and meaning. Social rejection may also interfere with the important human capacity for self-regulation. Friends foster our sense of self-worth and responsibility. They also help us evaluate our beliefs and guide our behavior. Recognizing that social influence can be either constructive or destructive, wise people choose friends carefully.

Features of Friendship

Our friends may be unique, but as we will see, there are a number of features most of us expect in someone we call "friend."

Defining Friendship

Let's first focus on how we define a friend. Reflect carefully before answering the following question for yourself.

What Is a Friend?

What do you think are the important characteristics of friendship? Complete the sentence "A friend is someone…" in five different ways.

1. _____

2. _____

3. _____

4. _____

5. _____

Answers from professional men and women in several large urban centers fell into the following eight categories, from most to least frequent (Sapadin, 1988). A friend is someone:

• With whom we are intimate

• Whom we trust

• On whom we can depend

• Who shares

• Who is accepting

• Who is caring

• With whom we are close

• Whom we enjoy

What about the friend who is closest to us? Do you have a *best* friend? Complete the following exercise to give that relationship some thought.

 SELF-ASSESSMENT

Intimate Friendship Scale

This scale suggests that our closest friendships reflect eight dimensions. Thinking of your best friend, how many items are true?

T   F   **1.** I feel free to talk with him/her about almost anything.

T   F   **2.** I know what kinds of books, games, and activities he/she likes.

T   F   **3.** When he/she is not around, I miss him/her.

T   F   **4.** The most exciting things happen when I am with him/her and nobody else is around.

T　F　**5.** Whenever he/she wants to tell me about a problem I stop what I am doing and listen for as long as he/she wants.

T　F　**6.** I can be sure he/she will help me whenever I ask for it.

T　F　**7.** I like to do things with him/her.

T　F　**8.** I know that whatever I tell him/her is kept secret between us.

Each of the statements in the Intimate Friendship Scale assesses a different dimension of close friendship:

1. **Frankness and spontaneity.** Your relationship includes honest self-disclosure of strengths and weaknesses as well as frank feedback about the other's actions.

2. **Sensitivity and knowing.** Understanding and empathy counterbalance frankness.

3. **Attachment.** Closeness and liking produce feelings of connection to the friend.

4. **Exclusiveness.** Unique qualities in the relationship lead to its elevation over other relationships.

5. **Giving.** You and your friend provide one another with material goods as well as social support.

6. **Imposition.** You and your friend stand ready to seek and accept each other's help.

7. **Common activities.** You enjoy time spent together in joint activities.

8. **Trust and loyalty.** You can hold each other's disclosures in confidence and will defend one another from outside attack.

Beverly Fehr summarizes the survey literature on friendship with a helpful definition. Friendship, she suggests, is a "voluntary, personal relationship, typically providing intimacy and assistance, in which the two parties like one another and seek each other's company (1996, p. 20)." Sharing (intimacy) and caring (assistance) seem to be the central, perhaps even the defining, features of friendship.

Sharing

"A friend is a person with whom I may be sincere," wrote Ralph Waldo Emerson (Emerson, et al., 1980, p. 119). "Before him I may think aloud" (Thoreau & Emerson, 2008, p. 40). And the result of such honesty? "Your friend," observed nineteenth-century physician and author Elbert Hubbard, "is the person who knows all about you and still likes you" (cited in Chang, 2006, p. 324).

Self-Concealment Scale

Respond to each of the following statements using a scale from 1 (strongly disagree) to 5 (strongly agree).

_____ **1.** I have an important secret that I haven't shared with anyone.

_____ **2.** If I shared all my secrets with my friends, they'd like me less.

_____ **3.** There are lots of things about me that I keep to myself.

_____ **4.** Some of my secrets have really tormented me.

_____ **5.** When something bad happens to me, I tend to keep it to myself.

_____ **6.** I'm often afraid I'll reveal something I don't want to.

_____ **7.** Telling a secret often backfires and I wish I hadn't told it.

_____ **8.** I have a secret that is so private I would lie if anybody asked me about it.

_____ **9.** My secrets are too embarrassing to share with others.

_____ **10.** I have negative thoughts about myself that I would never share with anyone.

Source: Larson & Chastain 1990. Copyright © 1990 Guilford Publications Inc. Reprinted by permission.

The Self-Concealment Scale was designed to measure the extent to which people typically share or disclose personal information that they perceive as distressing or negative. Total scores, which can range from 10 to 50, are obtained by summing the numbers placed before all the items. In this case, higher scores reflect a stronger tendency toward self-concealment and lower scores reflect more sharing. The mean score obtained from a group of 306 respondents, which included human service workers and graduate students in counseling psychology, was 25.92.

Higher scores on the Self-Concealment Scale predict anxiety, depression, and a variety of physical symptoms. Higher levels of self-concealment are also positively associated with reported pain among both chronically ill and healthy groups of people (Uysal & Lu, 2011). Sharing mends both body and soul. Disclosing to a friend stressful events and problems that threaten our self-esteem can be liberating. Those who write about personal trauma in a diary enjoy better physical health than those who don't (Baddeley & Pennebaker, 2011), but talking to a friend is even more beneficial (Smyth, Pennebaker, & Arigo, 2012). As we have already seen, benefits from our friends include everything from medical assistance to the bolstering of our self-esteem. Sometimes the benefit may be simply in knowing that our situation is not unique, that others experience the same distress. The act of not discussing or confiding in another about a stressful event may be more damaging than the event itself (Pennebaker, 1985, 2002).

Caring

Given human interdependence, it is not surprising that we may come to think of interpersonal relationships in terms of social economics, or an exchange of favors. A "tit for tat" exchange of favors is in fact one important way casual acquaintances maintain their relationships. From coworkers in a carpool taking turns driving to students exchanging lecture notes for the class days they missed, people trade similar benefits. Is this how you operate? Consider the following questions.

✓ SELF-ASSESSMENT

Exchange Orientation Scale

Do you tend to agree or disagree with the following statements?

1. When I give something to another person, I generally expect something in return.
   ____ Agree ____ Disagree

2. When someone buys me a gift, I try to buy that person as comparable a gift as possible.
   ____ Agree ____ Disagree

3. When people receive benefits from others, they ought to repay those others right away.
   ____ Agree ____ Disagree

4. It's best to make sure that things are always kept "even" between two people in a relationship.
   ____ Agree ____ Disagree

Source: From Mills, J., & Clark, M. S., "Communal and exchange relationships: Controversies and research," in R. Erber & R. Gilmour (Eds.), *Theoretical Frameworks for Personal Relationships* (pp. 29–42). Copyright © 1994 Taylor & Francis. Reprinted by permission.

Agreement with the statements reflects a stronger exchange orientation—seeing interpersonal relationships as structured on the giving and receiving of favors.

Research findings indicate that those with a strong exchange orientation:

- Are motivated by a desire to have "fair" relationships

- Expect benefits given or received to be repaid immediately

- Monitor individual inputs into tasks for which there will be a joint reward

- Keep track of another person's needs only when they expect the person to have an opportunity in the near future to reciprocate in taking care of their own needs

- Show little change in mood or self-evaluation when they help another person

This orientation seems to work well with strangers, casual acquaintances, and business partners. As friendships develop, however, we should be less concerned with instant repayment. True friends show a communal orientation—they respond to each others' needs without expecting immediate repayment (Morrow, 2009).

People vary in the strength of their communal orientation. How about you? Consider the following.

CHAPTER 10

 **SELF-ASSESSMENT**

Communal Orientation Scale

Do you tend to agree or disagree with the following statements?

1. It bothers me when other people neglect my needs.

____ Agree ____ Disagree

2. When making a decision, I take other people's needs and feelings into account.

____ Agree ____ Disagree

3. When I have a need, I turn to others I know for help.

____ Agree ____ Disagree

4. I often go out of my way to help another person.

____ Agree ____ Disagree

Source: From Mills, J., & Clark, M. S., "Communal and exchange relationships: Controversies and research," in R. Erber & R. Gilmour (Eds.), *Theoretical Frameworks for Personal Relationships* (pp. 29–42). Copyright © 1994 Taylor & Francis. Reprinted by permission.

Agreement with the statements reflects a tendency to watch out for others' welfare as well as the expectation that others will watch out for yours.

Research indicates that those with a strong communal orientation:

- Are motivated by a desire to please others

- Dislike immediate repayment for favors

- Do not monitor individual contributions to a relationship

- Keep track of another person's needs even when that person is unlikely to have an opportunity in the near future to reciprocate

- Are more cheerful and have a heightened self-evaluation when they help another person

"Friendship is based on what it gives, not what it gets. It is motivated by love, not debt, and is willing to sacrifice without seeing or expecting a return," explain John Maxwell and Dan Reiland (1999, p. 73). Friendship is a communal relationship in which partners are oriented toward each other's needs (Mills & Clark, 1994; see also Harvey & Wenzel, 2006). Only when the benefits are voluntary, when partners freely give and receive, do we tend to view a relationship as true friendship or love.

In fact, while tit-for-tat exchanges increase people's liking when the relationship is relatively formal, the same social economics decreases liking when two people seek true friendship (Clark & Mills, 1993).

Gender Differences in Friendship

Women show a stronger tendency than men to think of themselves in terms of their close relationships. They are more likely to define themselves in terms of their social connections rather than their independence. Indeed, when asked to provide photos that reflect who they are, women, more than men, include pictures of themselves with others.

Consider this fascinating dilemma: Suppose you had to spend the rest of your life on a small island with only one other human being. Further, suppose that you couldn't choose the specific individual with whom you'd be sharing the island but that you could specify what this person's sex would be. What sex would your island-mate be?

The response of most men and women is "Female!" (Weber, 1984). Why?

Early in life, females more than males give priority to relationships (see Myers, 2000a, for a review). Boys strive for independence. Girls embrace their interdependence. Although both sexes enjoy group activity, girls play in smaller groups involving more intimate sharing and less aggression. As teens, girls tend to spend more time with friends and less time alone than do boys. And in college, women more than men say it is very important to "help others who are in difficulty."

Humorist Dave Barry characterizes gender differences in friendship in the following account:

> It seems that some winters ago, Mark and Bob were sitting around a gas station with not much to do. If Mark and Bob had been women, they probably would have passed the time in some nonproductive matter, such as nurturing their friendship, exploring their innermost feelings or helping each other gain significant insights into the important relationships in their lives. But fortunately for humanity, Mark and Bob are not women. Mark and Bob are guys and what they did is invent snowplow hockey (1995, p. C4).

Putting the tongue-in-cheek value judgment of "productivity" aside, do you think Barry's portrayal of gender differences, at least in same-sex friendships, is accurate?

Several studies (for a review, see Brehm et al., 2002) suggest that women's friendships are more often characterized by emotional sharing. In contrast, male friendships are usually linked to shared interests and activities—doing things together (Fehr, 2009). But don't be too quick to stereotype here, as both men and women like trust, intimacy, and self-disclosure with their friends (Winstead, 2009).

In comparison with men, women:

- Self-disclose more
- Show stronger social support, especially emotional support
- Are more likely to express feelings of love and affection

- Tend to have closer friendships
- Are more likely to talk about relationships and personal issues
- Are more likely to have "all purpose" friendships covering many areas of experience (men are more likely to have different friends for different activities)

Researchers do not all agree on the size of gender differences. Some see them as pervasive, others as small and perhaps due to factors other than gender. Thus, the research continues. One research analysis (Wright, 1998) suggests that gender differences in agency (for example, activities) are relatively small whereas differences in communion (for example, intimacy, expressiveness, and self-disclosure) are larger.

⇛ I N   R E V I E W

> People regard trust, honesty, and understanding as important features in their closest relationships. One popular definition of friendship regards intimacy and assistance as its core ingredients. Disclosing stressful events to a close friend can be liberating. Friends share a communal relationship in which they are mutually responsive to each other's needs. Research on gender differences suggests that male and female friendships may differ more in terms of affect than in terms of activity.

Forming and Maintaining Friendships

In his best-selling book *The Friendship Factor*, Alan Loy McGinnis explains the importance of friendship:

> In research at our clinic, my colleagues and I have discovered that friendship is the springboard to every other love. Friendships spill over onto the other important relationships of life. People with no friends usually have a diminished capacity for sustaining any kind of love. They tend to go through a succession of marriages, be estranged from various family members, and have trouble getting along at work. On the other hand, those who learn how to love their friends tend to make long and fulfilling marriages, get along well with the people at work, and enjoy their children (2004, p. 9).

However, making friends is not a high priority for many of us. "We take care of our health," noted Ralph Waldo Emerson, "we lay up money, we make our rooms tight, and our clothing sufficient; but who provides wisely that he shall not be wanting in the best property of all—friends?" (cited in Barnes, 2008, p. 188). The seventeenth-century French writer François de La Rochefoucauld agreed. "A true friend," he lamented, "is the most precious of possessions and the one we take least thought about acquiring" (cited in Trehan & Trehan, 2010, p.139).

Perhaps we think that friendship, unlike other strengths such as commitment, compassion, and self-control, "just happens." Those who enjoy close social connections are simply luckier than others. Or maybe we assume that the ability to form friendships is an inherent strength: "Others are extroverts but I'm an introvert—always have been, always will be."

However, friendship can be cultivated just as much as the other strengths. It's not a matter of suddenly becoming the life of the party. Rather, friendship involves the challenge of developing meaningful, intimate relationships with a few other people. "True happiness," according to seventeenth-century playwright Ben Jonson, "consists not in the multitude of friends but in the worth and choice" (cited in Demakis, 2012, p. 173). In our age of social media, it's too easy to quantify how many friends we have on Facebook or Twitter or the like—can you really say you have 300 or 400 "friends" you know *well*? The quality of our interpersonal connections, not the quantity, is what matters and what we should focus on when we think about our truly close friends.

So how do we foster friendship? Both the wisdom of the ages and the advice of contemporary students of friendship, such as McGinnis (2004), help us. Guidelines for deepening relationships and for cultivating intimacy include the following.

1. **Assign priority to close relationships.** Friendship doesn't merely happen. It unfolds when we recognize its importance and commit our lives to it.

   Friendship is a basic source of happiness, and it is worth developing a life-style that allows time for close relationships. In making connections, look for a few people who interest you, begin to communicate care to them in small ways, and invest in their lives. Friendship often begins with a simple show of interest or word of encouragement. You make more friends in 2 months, observed popular author and speaker Dale Carnegie, by becoming more interested in other people than you can in 2 years by trying to get people interested in you. The secret to being interesting is to be interested (McGinnis, 2004).

   Once a relationship is established, make getting together with your friends a priority along with work, school, family, and recreation. If necessary, schedule a regular get-together such as a weekly lunch, a movie night, or a book club. If you are really pressed for time, combine what you must do with meeting each other. For example, you might exercise together, share a vacation, or jointly enroll in an evening class. If your friend attends another school or lives in another part of the country, you do have your work cut out for you. Still, social media—texting, Facebook—or regular communication—an old-fashioned phone call or, better yet, calling by Skype—can help maintain a close connection. With a schedule, friends won't fall by the wayside. Ritual, anthropologists remind us, is one of the most important ingredients in good relationships.

2. **Practice transparency.** Allow people to see what is in your heart. We form friendships with windows, not walls. Such honesty does not come easily. We long

to be known, but also to remain hidden. When we are transparent, we risk rejection. However, only honesty promotes intimacy, a central feature of friendship.

Like affection itself, self-disclosure tends to be reciprocated. If you take the initiative in revealing yourself to a friend, the friend is more likely to disclose secrets to you. There are, of course, important caveats. Intimacy does not occur instantaneously. It is a process, not an event. People who empty their hearts and let it all hang out in the first hour of acquaintance will surely be viewed as indiscreet and unstable. Rather, intimacy, observes David Myers, "progresses like a dance: I reveal a little, you reveal a little—but not too much. You then reveal more, and I reciprocate" (2002, p. 458).

Such disclosure pays an unexpected dividend, suggests McGinnis (2004). Expanding the familiar counsel "Know yourself," he writes, "Make yourself known, and you will then know yourself" (2003, p. 30). By revealing ourselves to others, we come to know ourselves better. One thing: More emotionally evaluative self-disclosure (how you feel about a mutual friend, for example) will promote feelings of closeness, whereas factual-descriptive disclosure (that you've know this mutual friend since third grade) will not (Laurenceau, Barrett, & Rovine, 2005).

3. **Learn to listen.** Listening is the other half of intimacy—the corollary to making oneself known. It's an important route to forming as well as strengthening friendship. "The road to the heart," observed Voltaire, "is the ear." Listening attentively pays the highest compliment. Just don't engage in *pseudolistening*, where you are more or less pretending to actively listen but are actually thinking about other (nonrelated) things while waiting your turn to speak (O'Keefe, 2002).

Our whole body conveys the intensity of our interest. In Western cultures, eye contact is one of the surest signs of a good listener. Looking others directly in the eye, allowing nothing to distract, conveys strong interest and is a powerful social magnet. Listening attentively pays the highest compliment.

Sympathetic listeners, adds McGinnis, dispense advice sparingly. Merely acknowledging another's statement is enough to complete the communication loop. Often, troubled friends are not seeking advice. They simply want to unburden themselves and thank you for being there. Once they have expressed themselves, they often see their problem more clearly and are able to arrive at their own solution. Merely expressing gratitude that another trusted you enough to divulge a secret builds intimacy.

4. **Communicate warmth.** Dare to talk about your affection and express your admiration. "Many a friendship," observes English theologian Frederick Faber, "long, loyal, and self-sacrificing, rests on no thicker a foundation than a kind word" (cited in Chang, 2006, p. 324).

Communicating affection does not come easily. Sometimes fear of sentimentality gets in the way. Other times we may be afraid that our warmth will not be reciprocated. Perhaps we even worry that we'll be ridiculed. The words "I care about you" may be especially difficult. A good alternative is to tell your friend you missed seeing him or her, or that it means a lot to get together or that your friendship is a wonderful thing.

Be as liberal with praise as you are cautious with criticism. We have enormous ability to motivate people with our admiration. "The deepest principle in human nature," noted early psychologist William James, "is the craving to be appreciated" (cited in Levine, 2003, p. 81). Some of the best ways to feed friendship include writing a heartfelt note or just calling to say how much you care.

The expression of admiration affects both the admirer and the recipient. In spite of our fears of rejection, liking is usually mutual. Experiments show that people who are told that certain others like or admire them usually feel a reciprocal affection (Berscheid & Walster, 1978). Emerson was right: "To have a friend one must be a friend" (cited in Hall & Hall, 2009, p. 139).

Of course, it's not empty flattery that marks friendship. Rather, "The more we love our friends," argued playwright Jean-Baptiste Molière, "the less we flatter them; it is by excusing nothing that pure love shows itself." True friends are honest with each other, but even when they reveal their foibles, they do so against the backdrop of unconditional acceptance. There is tremendous relief in being known and still being accepted. In telling the truth, friends spur us to growth. Most important, true friends bring out the best in us. They bring to light strengths that no one else looks hard enough to find.

5. **Create space in your friendships.** Intimacy is important, but it is equally important to recognize the role of freedom in friendship. "There can be no friendship," observed American statesman William Penn, "where there is no freedom" (cited in Zubko, 2004, p. 177). Lasting friendships combine the need to belong with the need for space.

Consider relationships you've had that never became friendships. Were the relationships you dropped with people who were controlling, manipulative, and/or judgmental? Here are some more painful questions (McGinnis, 2004): Do you have a tendency to want to control others? Do you usually go to the restaurant or movie you prefer? Do you enjoy correcting factual errors in other people's conversation? Do you use humor to put down friends? Do you have to know more about a topic than others to feel comfortable discussing it?

In true friendship, no one has the upper hand. In helping true friends to realize their dreams, we will permit, even encourage, them to develop other relationships, and we will always leave room for solitude.

6. **Be loyal.** "Loyalty" and "devotion" are among the qualities we admire most in friends. Our friends suffer alongside us even when many others find us insufferable.

In long-term relationships, there will be times when friends are not functioning well. They give nothing to the friendship and test our staying power (McGinnis, 2004). Friendship is not founded on reciprocity but instead on genuine caring. Demanding a return on our investment can undermine the friendship. Perseverance keeps us connected through tough times.

Although we may imagine that the greatest strain comes when our friends are down and troubled, this may actually be one of the easier times (Langer, 2002). Listening to another's woes can make us feel superior. This makes it easy to find a sympathetic ear. It may actually be more challenging to maintain friendship in times of triumph.

In one study, research participants were asked to provide clues to help others complete a task (Langer, 2002). When described as a game, participants were more helpful to their friends than they were to strangers. However, when the task was presented as serious, participants were more helpful to strangers than they were to their friends.

Unfortunately, we can feel threatened by our friends' successes. English statesman Lord Chesterfield declared, "Most people enjoy the inferiority of their best friends" (cited in Murray, 2007, p. 161). Think about it: Would you prefer that a stranger or a friend wins the lottery? Would the friend still need you? Would he or she still want you as a friend? Although it may be easy to say, "I'm happy for you," can we really listen to the details of another's success?

True friends are loyal in good times as well as bad. Friendship aims to transcend envy. "A real friend," concludes Langer, "can be happy for someone independent of his or her own life experiences.... Sharing someone's happiness can be its own positive experience and enable us to enjoy and relive it together. Attention to this mutual, positive need will likely be noticed, and in the long run, better serve the friendship" (2002, p. 74).

Finally, being loyal means never breaking confidence. Perhaps nothing shakes relationships more than learning that a friend has revealed a secret.

7. **Follow the universal rules of friendship.** Are there universal norms to follow in maintaining friendships? Adults in various countries indicated which of 43 possible friendship rules they would endorse (Argyle & Henderson, 1984). Interestingly, Japanese participants endorsed the fewest, participants from Britain and Hong Kong the most. Overall, the researchers found the following rules to be strongest:

   1. Volunteer help in time of need.

   2. Respect the friend's privacy.

   3. Keep confidences.

   4. Trust and confide in each other.

5. Stand up for the person in their absence.

6. Don't criticize each other in public.

7. Show emotional support.

8. Strive to make him/her happy while in each other's company.

9. Don't be jealous or critical of a friend's other relationships.

10. Be tolerant of each other's friends.

11. Share news of success with the other.

12. Don't nag.

13. Try to repay debts, favors, and compliments.

When people compare their current and former friendships, they remember following the rules of friendship less regularly in the latter than the former (Argyle & Henderson, 1984).

8. **Don't forget to capitalize on your friend's good fortune!** As we learned back in Chapter 6, be sure to celebrate your friends' successes, whether they are major or minor events. Be warm and sincere in your interest and genuine in your praise for their achievements. They, in turn, will respond with enthusiasm when your turn at good news arrives. Remember, to have a good friend—one who will help you flourish—you have to be a good friend in return. Be attentive, listen closely, and express pleasure—friendship dividends are sure to follow!

In pursuing close relationships, we quickly discover how fundamental friendship is to flourishing. As the people closest to us meet our basic needs for belonging, meaning, and self-worth, we probably echo Helen Keller's grateful lament, "With the death of every friend I love, a part of me has been buried…but their contribution to my being of happiness, strength, and understanding remains to sustain me in my altered world" (cited in Kinnaman, 1996, p. 13).

⇒ IN REVIEW

The ability to form and maintain friendship may predict success in other interpersonal relationships. Like the other strengths, friendship can be cultivated. Assigning priority to close relationships, practicing transparency, and developing good listening skills are important first steps. Daring to express one's affection and admiration strengthens bonds. The road to friendship is paved with small kindnesses. True friends allow space for the development of other relationships as well as simple solitude. They are loyal in times of triumph as well as trial, and follow what seem to be universal rules of friendship.

Epilogue: Meaning and Flourishing

Life Is Pretty Meaningful

Flourishing in the Future

What's Ahead? Mindful Mindsets Matter

Lives may be experienced as meaningful when they are felt to have significance beyond the trivial or momentary, or to have purpose, or to have a coherence that transcends chaos. —LAURA KING AND COLLEAGUES, 2006

I believe it is within our capacity that by the year 2051 that 51 percent of the human population will be flourishing. That is my charge. —MARTIN SELIGMAN, 2010

Among many of the things that human beings do is to make meaning. Whether we encounter good things or bad things, we often search for a reason for why they happened and what they mean for us. Consider the following events related by Konika Banerjee and Paul Bloom:

> On April 15, 2013, James Costello was cheering on a friend near the finish line at the Boston Marathon when the bombs exploded, severely burning his arms and legs and sending shrapnel into his flesh. During the months of surgery and rehabilitation that followed, Mr. Costello developed a relationship with one of his nurses, Krista D'Agostino, and they soon became engaged. Mr. Costello posted a picture of the ring on Facebook. "I now realize why I was involved in the tragedy," he wrote. "It was to meet my best friend, and the love of my life" (2014, p. SR12).

Good came from bad, and Costello attached positive meaning and purpose to it. Konika Banerjee and Paul Bloom note that we are all like Mr. Costello: We, too, find meaning in life events, great or small, expected or unexpected, happy or sad. Think about it: Doesn't it often feel like things "happen for a reason"?

Research conducted by Konika Banerjee and Paul Bloom finds that people—including young children—believe that an underlying pattern exists in their affairs, that things unfold as they do because they are apparently supposed to. Humans are truly "sense makers." The good news is that highly empathetic people (recall Chapter 3)—the ones who care about emotions, goals, and the experiences of others—are especially likely to see the world as ordered by a certain fate. Sadly, so do people who display paranoia, as they are endlessly preoccupied by the hidden intentions or imagined motives of others.

Are there any challenges with making meaning out of what might actually be coincidence or quasi-random occurrences? Konika Banerjee and Paul Bloom (2014) suggest that if we see the world as being a fair and just place where things happen for a reason (recall the "just world" view from Chapter 3), we risk reaching some erroneous conclusions, such as believing that people who suffer, are poor, or are victimized in some way are deserving of their fate. Better to see a benevolent pattern in the presence of good things and to work to change bad things. After all, what could be a better display of positive meaning, as well as an active exercise in positive psychology, than working to reduce poverty and inequality, eliminating oppression, and helping others achieve happiness? As Konika Banerjee and Paul Bloom suggested in their thoughtful editorial, "...the events of human life unfold in a fair and just manner only when individuals and society work hard to make this happen..." (p. SR12).

Thus, finding meaning is important because you can see good things in your own experience or you can be motivated to work for them in the lives of others.

Life Is Pretty Meaningful

We know people readily find or make meaning all the time, but do they see their own lives as meaningful? *Meaning in life* can be defined in any number of ways, but according to psychologists Samantha Heintzelman and Laura King (2014), three themes are usually present:

- A meaningful life is one with a sense of *purpose*.

- A meaningful life is one that matters or possesses some *significance*.

These two qualities are motivational, that is, when they are present, people behave in ways that are goal directed.

What about the third quality?

- A meaningful life *makes sense* to the individual, who sees his or her experience in the world as predictable and marked by regularity.

This third theme is more cognitive than motivational, and is based on how people reflect on and construe their individual lives.

What about you? Do you see your life as meaningful? Find out by completing the Meaning in Life Questionnaire (MLQ).

Meaning in Life Questionnaire (MLQ)

Please take a moment to think about why your life and existence feel important and significant to you. Please respond to the following statements as truthfully and accurately as you can, and also please remember that these are very subjective questions and that there are no right or wrong answers. Please answer according to the scale below:

1 = Absolutely untrue   2 = Mostly untrue   3 = Somewhat untrue   4 = Can't say true or untrue   5 = Somewhat true   6 = Mostly true   7 = Absolutely true

_____ **1.** I understand my life's meaning.

_____ **2.** I am looking for something that makes my life feel meaningful.

_____ **3.** I am always looking to find my life's purpose.

_____ **4.** My life has a clear sense of purpose.

_____ **5.** I have a good sense of what makes my life meaningful.

_____ **6.** I have discovered a satisfying life purpose.

_____ **7.** I am always searching for something that makes my life feel significant.

_____ **8.** I am seeking a purpose or mission for my life.

_____ **9.** My life has no clear purpose.

_____ **10.** I am searching for meaning in my life.

Source: Copyright © 2006 by the American Psychological Association. Reproduced with permission. Appendix, p. 93, from Steger, M. F., Frazier, P., Oishi, S., & Kaler, M. (2006). The meaning in life questionnaire: Assessing the presence of and search for meaning in life. *Journal of Counseling Psychology, 53(1)*, 80–93. No further reproduction or distribution is permitted without written permission from the American Psychological Association.

Scoring: The MLQ has two subscales, the Presence subscale and the Search subscale. To determine your Presence score, add items 1, 4, 5, and 6, as well as item 9, which is reverse recoded (i.e., 1 = 7, 2 = 6, 3 = 5, 4 = 4, 5 = 3, 6 = 2, and 7 = 1). The Search score is determined by adding items 2, 3, 7, 8, and 10.

Presence of Meaning score _____

Search for Meaning score _____

The Presence of Meaning subscale measures how full respondents feel their lives are of meaning. The Search for Meaning subscale measures how engaged and motivated respondents are in efforts to find meaning or deepen their understanding of meaning in their lives. Presence is positively related to well-being, intrinsic religiosity, extroversion and agreeableness, and negatively related to anxiety and depression. Search is positively related to religious quest, rumination, past-negative and present-fatalistic time perspectives, negative affect, depression, and neuroticism, and negatively related to future time perspective, close-mindedness (i.e., dogmatism), and well-being. Presence is also related to personal growth self-appraisals, and altruistic and spiritual behavior.

Heintzelman and King (2014) found that believing that one's own life is a meaningful one is associated with a variety of positive qualities or outcomes. These associations are largely correlational; however, their degree of consistency suggests that interesting and beneficial things are somehow linked with believing one has a meaningful life, including:

- Positive rather than negative moods (Hicks & King, 2009)
- Lower incidence of psychological disorders (Steger & Kashdan, 2009)
- Higher quality of life (Krause, 2007) and self-reported health (Steger et al., 2009)
- Decreased rates of mortality (Boyle et al., 2009)
- Lower rates of loneliness or social exclusion (Williams, 2007)
- Slower age-related cognitive decline and lower risk for Alzheimer's disease (Boyle et al., 2010)

People who see their lives as meaningful tend to be better adjusted to their work and career lives than those who find less meaning (Littman-Ovadia & Steger, 2010). People who rate their lives as meaningful tend to be viewed by others as being more socially appealing than those who do not see their lives as meaningful (Stillman et al., 2011). And when the going gets tough, people who see their lives as meaningful appear to deal with obstacles and challenges by using adaptive coping strategies (Thompson et al., 2003).

According to Heintzelman and King (2014), the good news is that a variety of studies reveal that seeing life as meaningful is widespread. Rather than being something that is reserved for a chosen few, most people appear to believe their lives are indeed significant. Belief in such meaning is adaptive; that is, it promotes our species' survival.

We hope that you are like many of the participants in studies on meaning (see Heintzelman & King, 2014), whose thoughts, feelings, and actions indicate, "What I do has purpose. What I do has significance. My life matters in a way that will outlast my physical existence" (p. 569).

Flourishing in the Future

What does it mean to flourish? Why is flourishing important?

You have read this book and completed a host of self-reflective and critical thinking exercises and assessments aimed at helping you realize your potential while also enhancing your life. As we learned in Chapter 7, being happy is important, but most of us would like to be satisfied in all of our life domains. Ed Diener and Robert Biswas-Diener (2008) refer to this state as *consummate happiness*, one in which the affected individual is happy about relationships, work or career, health, and recreation or leisure—in short, in virtually all areas of living. More to the point, consummate happiness also entails feelings of accomplishment, competence, and being respected by others. When all these core areas are positive, a person can be said to be *flourishing* or to be living a meaningful and fulfilling life.

According to Corey L. M. Keyes (2003, 2009), part of flourishing is to be mentally healthy; that is, to be free of mental illness and to be functioning well in both the social and private areas of one's life. People who *flourish* have high levels of well-being and low levels of mental illness (Keyes & Lopez, 2002). Those who are *struggling* experience high levels of both well-being and mental illness. *Floundering* occurs when a person experiences low levels of well-being and high levels of mental illness. Low levels of well-being and low levels of mental illness indicate an individual is *languishing*.

Flourishing, then, goes beyond just experiences of enjoyment or pleasure or even beauty—it's about holding the view that your actions serve a greater purpose and are vitally engaging for you. When people flourish, they also display high emotional well-being, high social well-being, and high psychological well-being (Keyes & Lopez, 2002).

When you began to read this book, you completed the Flourishing Scale in Chapter 1. Now, 10 chapters later, at the end of the book, it's time to complete the same scale once more to see if your self-explorations have led to greater flourishing than when you started the book. We hope so, but if not, then you might be able to think about making some changes in your life in order to enhance your flourishing for the future.

 **SELF-ASSESSMENT**

Flourishing Scale

Below are eight statements with which you may agree or disagree. Using the 1–7 scale below, indicate your agreement with each item by indicating that response for each statement.

7 = Strongly agree   6 = Agree   5 = Slightly agree   4 = Neither agree nor disagree   3 = Slightly disagree   2 = Disagree   1 = Strongly disagree

_____ **1.** I lead a purposeful and meaningful life.

_____ **2.** My social relationships are supportive and rewarding.

_____ **3.** I am engaged and interested in my daily activities.

_____ **4.** I actively contribute to the happiness and well-being of others.

_____ **5.** I am competent and capable in the activities that are important to me.

_____ **6.** I am a good person and live a good life.

_____ **7.** I am optimistic about my future.

_____ **8.** People respect me.

Source: Diener, E., Wirtz, D., Tov, W., Kim-Prieto, C., Choi, D., Oishi, S., & Biswas-Diener, R. (2009). New measures of well-being: Flourishing and positive and negative feelings. _Social Indicators Research, 39,_ 247–266.

Scoring: Add the responses, varying from 1 to 7, for all eight items. The possible range of scores is from 8 (lowest possible) to 56 (highest possible). A high score represents a person with many psychological resources and strengths.

_Flourishing score _____

Turn back to Chapter 1 to check your baseline flourishing score. Did your flourishing score change from then to now? If yes, did it increase? What particular changes do you believe occurred in your thoughts, feelings, and behaviors that enhanced your positive well-being?

If your flourishing score didn't change—it stayed more or less the same—why do you think it remained relatively stable? Were you flourishing well before you read this book?

If your score went down, has anything happened in your life recently that changed how you feel about yourself or any of your key life domains? If there has been a change, is there anything you can do in your daily life to enhance your flourishing? We hope that there is and that you can continue to use this book to enhance your outlook.

What's Ahead? Mindful Mindsets Matter

Positive psychology and the study of human strengths are still rather new. Promising research is now being done that helps to identify ways in which outlook can be modified to positively influence well-being. As this chapter was being completed, a story about social psychologist Ellen Langer's latest research appeared in the _New York Times Magazine_ (Grierson, 2014). For decades, Langer has cleverly demonstrated that health, illness, and even age-related behaviors are rooted in how we think about ourselves as we experience the world. Just as we label other people as "old," for example, because we recognize characteristics we associate with aging in the way they behave, we can turn the same critical lens onto ourselves. The problem is that we then often end up being mindlessly led by the power of the label. If you start to think of yourself as "old" (or "sick" or "helpless" or whatever), you can begin to confirm the belief (see Hsu & Langer, 2013; see also Crum & Langer, 2007).

But it isn't just a self-fulfilling prophecy that Langer worries about—it's how we think. In contrast to "mindless" thinking (i.e., adopting and confirming a label), mindful people continually notice details in the world around them and actively perceive—and pursue—the choices available to them. Langer suggests that we should "actively mak[e] new distinctions, rather than relying on habitual" ways of categorizing the things around us (Grierson, 2014). Making new distinctions—seeing and thinking about new details that are already there or adopting new perspectives—can promote health and well-being. In one series of studies, for example, Hsu, Chung, and Langer (2010) demonstrated that women who think they look younger after having had their hair colored and cut displayed a decrease in blood pressure. Moreover, when they were photographed (and their hair was cropped out of the pictures), a group of independent raters coded them as younger than women in a control group. In another study, Langer and her colleagues noted that baldness is a cue that triggers the use of old-age labels. They found that men who go bald prematurely view an "older self" and thus age faster. The intriguing problem is that prematurely bald men also have an excess risk of being diagnosed with prostate cancer and coronary heart disease than men who do not go prematurely bald (see Hsu, Chung, & Langer, 2010).

Consider a more dramatic example: Langer and her colleagues (2010) had two groups of participants use a flight simulator. One group was told to regard themselves as Air Force pilots and were given flight suits to wear as they guided their simulated flights. A second group was told the simulator was broken and that they should just pretend they were flying a plane. After the exercise, the members of each group were given an eyesight test. Those who piloted the simulated flight performed 40 percent better on the eye exam than those in the control group.

Think about it: When we are properly primed with "mindful" mindsets, as Langer and her colleagues have shown, we may be able to challenge adopted beliefs that weigh us down ("I'm old"), hold us back, or otherwise compromise our health and well-being. As Langer said regarding the flight simulator study, "mind-set manipulation can counteract presumed physiological limits" and a desirable goal is to "return the control of our health back to ourselves" (Grierson, 2014). This exciting research suggests (if you will pardon me) that the sky is the limit where the power of the human mind is concerned. Clearly, carefully and thoughtfully designed positive psychological interventions can turn back the clock of aging for many people, just as they have great promise for dealing with a variety of health problems. At present, Langer and her colleagues are exploring whether mindsets can influence the course of cancer, including shrinking tumors (see Grierson, 2014). Stay tuned to results from the field of positive psychology: What we know about the benefits of human strengths will expand in the near future—the subfield's most powerful findings are ahead!

After reading and reflecting on the contents of this book, you now have a wide variety of tools at your disposal for pursuing human strengths. Use them to flourish and to enhance your daily life and the lives of those around you. Good luck to you for the future and enjoy the journey.

⇒ IN REVIEW

Life is meaningful, as most people will attest. Having meaning in life gives individuals a sense of purpose, allows them to see significance in their affairs, and makes sense, so events seem to be predictable. People flourish in their lives when they believe daily existence has meaning and provides them with fulfillment. Comparing one's level of flourishing here with that assessed in Chapter 1 can point to acquired strengths or suggest positive changes for the future. Maintaining strengths can be achieved by developing "mindful" mindsets, thereby avoiding reliance on or conforming to behavioral labels that curb our positive growth.

References

Adams, G. (2012). Context in person, person in context: A cultural psychology approach to social-personality psychology. In K. Deaux & M. Snyder (Eds.), *The Oxford handbook of personality and social psychology* (pp. 182–208). New York, NY: Oxford University Press.

Adams, J. M., & Jones, W. H. (1997). The conceptualization of marital commitment: An integrative analysis. *Journal of Personality and Social Psychology, 72,* 1177–1196.

Ainsworth, M. D. S., Blehar, M. C., Waters, E., & Wall, S. (1978). *Patterns of attachment: A psychological study of the strange situation.* Hillsdale, NJ: Erlbaum.

Aknin, L. B., Barrington-Leigh, C. P., Dunn, E. W., Helliwell, J. F., Biswas-Diener, R., Kemeza, I., & ... Norton, M. I. (2010). *Prosocial spending and well-being: Cross-cultural evidence for a psychological universal.* No. 16415, NBER Working Papers, National Bureau of Economic Research.

Andersen, S. M. (1998). *Service learning: A national strategy for youth development.* Position paper issued by the Task Force on Education Policy. Washington, DC: Institute for Communitarian Policy Studies, George Washington University.

Andrews, F. M., & Withey, S. B. (1976). *Social indicators of well-being: Americans' perception of life quality.* New York, NY: Plenum.

Anik, L., Aknin, L. B., Norton, M. L., & Dunn, E. W. (2011). Feeling good about giving: The benefits (and costs) of self-interested charitable behavior. In D. M. Oppenheimer & C. Y. Olivola (Eds.), *The science of giving: Experimental approaches to the study of charity* (pp. 3–13). New York, NY: Psychology Press.

Argyle, M., & Henderson, M. (1984). The rules of friendships. *Journal of Social and Personal Relationships, 1,* 211–237.

Aron, A., Aron, E. N., & Smollan, D. (1992). Inclusion of other in the Self Scale and the structure of interpersonal closeness. *Journal of Personality and Social Psychology, 63,* 596–612.

Aron, A., Norman, C. C., & Aron, E. N. (2001). Shared self-enhancing activities as a means of maintaining and enhancing close romantic relationships. In J. H. Harvey & A. Wenzel (Eds.), *Close romantic relationships: Maintenance and enhancement* (pp. 47–66). Mahwah, NJ: Erlbaum.

Aron, A., & Westbay, L. (1996). Dimensions of the prototype of love. *Journal of Personality and Social Psychology, 70,* 53–55.

Aronson, E., & Bridgeman, D. (1979). Jigsaw groups and the desegregated classroom: In pursuit of common goals. *Personality and Social Psychology Bulletin, 5,* 438–446.

Aronson, E., & Patnoe, S. (2011). *Cooperation in the classroom: The jigsaw method* (3rd ed). London, England: Pinter & Martin.

Aronson, E., Willerman, B., & Floyd, J. (1966). The effect of a pratfall on increasing interpersonal attractiveness, *Psychonomic Science, 4,* 227–228.

Aspinwall, L. G., & Brunhart, S. M. (1996). Distinguishing optimism from denial: Optimistic beliefs predict attention to health threats. *Personality and Social Psychology Bulletin, 22,* 993–1003.

Aspinwall, L. G., & Staudinger, U. M. (Eds.). (2002). *A psychology of human strengths: Fundamental questions and future directions for a positive psychology.* Washington, DC: American Psychological Association.

Aspinwall, L. G., & Taylor, S. E. (1992). Modeling cognitive adaptation: A longitudinal investigation of the impact of individual differences and coping on college adjustment and performance. *Journal of Personality and Social Psychology, 63,* 989–1003.

Baddeley, J. L., & Pennebaker, J. W. (2011). The expressive writing method. In L. L'Abate, L. G. Sweeney (Eds.), *Research on writing approaches in mental health* (pp. 85–92). Bingley, United Kingdom: Emerald Group Publishing.

Baltes, P. B., Glück, J., & Kunzmann, U. M. (2002). Wisdom: Its structure and function in regulating successful life span development. In C. R. Snyder & S. J. Lopez (Eds.), *Handbook of positive psychology* (pp. 327–347). New York, NY: Oxford University Press.

Baltes, P. B., & Smith, J. (1990). The psychology of wisdom and its ontogenesis. In R. J. Sternberg (Ed.), *Wisdom: Its nature, origins, and development* (pp. 87–120). New York, NY: Cambridge University Press.

Baltes, P. B., & Staudinger, U. M. (2000). Wisdom: A meta-heuristic (pragmatic) to orchestrate mind and virtue toward excellence. *American Psychologist, 55,* 122–135.

Banerjee, K., & Bloom, P. (2014, October 19). Does everything happen for a reason? *New York Times, Sunday Review,* 12.

Barnes, E. (2008). *Walk with me today, Lord: Inspiring devotions for women.* Eugene, OR: Harvest House.

Barry, D. (1995, January 9). Hockey like you've never seen. *Winnipeg Free Press,* p. C4.

Batson, C. D. (1991). *The altruism question: Toward a social-psychological answer.* Hillsdale, NJ: Erlbaum.

Batson, C. D. (2002). Empathy and altruism. In C. R. Snyder & S. J. Lopez (Eds.), *Handbook of positive psychology* (pp. 485–498). New York, NY: Oxford University Press.

Batson, C. D. (2010). Empathy-induced altruistic motivation. In M. Mikulincer, P. R. Shaver (Eds.), *Prosocial motives, emotions, and behavior: The better angels of our nature* (pp. 15–34). Washington, DC: American Psychological Association. doi:10.1037/12061-001

Batson, C. D., Ahmad, N., & Lishner, D. A. (2009). Empathy and altruism. In S. J. Lopez & C. R. Snyder (Eds.), *Oxford handbook of positive psychology* (2nd ed.) (pp. 417–426). New York, NY: Oxford University Press.

Batson, C. D., Duncan, B. D., Ackerman, P., Buckley, T., & Birch, K. (1981). Is empathic emotion a source of altruistic motivation? *Journal of Personality and Social Psychology, 40,* 290–302.

Baumeister, R. F. (1996). Should schools try to boost self-esteem? Beware the dark side. *American Educator, 20,* 14–19, 43.

Baumeister, R. F. (1999). The nature and structure of the self: An overview. In R. F. Baumeister (Ed.), *The self in social psychology* (pp. 1–20). Philadelphia, PA: Psychology Press.

Baumeister, R. F. (2002a, August). *Psychology of evil and violence.* Paper presented at the 110th Annual Convention of the American Psychological Association, Chicago, IL.

Baumeister, R. F. (2002b). Ego depletion and self-control failure: An energy model of the self's executive function. *Self and Identity, 1*(2), 129–136. doi:10.1080/152988602317319302

Baumeister, R. F. (2010). The self. In R. A. Baumeister & E. J. Finkel (Eds.), *Advanced social psychology: The state of the science* (pp. 5–25). New York, NY: Oxford University Press.

Baumeister, R. F., Bratslavsky, E., Muraven, M., & Tice, D. M. (1998). Ego depletion: Is the active self a limited resource? *Journal of Personality and Social Psychology, 74*(5), 1252–1265. doi:10.1037/0022-3514.74.5.1252

Baumeister, R. F., & Bushman, B. J. (2011). *Social psychology and human nature* (2nd ed.). Belmont, CA: Wadsworth/Cengage.

Baumeister, R. F., Campbell, J. D., Krueger, J. I., & Vohs, K. D. (2003). Does high self-esteem cause better performance, interpersonal success, happiness, or healthier lifestyles? *Psychological Science in the Public Interest, 4,* 1–44.

Baumeister, R. F., & Exline, J. J. (1999). Virtue, personality, and social relations: Self-control as the moral muscle. *Journal of Personality, 67,* 1165–1194.

Baumeister, R. F., Heatherton, T. F., & Tice, D. M. (1994). *Losing control: How and why people fail at self-regulation.* San Diego, CA: Academic Press.

Baumeister, R. F., & Ilko, S. A. (1995). Shallow gratitude: Public and private acknowledgement of external help in accounts of success. *Basic and Applied Social Psychology, 16,* 191–209.

Baumeister, R. F., Smart, L., & Boden, J. M. (1996). Relation of threatened egotism to violence and aggression: The dark side of high self-esteem. *Psychological Review, 103,* 5–33.

Baumeister, R. F., Tice, D. M., & Hutton, D. G. (1989). Self-presentational motivations and personality differences in self-esteem. *Journal of Personality, 57,* 547–579.

Baumeister, R. F., Zell, A. L., & Tice, D. M. (2007). How emotions facilitate and impair self-regulation. In J. J. Gross (Ed.), *Handbook of emotion regulation* (pp. 408–426). New York, NY: Guilford Press.

Beecher, H. W. (1875). *Sunshine in the soul.* London, England: Darling and Son.

Bennett, W. J. (2013). *The book of man: Readings on the path to manhood.* Nashville, TN: Thomas Nelson, HarperCollins Christian Publishing.

Bent, S. A. (1887). *Familiar short sayings of great men with historical and explanatory notes.* Boston, MA: Ticknor and Company.

Berg, J. M., Dutton, J. E., & Wrzesniewski, A. (2013). Job crafting and meaningful work. In B. J. Dik, Z. S. Byrne, & M. F. Steger (Eds.), *Purpose and meaning in the workplace* (pp. 81–104). Washington, DC: American Psychological Association. doi:10.1037/14183-005

Berg, M. B., Janoff-Bulman, R., & Cotter, J. (2001). Perceiving value in obligations and goals: Wanting to do what should be done. *Personality and Social Psychology Bulletin, 27,* 982–995.

Berman, M. G., Jonides, J., & Kaplan, S. (2008). The cognitive benefits of interacting with nature. *Psychological Science, 19,* 1207–1212.

Berman, M. G., Kross, E., Krpan, K. M., Askren, M. K., Burson, A., Deldin, P. J., & … Jonides, J. (2012). Interacting with nature improves cognition and affect for individuals with depression. *Journal of Affective Disorders.* doi: 10.1016/j.jad.2012.03.012

Berry, J. W., Worthington, E. L., Jr., Parrott, L., III, O'Connor L. E., & Wade, N. G. (2001). Dispositional forgiveness: Development and construct validity of the Transgression Narrative Test of Forgivingness (TNTF). *Personality and Social Psychology Bulletin, 27,* 1277–1290.

Berscheid, E. (2003). The human's greatest strength: Other humans. In L. A. Aspinwall & U. M. Staudinger (Eds.), *A psychology of human strengths: Fundamental questions and future directions for a positive psychology* (pp. 37–48). Washington, DC: American Psychological Association.

Berscheid, E., & Meyers, S. A. (1996). A social categorical approach to a question about love. *Personal Relationships 3,* 19–43.

Berscheid, E., & Walster, E. H. (1978). *Interpersonal attraction* (2nd ed.). Reading, MA: Addison-Wesley.

Bettelheim, B. (1960). *The informed heart.* New York, NY: Free Press.

Blanchard, F. A., & Cook, S. W. (1976). Effects of helping a less competent member of a cooperating interracial group on the development of interpersonal attraction. *Journal of Personality and Social Psychology, 34,* 1245–1255.

Block, J. R., & Yuker, H. (1989). *Can you believe your eyes?* New York, NY: Gardner Press.

Blum, D. (2002). *Love at Goon Park: Harry Harlow and the science of affection.* Cambridge, MA: Perseus.

Bolt, R. (1960). *A man for all seasons: A play in two acts.* New York, NY: Random House.

Bonanno, G. A. (2004). Loss, trauma, and human resilience: Have we underestimated the human capacity to thrive after extremely aversive events? *American Psychologist, 59*(1), 20–28. doi:10.1037/0003-066X.59.1.20

Bonanno, G. A. (2009). *The other side of sadness: What the new science of bereavement tells us about life after loss.* New York, NY: Basic Books.

Bono, G., Emmons, R. A., & McCullough, M. E. (2004). Gratitude in practice and the practice of gratitude. In P. A. Linley

& S. Joseph (Eds.), *Positive psychology in practice* (pp. 464–484). Hoboken, NJ: Wiley.

Borba, M. (2001). *Building moral intelligence: The seven essential virtues that teach kids to do the right thing.* San Francisco, CA: Jossey-Bass.

Bowlby, J. (1988). *A secure base: Parent-child attachment and healthy human development.* New York, NY: Basic Books.

Boyle, P. A., Barnes, L. L., Buchman, A. S., & Bennett, D. A. (2009). Purpose in life is associated with mortality among community-dwelling older persons. *Psychosomatic Medicine, 71,* 574–579.

Boyle, P. A., Buchman, A. S., Barnes, L. L., & Bennett, D. A. (2010). Effect of a purpose in life on risk of incident Alzheimer disease and mild cognitive impairment in community-dwelling older persons. *Archives of General Psychiatry, 67,* 304–310.

Breathnach, S. B. (1995). *Simple abundance: A daybook of comfort and joy.* New York, NY: Warner Books.

Brehm, S. S., & Brehm, J. W. (1981). *Psychological reactance: A theory of freedom and control.* New York, NY: Academic Press.

Brehm, S. S., Miller, R. S., Perlman, D., & Campbell, S. M. (2002). *Intimate relations* (3rd ed.). New York, NY: McGraw-Hill.

Brehony, K. A. (1999). *Ordinary grace: An examination of the roots of compassion, altruism, and empathy, and the ordinary individuals who help others in extraordinary ways.* New York, NY: Penguin.

Breslau, N., Peterson, E., Schultz, L., Andreski, P., & Chilcoat, H. (1996). Are smokers with alcohol disorders less likely to quit? *American Journal of Public Health, 86,* 985–990.

Brickman, P. (1987). *Commitment, conflict, and caring.* Englewood Cliffs, NJ: Prentice Hall.

Brissette, I., Scheier, M. F., & Carver, C. S. (2002). The role of optimism in social network development, coping, and psychological adjustment during a life transition. *Journal of Personality and Social Psychology, 82,* 102–111.

Brown, H. J. (1991). *Life's little instruction book.* Nashville, TN: Rutledge Hill Press.

Brown, H. J. (1997). *Life's little instruction book: 511 suggestions, observations, and reminders on how to live a happy and rewarding life.* Nashville, TN: Thomas Nelson.

Brown, J. D. (1998). *The self.* New York, NY: McGraw-Hill.

Brown, K. W., & Ryan, R. M. (2003). The benefits of being present: Mindfulness and its role in psychological well-being. *Journal of Personality and Social Psychology, 84,* 822–848.

Brown, S. L., Nesse, R. M., Vinokur, A. D., & Smith, D. M. (2003). Providing social support may be more beneficial than receiving it: Results from a prospective study of mortality. *Psychological Science, 14,* 320–327.

Bryant, F. (1989). A four-factor model of perceived control: Avoiding, coping, obtaining, and savoring. *Journal of Personality, 57,* 773–797.

Bryant, F. B., & Veroff, J. (2007). *Savoring: A new model of positive experience.* Mahwah, NJ: Erlbaum.

Bushman, B. J., & Baumeister, R. F. (1998). Threatened egotism, narcissism, self-esteem, and direct and displaced aggression: Does self-love or self-hate lead to violence? *Journal of Personality and Social Psychology, 75,* 219–229.

Bushman, B. J., DeWall, C. N., Pond, R. S., Jr., & Hanus, M. D. (2014). Low glucose relates to greater aggression in married couples. *Proceedings of the National Academy of Sciences of the United States of America, 111* (17), 6254–6257. doi: 10.1073/pnas.1400619111

Burger, J. M. (2004). *Personality* (6th ed.). Belmont, CA: Wadsworth/Thomson.

Burger, J. M., & Burns, L. (1988). The illusion of unique invulnerability and the use of effective contraception. *Personality and Social Psychology Bulletin, 14,* 264–270.

Buss, D. M. (1989). Sex differences in human mate preferences: Evolutionary hypotheses tested in 37 cultures. *Behavioral and Brain Sciences, 12,* 1–49.

Buss, D. M. (2006). The evolution of love. In R. J. Sternberg & K. Weis (Eds.), *The new psychology of love* (pp. 65–86). New Haven, CT: Yale University Press.

Buss, D. M., & Schmitt, D. P. (1993). Sexual strategies theory: An evolutionary perspective on human mating. *Psychological Review, 100,* 204–232.

California Task Force to Promote Self-Esteem and Personal and Social Responsibility (1990). *Toward a state of self-esteem.* Sacramento, CA: California State Department of Education.

Campbell, A. (1981). *The sense of well-being in America.* New York, NY: McGraw-Hill.

Campbell, J. D. (1990). Self-esteem and the clarity of the self-concept. *Journal of Personality and Social Psychology, 59,* 538–549.

Campbell, J. D., & Lavallee, L. F. (1993). Who am I? The role of self-concept confusion in understanding the behavior of people with low self-esteem. In R. F. Baumeister (Ed.), *Self-esteem: The puzzle of low self-regard* (pp. 3–20). New York, NY: Plenum.

Carvajal, S. C., Clair, S. D., Nash, S. G., & Evans, R. I. (1998). Relating optimism, hope, and self-esteem to social influences in deterring substance use in adolescents. *Journal of Social and Clinical Psychology, 17,* 443–465.

Carver, C. S., & Gaines, J. G. (1987). Optimism, pessimism, and postpartum depression. *Cognitive Therapy and Research, 11,* 449–462.

Carver, C. S., Pozo, C., Harris, S. D., Noriega, V., Scheier, M. F., Robinson, D. S., ... Clark, K. C. (1993). How coping mediates the effect of optimism on distress: A study of women with early-stage breast cancer. *Journal of Personality and Social Psychology, 65,* 375–390.

Carver, C. S., & Scheier, M. F. (1981). *Attention and self-regulation: A control theory approach to human behavior.* New York, NY: Springer-Verlag.

Carver, C. S., & Scheier, M. F. (1999). Optimism. In C. R. Snyder (Ed.), *Coping: The psychology of what works* (pp. 182–204). New York, NY: Oxford University Press.

Carver, C. S., Scheier, M. F., Miller, C. J., & Fulford, D. (2009). Optimism. In C. R. Snyder & S. J. Lopez (Eds.), *Oxford handbook of positive psychology* (2nd ed., pp. 303–311). New York, NY: Oxford University Press.

Carver, C. S., Scheier, M. F., & Segerstrom, S. C. (2010). Optimism. *Clinical Psychology Review, 30*, 879–889.

Caza, B., & Wrzesniewski, A. (2013). How work shapes well-being. In S. A. David, I. Boniwell, & A. Conley Ayers (Eds.), *The Oxford handbook of happiness* (pp. 693–710). New York, NY: Oxford University Press.

Chang, L. (2006). *Wisdom for the soul: Five millennia of prescriptions for spiritual healing.* Washington, DC: Gnosophia.

Cialdini, R. B. (2009). *Influence: Science and practice* (5th ed.). New York, NY: Pearson-Longman.

Clark, M. S., & Mills, J. (1993). The difference between communal and exchange relationships: What it is and is not. *Personality and Social Psychology Bulletin, 19*, 684–691.

Coats, E. J., Janoff-Bulman, R., & Alpert, N. (1996). Approach versus avoidance goals: Differences in self-evaluation and well-being. *Personality and Social Psychology Bulletin, 22*, 1057–1067.

Collins, J. (2001). *Good to great: Why some companies make the leap…and others don't.* New York, NY: Harper-Collins.

Cooper, M. L., Albino, A. W., Orcutt, H. K., & Williams, N. (2004). Attachment styles and intrapersonal adjustment: A longitudinal study from adolescence into young adulthood. In W. S. Rholes & J. A. Simpson (Eds.), *Adult attachment: Theory, research, and clinical implications* (pp. 438–466). New York, NY: Guilford.

Crane, F. (1914). Plain talk for plain people. *Syracuse Herald.*

Crocker, J., & Knight, K. M. (2005). Contingencies of self-worth. *Current Directions in Psychological Science, 14*(4), 200–203. doi:10.1111/j.0963-7214.2005.00364.x

Crocker, J., Luhtanen, R., & Bouvrette, S. (2001). Contingencies of self-worth in college students: Predicting freshman year activities. Unpublished manuscript, University of Michigan, Ann Arbor, MI.

Crocker, J., Luhtanen, R., Cooper, M. L., & Bouvrette, S. (2003). Contingencies of self-worth in college students: Theory and measurement. *Journal of Personality and Social Psychology, 85*, 894–908.

Crocker, J., & Park, L. E. (2004). The costly pursuit of self-esteem. *Psychological Bulletin, 130*, 392–414.

Crocker, J., & Park, L. E. (2012). Contingencies of self-worth. In M. R. Leary & J. Tangney (Eds.), *Handbook of self and identity* (2nd ed.) (pp. 309–326). New York, NY: Guilford Press.

Crocker, J., & Wolfe, C. T. (2001). Contingencies of self-worth. *Psychological Review, 108*, 593–623.

Crum, A. J., & Langer, E. J. (2007). Mind-set matters: Exercise and the placebo effect. *Psychological Science, 18*, 165–171. doi:10.1111/j.1467-9280.2007.01867.x

Csikszentmihalyi, M. (1990). *Flow: The psychology of optimal experience.* New York, NY: Harper and Row.

Csikszentmihalyi, M. (1997). *Finding flow.* New York, NY: Basic Books.

Csikszentmihalyi, M. (1999). If we are so rich, why aren't we happy? *American Psychologist, 54*, 821–827.

Csikszentmihalyi, M. (2003). *Good business: Leadership, flow, and the making of meaning.* New York, NY: Viking.

Csikszentmihalyi, M., & Nakamura, J. (2011). Positive psychology: Where did it come from, where is it going? In K. M. Sheldon, T. B. Kashdan, & M. F. Steger (Eds.), *Designing positive psychology: Taking stock and moving forward* (pp. 3–8). New York, NY: Oxford University Press.

Csikszentmihalyi, M., Rathunde, K., & Whalen, S. (1993). *Talented teenagers: The roots of success and failure.* New York, NY: Cambridge University Press.

Cytowic, R. E. (1993). *The man who tasted shapes.* New York, NY: Plenum.

Daloz, L. A., Keen, C. H., Keen, J. P. & Parks, S. D. (1997). *Common fire: Lives of commitment in a complex world.* New York, NY: Beacon Press.

Danner, D. D., & Snowdon, D. A. (2001). Positive emotions in early life and longevity: Findings from the Nun Study. *Journal of Personality and Social Psychology, 80*, 804–873.

Dar-Nimrod, I., Rawn, C. D., Lehman, D. R., & Schwartz, B. (2009). The maximization paradox: The costs of seeking alternatives. *Personality and individual differences, 46*(5–6), 631–635. doi:10.1016/j.paid.2009.01.007

Davis, M. H. (1980). A multidimensional approach to individual differences in empathy. *Catalog of Selected Documents in Psychology, 10*, 85.

Davis, S. (2014, January 15). "Miracle on the Hudson" was "life-changing," captain says five years later. *CBS This Morning.* Retrieved http://www.cbsnews.com/news/five-years-later-captain-and-first-officer-recall-emergency-landing/

Deci, E. L. (1995). *Why we do what we do: The dynamics of personal autonomy.* New York, NY: Putnam.

Deci, E. L., Eghrari, H., Patrick, B. C., & Leone, D. R. (1994). Facilitating internalization: The self-determination theory perspective. *Journal of Personality, 62*, 119–142.

Deci, E. L., & Ryan, R. M. (1995). Human autonomy: The basis for true self-esteem. In M. H. Kemis (Ed.), *Efficacy, agency, and self-esteem* (pp. 31–49). New York, NY: Plenum.

Demakis, J. (2012). *The ultimate book of quotations.* South Carolina: CreateSpace.

Demir, M., & Özdemir, M. (2010). Friendship, need satisfaction and happiness. *Journal of Happiness Studies, 11*, 243–259.

DeNeve, K. M. (1999). Happy as an extraverted clam? The role of personality for subjective well-being. *Current Directions in Psychological Science, 8*, 141–144.

DeNeve, K. M., & Cooper, H. (1998). The happy personality: A meta-analysis of 137 personality traits and subjective well-being. *Psychological Bulletin, 124*, 197–229.

DePaulo, B. M. (2006). *Singled out: How singles are stereotyped, stigmatized, and ignored, and still live happily ever after.* New York, NY: St. Martin's Griffin.

DePaulo, B. M., & Morris, W. L. (2005). Singles in society and in science. *Psychological Inquiry, 16,* 57–83.

Dermer, M., Cohen, S. J., Jacobsen, E., & Anderson, E. A. (1979). Evaluative judgments of aspects of life as a function of vicarious exposure to hedonic extremes. *Journal of Personality and Social Psychology, 37,* 247–260.

DeWall, C. N. (2013). *The Oxford handbook of social exclusion.* New York, NY: Oxford University Press.

Diener, E. (2000). Subjective well-being: The science of happiness and a proposal for a national index. *American Psychologist, 55,* 34–43.

Diener, E. (2001, February). *Subjective well-being.* Address presented at the annual meeting of the Society for Personality and Social Psychology, San Antonio, TX.

Diener, E. (2012). New findings and future directions for subjective well-being research. *American Psychologist, 67,* 591–597.

Diener, E., & Biswas-Diener, R. (2008). *Happiness: Unlocking the mysteries of psychological wealth.* Malden, MA: Blackwell.

Diener, E., Emmons, R. A., Larsen, R. J., & Griffen, S. (1985a). The Satisfaction with Life Scale. *Journal of Personality Assessment, 49,* 71–75.

Diener, E., Horwitz, J., & Emmons, R. A. (1985b). Happiness of the very wealthy. *Social Indicators, 16,* 263–274.

Diener, E., Oishi, S., & Lucas, R. E. (2009). Subjective well-being: The science of life satisfaction. In S. J. Lopez & C. R. Snyder (Eds.), *Oxford handbook of positive psychology* (2nd ed., pp. 187–194). New York, NY: Oxford University Press.

Diener, E., & Scollon, C. N. (2014). The what, why, when, and how of teaching the science of subjective well-being. *Teaching of Psychology, 41,* 175–183.

Diener, E., & Seligman, M. E. P. (2002). Very happy people. *Psychological Science, 13,* 81–84.

Diener, E., Wirtz, D., Tov, W., Kim-Prieto, C., Choi, D., Oishi, S., & Biswas-Diener, R. (2009). New measures of well-being: Flourishing and positive and negative feelings. *Social Indicators Research, 39,* 247–266.

Dillard, A. J., Schiavone, A., & Brown, S. L. (2008). Helping behavior and positive emotions: Implications for health and well-being. In S. J. Lopez (Ed.), *Positive psychology: Exploring the best in people, vol. 2: Capitalizing on emotional experiences* (pp. 101–114). Westport, CT: Praeger.

Dittes, J. E. (1959). Justification by faith and the experimental psychologist. *Religion in Life, 28,* 567–576.

Drigotas, S. M. (2002). The Michelangelo phenomenon and personal well-being. *Journal of Personality, 70,* 58–77.

Driscoll, R., Davis, K. E., & Lipetz, M. E. (1972). Parental interference and romantic love: The Romeo and Juliet effect. *Journal of Personality and Social Psychology, 24*(1), 1–10. doi:10.1037/h0033373

Duck, S. (1983). *Friends, for life: The psychology of close relationships.* New York, NY: St. Martin's Press.

Duckworth, A. L., Peterson, C., Matthews, M. D., & Kelly, D. R. (2007). Grit: Perseverance and passion for long-term goals. *Journal of Personality and Social Psychology, 92,* 1087–1101.

Duckworth, A., Kirby, T. A., Tsukayama, E., Berstein, H., & Ericsson, K. (2011). Deliberate practice spells success: Why grittier competitors triumph at the National Spelling Bee. *Social Psychological and Personality Science, 2*(2), 174–181. doi:10.1177/1948550610385872

Duckworth, A. L., Tsukayama, E., & Kirby, T. A. (2013). Is it really self-control? Examining the predictive power of the delay of gratification task. *Personality and Social Psychology Bulletin, 39*(7), 843–855.

Dutton, D. G., & Aron, A. P. (1974). Some evidence for heightened sexual attraction under conditions of high anxiety. *Journal of Personality and Social Psychology, 30,* 510–517.

Dunn, D. S., & Brody, C. (2008). Defining the good life following acquired physical disability. *Rehabilitation Psychology, 53,* 413–425.

Dunn, D. S., & Wilson, T. D. (1990). When the stakes are high: A limit to the illusion-of-control effect. *Social Cognition, 8,* 305–323. doi: 10.1521/soco.1990.8.3.305

Dunn, E. W., Aknin, L. B., & Norton, M. I. (2008, March 21). Spending money on others promotes happiness. *Science, 319,* 1687–1688. doi: 10.1126/science/1150952

Dunn, E. W., & Norton, M. (2013). *Happy money: The science of smarter spending.* New York, NY: Simon & Schuster.

Dunn, E. W., Gilbert, D. T., & Wilson, T. D. (2011). If money doesn't make you happy, you probably aren't spending it right. *Journal of Consumer Psychology, 2,* 115–125.

Dunning, D. (2011). The Dunning-Kruger effect: On being ignorant of one's own ignorance. In J. M. Olson, M. P. Zanna (Eds.), *Advances in experimental social psychology* (Vol. 44, pp. 247–296). San Diego, CA: Academic Press. doi:10.1016/B978-0-12-385522-0.00005-6

Dunning, D., Heath, C., & Suls, J. M. (2004). Flawed self-assessment: Implications for health, education, and the workplace. *Psychological Science in the Public Interest, 5*(3), 69–106.

Duval, S., & Wicklund, R. A. (1972). *A theory of objective self awareness.* Oxford, England: Academic Press.

Dweck, C. S. (1999). *Self-theories: Their role in motivation, personality and development.* Philadelphia, PA: Psychology Press.

Dweck, C. (2000). *Self-theories: Their role in motivation, personality, and development.* Philadelphia, PA: Psychology Press.

Dweck, C. (2008). Can personality be changed? The role of beliefs in personality and change. *Current Directions in Psychological Science, 17,* 391–394. doi: 10.1111/j.1467-8721.2008.00612.x

Dweck, C. S. (2002). Beliefs that make smart people dumb. In R. J. Sternberg (Ed.), *Why smart people can be so stupid* (pp. 24–41). New Haven, CT: Yale University Press.

Eagan, K., Lozano, J. B., Hurtado, S., & Case, M. H. (2013). *The American freshman: National norms fall 2013.* Los Angeles, CA: Higher Education Research Institute, UCLA.

Edelman, S. (2012). *The happiness of pursuit: What neuroscience can teach us about the good life.* New York, NY: Basic Books.

Elias, M. (2002, November 11). A generous spirit may yield generous life span. *USA Today,* p. 4A.

Elias, M. (2002, December 9). Ask "Dr. Happiness." *USA Today,* p. 11D.

Eliot, T. S. (1998). *The Wasteland, Prufrock, and other poems.* Mineola, NY: Dover.

Elliot, A. J., & Sheldon, K. M. (1998). Avoidance, personal goals, and the personality-illness relationship. *Journal of Personality and Social Psychology, 75,* 1282–1299.

Elliot, A. J., Sheldon, K. M., & Church, M. (1997). Avoidance, personal goals, and subjective well-being. *Personality and Social Psychology Bulletin, 23,* 915–927.

Ellis, A. (1989). Rational-emotive therapy. In R. J. Corsini (Ed.), *Current psychotherapies* (4th ed.). Itasca, IL: Peacock.

Emerson, R. W., Slater, J., Ferguson, A. R., & Carr, J. F. (1980). *Collected works of Ralph Waldo Emerson, Vol. II: Essays: First series.* Cambridge, MA: Belknap Press of Harvard University Press.

Emmons, R. A. (1996). Striving and feeling: Personal goals and subjective well-being. In P. M. Gollwitzer & J. A. Bargh (Eds.), *The psychology of action: Linking cognition and motivation to behavior* (pp. 313–337). New York, NY: Guilford Press.

Emmons, R. A. (1999). *The psychology of ultimate concerns.* New York, NY: Guilford.

Emmons, R. A. (2005). Giving thanks: Psychological research on gratitude and praise. In C. L. Harper Jr. (Ed.), *Spiritual formation: 100 perspectives* (pp. 451–456). Philadelphia, PA: Templeton Foundation Press.

Emmons, R. A., & Kaiser, H. (1996). Goal orientation and emotional well-being: Linking goals and affect through the self. In A. Tesser & L. Martin (Eds.), *Striving and feeling: Interactions among goals, affect, and self-regulation* (pp. 79–98). New York, NY: Plenum.

Emmons, R. A., & McCullough, M. E. (2003). Counting blessings versus burdens: An experimental investigation of gratitude and subjective well-being in daily life. *Journal of Personality and Social Psychology, 84,* 377–389.

Enright, R. D. (2001). *Forgiveness is a choice: A step-by-step process for resolving anger and restoring hope.* Washington, DC: American Psychological Association.

Erikson, E. (1963). *Childhood and society.* New York, NY: Norton.

Erikson, M. G. (2007). The meaning of the future: Toward a more specific definition of possible selves. *Review of General Psychology, 11,* 348–358.

Exline, J., & Geyer, A. L. (2004). Perceptions of humility: A preliminary study. *Self and Identity, 3*(2), 95–114. doi:10.1080/13576500342000077

Exline, J. J., & Hill, P. C. (2012). Humility: A consistent and robust predictor of generosity. *The Journal of Positive Psychology, 7*(3), 208–218. doi:10.1080/17439760.2012.671348

Fehr, B. (1988). Prototype analysis of the concepts of love and commitment. *Journal of Personality and Social Psychology, 55,* 557–579.

Fehr, B. (1996). *Friendship processes.* Thousand Oaks, CA: Sage.

Fehr, B. (2009). Friendship formation and development. In H. T. Reis & S. Sprecher (Eds.), *Encyclopedia of human relationships* (Vol. 1, pp. 706–710). Los Angeles, CA: Sage.

Fiske, S. T. (2014). *Social beings: Core motives in social psychology.* Hoboken, NJ: Wiley.

Fitzgerald, T. E., Tennen, H., Affleck, G., & Pransky, G. S. (1993). The relative importance of dispositional optimism and control appraisals in quality of life after coronary artery bypass surgery. *Journal of Behavioral Medicine, 16,* 25–43.

Fordyce, M. W. (1977). Development of a program to increase personal happiness. *Journal of Counseling Psychology, 24,* 511–521.

Fraley, R. C. (2002). Attachment stability from infancy to adulthood: Meta-analysis and dynamic modeling of developmental mechanisms. *Personality and Social Psychology Review, 6*(2), 123–151.

Franklin, S. S. (2010). *The psychology of happiness: A good human life.* New York, NY: Cambridge University Press.

Frantz, S. (2003, June 5). Rap essay. Message posted to http://www.frostburg.edu/dept/psyc/southerly/tips.

Fredrickson, B. L. (2001). The role of positive emotions in positive psychology: The broaden-and-build theory of positive emotions. *American Psychologist, 56,* 218–226.

Fredrickson, B. L. (2007). The broaden-and-build theory of positive emotions. In F. Huppert, N. Baylis, & B. Keverne (Eds.), *The science of well-being* (pp. 217–240). New York, NY: Oxford University Press.

Freedman, J. (1978). *Happy people.* New York, NY: Harcourt, Brace, Jovanovich.

Freedman, J. S. (1965). Long-term behavioral effects of cognitive dissonance. *Journal of Experimental Social Psychology, 1,* 145–155.

Freud, S. (1930/1961). *Civilization and its discontents* (J. Strachey, Trans.). New York, NY: Norton.

Friedrich, J. (1996). On seeing oneself as less self-serving than others: The ultimate self-serving bias? *Teaching of Psychology, 23,* 107–109.

Gable, S. L., Reis, H. T., Impett, E. A., & Asher, E. R. (2004). What do you do when things go right? The intrapersonal and interpersonal benefits of sharing positive events. *Journal of Personality and Social Psychology, 87,* 228–245.

Gallup, G. H., Jr. (1998). *Thankfulness: America's saving grace.* Paper presented at the National Day of Prayer Breakfast, Thanks-Giving Square, Dallas, TX.

Gibbons, F. X., Eggleston, T. J., & Benthin, A. C. (1997). Cognitive reactions to smoking relapse: The reciprocal relation between dissonance and self-esteem. *Journal of Personality and Social Psychology, 72,* 184–195.

Gilbert, D. T., & Ebert, J. E. J. (2002). Decisions and revisions: The affective forecasting of changeable outcomes. *Journal of Personality and Social Psychology, 82*, 503–514.

Given, C. W., Stommel, M., Given, B., Osuch, J., Kurtz, M. E., & Kurtz, J. C. (1993). The influence of cancer patients' symptoms and functional states on patients' depression and family caregivers' reaction and depression. *Health Psychology, 12*, 277–285.

Glass, J. (2001, June–July). Nurturing empathy. *Parenting*, p. 72.

Goldman, J. L., & Sparks, A. N. (Eds.). (1996). *Webster's new world student's dictionary* (Rev. ed.). Cleveland, OH: Wiley.

Goleman, D. (1995). *Emotional intelligence.* New York, NY: Bantam Books.

Goleman, D. (1998). *Working with emotional intelligence.* New York, NY: Bantam Books.

Goleman, D. (2002, June 16). Could you be a leader? *Parade Magazine*, pp. 4–5.

Gollwitzer, P. M. (1999). Implementation intentions. *American Psychologist, 54*, 493–503.

Gollwitzer, P. M., & Brandstätter, V. (1997). Implementation intentions and effective goal pursuit. *Journal of Personality and Social Psychology, 73*, 186–199.

Gottfredson, M. R., & Hirschi, T. (1990). *A general theory of crime.* Stanford, CA: Stanford University Press.

Gottman, J. (1994). *Why marriages succeed or fail.* New York, NY: Fireside.

Gottman, J. M. (2011). *The science of trust: Emotional attunement for couples.* New York, NY: Norton.

Gottman, J., & Silver, N. (1999). *The seven principles for making marriage work.* New York, NY: Three Rivers.

Greenwald, A. G., Carnot, C. G., Beach, R., & Young, B. (1987). Increasing voting behavior by asking people if they expect to vote. *Journal of Applied Psychology, 72*, 315–318.

Grierson, B. (2014, October 22). What if age is nothing but a mind-set? *New York Times Magazine*. Retrieved from http://www.nytimes.com/2014/10/26/magazine/what-if-age-is-nothing-but-a-mind-set.html?_r=1

Haggerty, G., Hilsenroth, M. J., & Vala-Stewart, R. (2009). Attachment and interpersonal distress: Examining the relationship between attachment styles and interpersonal problems in a clinical population. *Clinical Psychology and Psychotherapy, 16*, 1–9.

Hall, M. R., & Hall, M. R. (2009). *The sky's the limit: Go for the gold!* Bloomington, IN: AuthorHouse.

Hamilton, T. F. (2001, December 2). *The right stuff.* Grand Rapids Press, p. J1.

Hanford, E. (2012). *Angela Duckworth and the research on "Grit."* Retrieved from http://americanradioworks.publicradio.org/features/tomorrows-college/grit/angela-duckworth-grit.html

Harker, L., & Keltner, D. (2001). Expressions of positive emotion in women's college yearbook pictures and their relationship to personality and life outcomes across adulthood. *Journal of Personality and Social Psychology, 80*, 112–124.

Harter, J. K., Schmidt, F. L., & Keyes, C. L. M. (2003). Well-being in the workplace and its relationship to business outcomes: A review of the Gallup studies. In C. L. M. Keyes & J. Haidt (Eds.), *Flourishing: Positive psychology and the life well-lived* (pp. 205–224). Washington, DC: American Psychological Association.

Harter, S. (2002). Authenticity. In C. R. Snyder & S. J. Lopez (Eds.), *Handbook of positive psychology* (pp. 382–394). New York, NY: Oxford University Press.

Hartup, W. W., & Stevens, N. (1997). Friendships and adaptation in the life course. *Psychological Bulletin, 121*, 355–370.

Harvey, J. H., & Omarzu, J. (1997). Minding the close relationship. *Personality and Social Psychology Review, 1*, 223–239.

Harvey, J. H., & Omarzu, J. (1999). *Minding the close relationship: A theory of relationship enhancement.* New York, NY: Cambridge University Press.

Harvey, J. H., & Omarzu, J. (2006). *Minding the close relationship: A theory of relationship enhancement.* New York, NY: Cambridge University Press.

Harvey, J. H., & Wenzel, A. (2006). Theoretical perspectives in the study of close relationships. In A. L. Vangelisti & D. Perlman (Eds.), *The Cambridge handbook of personal relationships* (pp. 35–49). New York, NY: Cambridge University Press.

Hashtroudian, J. (2003). Teaching stories: The Mullah Narudin. Retrieved November 3, 2003, from http://www.lifefocuscenter.com/teach.htm

Hatfield, E. (1988). Passionate and companionate love. In R. J. Sternberg & M. L. Barnes (Eds.), *The psychology of love* (pp. 191–217). New Haven, CT: Yale University Press.

Hatfield, E., & Rapson, R. L. (1987). Passionate love: New directions in research. In W. H. Jones & D. Perlman (Eds.), *Advances in personal relationships* (Vol. 1, pp. 109–139). Greenwich, CT: JAI Press.

Hazan, C., & Shaver, P. (1986). *Parental caregiving style questionnaire.* Unpublished manuscript.

Hazan, C., & Shaver, P. (1990). Love and work: An attachment-theoretical perspective. *Journal of Personality and Social Psychology, 59*, 270–280.

Hazan, C., & Shaver, P. (1994). Attachment as an organizational framework for research on close relationships. *Psychological Inquiry, 5*, 1–22.

Heider, F. (1958). *The psychology of interpersonal relations.* New York, NY: Wiley.

Heilman, M. (1976). Oppositional behavior as a function of influence attempt intensity and retaliation threat. *Journal of Personality and Social Psychology, 33*, 574–578.

Heimpel, S. A., Wood, J. V., Marshall, M. A., & Brown, J. D. (2002). Do people with low self-esteem really want to feel better? Self-esteem differences in motivation to repair negative moods. *Journal of Personality and Social Psychology, 82*, 128–147.

Heine, S. J., Lehman, D. R., Markus, H. R., & Kitiyama, S. (1999). Is there a universal need for positive self-regard? *Psychological Review, 106,* 766–795.

Heintzelman, S. J., & King, L. A. (2014). Life is pretty meaningful. *American Psychologist, 69,* 561–574. doi: 10.1037/a0035049

Herzog, A. R., Franks, X., Markus, H. R., & Holmberg, X. (1995). *The American self in its sociocultural variations.* Unpublished manuscript.

Hicks, J. A., & King, L. A. (2009). Meaning in life as a judgment and lived experience. *Social and Personality Psychology Compass, 3,* 638–653.

Hill, T., Smith, N. D., & Lewicki, P. (1989). The development of self-image bias: A real-world demonstration. *Personality and Social Psychology Bulletin, 15,* 205–211.

Hodges, B. H. (2000). Remapping psychology: A new look at values in scientific ontology. *Christian Scholar's Review, 29,* 471–497.

Hojjat, M., & Cramer, D. (Eds.). (2013). *Positive psychology of love.* New York, NY: Oxford University Press.

Holahan, C., & Moos, R. (1987). Personal and contextual determinants of coping strategies. *Journal of Personality and Social Psychology, 52,* 946–955.

Horvath, S., & Morf, C. C. (2010). To be grandiose or not to be worthless: Different routes to self-enhancement for narcissism and self-esteem. *Journal of Research in Personality, 44,* 585–592.

House, J. S., Landis, K. R., & Umberson, D. (1988). Social relationships and health. *Science, 241,* 540–545.

Hsu, L. M., Chung, J., & Langer, E. J. (2010). The influence of age-related cues on health and longevity. *Perspectives on Psychological Science, 5*(6), 632–648. doi:10.1177/1745691610388762

Hsu, L. M., & Langer, E. J. (2013). Mindfulness and cultivating well-being in older adults. In S. A. David, I. Boniwell, & A. Conley Ayers (Eds.), *The Oxford handbook of happiness* (pp. 1026–1036). New York, NY: Oxford University Press.

Huang, P. H., & Blumenthal, J. A. (2009). Positive institutions, law, and policy. In S. J. Lopez & C. R. Snyder (Eds.), *Oxford handbook of positive psychology* (2nd ed., pp. 589–597). New York, NY: Oxford University Press.

Hurley, D. B., & Kwon, P. (2012). Results of a study to increase savoring the moment: Differential impact on positive and negative outcomes. *Journal of Happiness Studies, 13,* 579–588.

Inglehart, R. (1990). *Culture shift in advanced industrial society.* Princeton, NJ: Princeton University Press.

Insel, P. M., & Roth, W. T. (2002). *Core concepts in health* (9th ed.). New York, NY: McGraw-Hill.

Isaacson, W. (2003, July 7). Citizen Ben's 7 great virtues. *Time,* pp. 40–53.

Isaacson, W. (2007). *Einstein: His life and universe.* New York, NY: Simon & Schuster.

Jackson, S. A., & Marsh, H. W. (1996). Development and validation of a scale to measure optimal experience: The flow state scale. *Journal of Sport and Exercise Psychology, 18,* 17–35.

Jackson, S. A., Eklund, R. C., & Martin, A. J. (2010). SHORT Flow State Scale. Retrieved from www.mindgarden.com

Johnston, M. M., & Finney, S. J. (2010). Measuring basic needs satisfaction: Evaluating previous research and conducting new psychometric evaluations of the Basic Needs Satisfaction in General Scale. *Contemporary Educational Psychology, 35,* 280–296.

Jose, P. E., Lim, B. T., & Bryant, F. B. (2012). Does savoring increase happiness? A daily diary study. *The Journal of Positive Psychology, 7,* 176–187.

Jourard, S. M. (1964). *The transparent self.* Princeton, NJ: Van Nostrand.

Jurors prefer lawyers who are well-prepared—and not arrogant (1993, February 22). *National Law Journal, 15,* 10.

Kahneman, D. (2011). *Thinking, fast and slow.* New York, NY: Farrar, Straus and Giroux.

Kasser, T. (2002). *The high price of materialism.* Cambridge, MA: MIT Press.

Kasser, T., & Ryan, R. M. (1993). A dark side of the American dream: Correlates of financial success as a central life aspiration. *Journal of Personality and Social Psychology, 65,* 410–422.

Kasser, T., & Ryan, R. M. (1996). Further examining the American dream: Differential correlates of intrinsic and extrinsic goals. *Personality and Social Psychology Bulletin, 22,* 280–286.

Katz, J., & Joiner, T. E. (2002). Being known, intimate, and valued: Global self-verification and dyadic adjustment in couples and roommates. *Journal of Personality, 70,* 33–58.

Keller, H. (1920). *Out of the dark: Essays, lectures, and addresses on physical and social vision.* Garden City, NY: Doubleday, Page.

Keller, H. (2009). *The story of my life: With her letters and a supplementary account of her education.* Auckland, New Zealand: Floating Press .

Keltner, D., & Haidt, J. (2003). Approaching awe, a moral, spiritual, and aesthetic emotion. *Cognition and Emotion, 17,* 297–314.

Kenrick, D. T., Neuberg, S. L., & Cialdini, R. B. (2002). *Social psychology: Unraveling the mystery* (2nd ed.). Boston, MA: Allyn and Bacon.

Keyes, C. L. M. (2003). Complete mental health: An agenda for the 21st century. In C. L. M. Keyes and J. Haidt (Eds.), *Flourishing: Positive psychology and the life well-lived* (pp. 293–312). Washington, DC: American Psychological Association.

Keyes, C. M. (2009). Toward a science of mental health. In S. J. Lopez & C. R. Snyder (Eds.), *Oxford handbook of positive psychology* (2nd ed., pp. 89–95). New York, NY: Oxford University Press.

Keyes, C. M., & Haidt, J. (Eds.). (2003). *Flourishing: Positive psychology and the life well-lived.* Washington, DC: American Psychological Association.

Keyes, C. L. M., & Lopez, S. J. (2002). Toward a science of mental health: Positive directions in diagnosis and interventions. In C. R. Snyder & S. J. Lopez (Eds.), *Handbook of positive psychology* (pp. 45–59). New York, NY: Oxford University Press.

Kim, Y., Butzel, J. S., & Ryan, R. M. (1998, June). *Interdependence and well-being: A function of culture and relatedness needs*. Paper presented at the annual meeting of the International Society for the Study of Personal Relationships, Saratoga Springs, NY.

King, L. A., & Emmons, R. A. (1991). Psychological, physical, and interpersonal correlates of emotional expressiveness, conflict, and control. *European Journal of Personality, 5,* 131–150.

Kinnaman, G. (1996). *My companion through grief: Comfort for your darkest hours.* Ventura, CA: Vine Books.

Kleiser, G. (2005). *Dictionary of proverbs.* New Delhi, India: A. P. H. Publishing.

Kohn, A. (1990). *The brighter side of human nature.* New York, NY: Basic Books.

Kotler, T. (1985). Security and autonomy within marriage. *Human Relations, 38,* 299–321.

Kramer, D. A. (2000). Wisdom as a classical source of human strength: Conceptualization and empirical inquiry. *Journal of Social and Clinical Psychology, 19,* 83–101.

Krause, N. (2007). Longitudinal study of social support and meaning in life. *Psychology and Aging, 22,* 456–469.

Kurtz, E. & Ketcham, K. (2009). *The spirituality of imperfection: Storytelling and the search for meaning.* New York, NY: Bantam.

Kurtz, J. L., & Lyubomirsky, S. (2008). Toward a durable happiness. In S. J. Lopez (Ed.), *Positive psychology: Exploring the best in people, vol. 4: Pursuing human flourishing* (pp. 21–36). Westport, CA: Prager.

Landers, A. (1990, March 14). Ann answers. *Detroit Free Press,* p. 2C.

Langer, E. J. (1977). The psychology of chance. *Journal for the Theory of Social Behavior, 7,* 185–208.

Langer, E. J. (2002, July/August). I'll be there. *Psychology Today,* p. 74.

Langer, E., Djikic, M., Pirson, M., Madenci, A., & Donohue, R. (2010). Believing is seeing: Using mindlessness (mindfully) to improve visual acuity. *Psychological Science, 21,* 661–666.

Larson, D. G., & Chastain, R. L. (1990). Self-concealment: Conceptualization, measurement, and health implications. *Journal of Social and Clinical Psychology, 9,* 439–455.

Larson, R. (2000). Toward a psychology of positive youth development. *American Psychologist, 55,* 170–183.

Larsen, R. J., & Buss, D. M. (2002). *Personality psychology: Domains of knowledge about human nature.* New York, NY: McGraw-Hill.

Larsen, R. J., & Ketelaar, T. (1991). Personality and susceptibility to positive and negative emotional states. *Journal of Personality and Social Psychology, 61,* 132–140.

Larson, R. W., & Bradney, N. (1988). Precious moments with family members and friends. In R. M. Milardo (Ed.), *Families and social networks* (pp. 107–126). Newbury Park, CA: Sage.

Laurenceau, J. P., Barrett, L. F., & Rovine, M. J. (2005). The interpersonal process model of intimacy in marriage: A daily-diary and multilevel modeling approach. *Journal of Family Psychology, 19,* 314–323.

Lawler, K. A., Younger, J. W., Piferi, R. L., Billington, E., Jobe, R., Edmondson, K. et al. (2003). A change of heart: Cardiovascular correlates of forgiveness in response to interpersonal conflict. *Journal of Behavioral Medicine, 26,* 373–393.

Legate, N., DeHaan, C. R., Weinstein, N., & Ryan, R. M. (2013). Hurting you hurts me too: The psychological costs of complying with ostracism. *Psychological Science, 24*(4), 583–588. doi:10.1177/0956797612457951

Lerner, M. J. (1980). *The belief in a just world.* New York, NY: Plenum.

Levenson, H. (1981). Differentiating among internality, powerful others, and chance. In H. M. Lefcourt (Ed.), *Research with the locus of control construct* (Vol. 1, pp. 1–63). New York, NY: Academic Press.

Levine, R. V. (2003). *The power of persuasion: How we're bought and sold.* Hoboken, NJ: Wiley.

Levy, B. R., Slade, M. D., Kunkel, S. R., & Kasl, S. V. (2002). Longevity increased by positive self-perceptions of aging. *Journal of Personality and Social Psychology, 83,* 261–270.

Lewis, C. S. (1949). *The weight of glory and other addresses.* New York, NY: Macmillan.

Lewis, C. S. (1960). *Mere Christianity.* New York, NY: Macmillan.

Linville, P. W. (1985). Self-complexity and affective extremity: Don't put all of your eggs in one cognitive basket. *Social Cognition, 3*(1), 94–120. doi:10.1521/soco.1985.3.1.94

Linville, P. W. (1987). Self-complexity as a cognitive buffer against stress-related illness and depression. *Journal of Personality and Social Psychology, 52*(4), 663–676. doi:10.1037/0022-3514.52.4.663

Littman-Ovadia, H., & Steger, M. (2010). Character strengths and well-being among volunteers and employees. *Journal of Positive Psychology, 5,* 419–430.

Lloyd, J., & Mitchinson, J. (2009). *If ignorance is bliss, why aren't there more happy people?: Smart quotes for dumb times.* New York, NY: Crown.

Logue, A. W. (1995). *Self-control: Waiting until tomorrow for what you want today.* Englewood Cliffs, NJ: Prentice Hall.

Lohr, J. M., Olatunji, B. O., Baumeister, R. F., & Bushman, B. J. (2007). The psychology of anger venting and empirically supported alternatives that do no harm. *The Scientific Review of Mental Health Practice, 5*(1), 53–64.

Lombardo, M. M., Ruderman, M. N., & McCauley, C. D. (1988). Explanations of success and derailment in upper-level management positions. *Journal of Business and Psychology, 2,* 199–216.

Lopes, P. N., Grewal, D., Kadis, J., Gall, M., & Salovey, P. (2006). Evidence that emotional intelligence is related to job performance and affect and attitudes at work. *Psichothema, 18,* 132–138.

Lopez, S. J. (2006a). *Giving positive psychology away: Ten strategies that promote student engagement.* Invited presentation at the 18th Annual Meeting of the Association for Psychological Science, New York, NY.

Lopez, S. J. (2006b). C. R. [Rick] Snyder [Obituary]. *American Psychologist, 61,* 719.

Lopez, S. J., & Snyder, C. R. (Eds.). (2009). *Oxford handbook of positive psychology* (2nd ed). New York, NY: Oxford University Press.

Luthans, F., & Youssef, C. M. (2009). Positive workplaces. In S. J. Lopez & C. R. Snyder (Eds.), *Oxford handbook of positive psychology* (2nd ed., pp. 579–588). New York, NY: Oxford University Press.

Lykken, D. (1999). *Happiness: The nature and nurture of joy and contentment.* New York, NY: St. Martin's Press.

Lyubomirsky, S. (2001). Why are some people happier than others? *American Psychologist, 56,* 239–249.

Lyubomirsky, S. (2007). *The how of happiness: A new approach to getting the life you want.* New York, NY: Penguin.

Lyubomirsky, S. (2008). *The how of happiness: A scientific approach to getting the life you want.* New York, NY: Penguin.

Lyubomirsky, S. (2013). *The myths of happiness: What should make you happy, but doesn't, what shouldn't make you happy, but does.* New York, NY: Penguin Press.

MacCann, C., Duckworth, A., & Roberts, R. D. (2009). Empirical identification of the major facets of conscientiousness. *Learning and Individual Differences, 19*(4), 451–458. doi:10.1016/j.lindif.2009.03.007

Maisel, N. C., & Gable, S. L. (2009). For richer…in good times…and in health: Positive processes in relationships. In C. R. Snyder & S. J. Lopez (Eds.), *Oxford handbooks of positive psychology* (pp. 455–462). New York, NY: Oxford University Press.

Malle, B. (2011). Attribution theories: How people make sense of behavior. In D. Chadee (Ed.), *Theories in social psychology* (pp. 72–95). Malden, MA: Wiley-Blackwell.

Malouff, J. M., Schutte, N. S., & Thorsteinsson, E. B. (2014). Trait emotional intelligence and romantic relationship satisfaction: A meta-analysis. *American Journal of Family Therapy, 42*(1), 53–66. doi:10.1080/01926187.2012.748549

Markus, H. R., & Kitayama, S. (1998). The cultural psychology of personality. *Journal of Cross-Cultural Psychology, 29,* 63–87.

Markway, B., & Markway, G. (2003). *Painfully shy: How to overcome social anxiety and reclaim your life.* New York, NY: St. Martin's Griffin.

Martin, A. J., & Debus, R. L. (1999). Alternative factor structure for the Revised Self-Consciousness Scale. *Journal of Personality Assessment, 72,* 266–282.

Maruta, T., Colligan, R. C., Malinchoc, M., & Offord, K. P. (2000). Optimism versus pessimism: Survival rate among medical patients over a 30-year period. *Mayo Clinic Proceedings, 75,* 140–143.

Marvin, N. (Producer), & Darabont, F. (Director). (1994). *The Shawshank redemption* [Motion picture]. United States: Warner Bros.

Maslow, B. G. (1972). *Abraham H. Maslow: A memorial volume.* Monterey, CA: Brooks/Cole.

Maxwell, J. C., & Reiland, D. (1999). *The treasure of a friend.* Nashville, TN: Nelson.

Mayer, J. D., Salovey, P., Caruso, D. R., & Cherkasskiy, L. (2011). Emotional intelligence. In R. J. Sternberg & S. Kaufman (Eds.), *The Cambridge handbook of intelligence* (pp. 528–549). New York, NY: Cambridge University Press.

McCrae, R. R., & Costa, P. T. (1990). *Personality in adulthood.* New York, NY: Guilford.

McCullough, M. E., Emmons, R. A., Tsang, J. (2002). The grateful disposition: A conceptual and empirical topography. *Journal of Personality and Social Psychology, 82,* 112–127.

McCullough, M. E., Pargament, K. I., & Thoresen, C. T. (2000). The psychology of forgiveness: History, conceptual issues, and overview. In M. E. McCullough, K. I. Pargament, & C. E. Thoresen (Eds.), *Forgiveness: Theory, research, and practice* (pp. 1–14). New York, NY: Guilford.

McCullough, M. E., Root, L. M., & Cohen, A. D. (2006). Writing about the personal benefits of a transgression facilitates forgiveness. *Journal of Consulting and Clinical Psychology, 74,* 887–897.

McCullough, M. E., Root, L. M., Tabak, B. A., & van Oyen Witvliet, C. (2009). Forgiveness. In S. J. Lopez & C. R. Snyder (Eds.), *Oxford handbook of positive psychology* (2nd ed., pp. 427–435). New York, NY: Oxford University Press.

McDermott, C., & Snyder, C. R. (1999). *Making hope happen: A workbook for turning possibilities into reality.* Oakland, CA: New Harbinger.

McGinnis, A. L. (2004). *The friendship factor: How to get closer to the people you care for.* Minneapolis, MN: Fortress Press.

McGuire, J. T., & Kable, J. W. (2013). Rational temporal predictions can underlie apparent failures to delay gratification. *Psychological Review, 120*(2), 395–410. doi:10.1037/a0031910

McQuaid, C. (Ed.). *Gambler's digest.* Chicago, IL: Digest Books, 1971.

Menninger, K. A., Mayman, M., & Pruyser, P. (1963). *The vital balance: The life process in mental health and illness.* New York, NY: Viking Press.

Metcalfe, J., & Mischel, W. (1999). A hot/cool system analysis of delay of gratification: Dynamics of willpower. *Psychological Review, 106,* 3–19.

Middlebrook, P. N. (1974). *Social psychology and modern life.* New York, NY: Knopf.

Mikulincer, M., & Shaver, P. R. (2003). The attachment behavioral system in adulthood: Activation, psychodynamics, and interpersonal processes. In M. P. Zanna (Ed.), *Advances in experimental social psychology* (Vol. 35, pp. 53–152). San Diego, CA: Academic Press.

Miller, L. C., Berg, J. H., & Archer, R. L. (1983). Openers: Individuals who elicit intimate self-disclosure. *Journal of Personality and Social Psychology, 44,* 1234–1244.

Miller, T. (1995). *How to want what you have.* New York, NY: Henry Holt.

Mills, J., & Clark, M. S. (1994). Communal and exchange relationships: Controversies and research. In R. Erber & R. Gilmour (Eds.), *Theoretical frameworks for personal relationships* (pp. 29–42). Hillsdale, NJ: Erlbaum.

Mischel, W. (1974). Processes in delay of gratification. In L. Berkowitz (Ed.), *Advances in experimental social psychology* (Vol. 7, pp. 249–292). New York, NY: Academic Press.

Mischel, W. (2014). *The marshmallow test: Mastering self-control.* New York, NY: Little, Brown and Co.

Mischel, W., Ayduk, O., Berman, M. G., Casey, B. J., Gotlib, I. H., Jonides, J., & ... Shoda, Y. (2011). 'Willpower' over the life span: Decomposing self-regulation. *Social Cognitive and Affective Neuroscience, 6*(2), 252–256. doi:10.1093/scan/nsq081

Mischel, W., Ebbesen, E. B., & Zeiss, A. R. (1972). Cognitive and attentional mechanisms in delay of gratification. *Journal of Personality and Social Psychology, 21,* 204–218.

Monks of New Skete. (1999). *In the spirit of happiness.* Boston, MA: Little, Brown.

Morris, H. J. (2001, September 3). New science shows how to inject real joy into your life. *U.S. News & World Report,* pp. 46–54.

Morrow, G. D. (2009). Exchange processes. In H. T. Reis & S. Sprecher (Eds.), *Encyclopedia of human relationships* (Vol. 1, pp. 551–555). Los Angeles, CA: Sage.

Mother Teresa. (1995). *A simple path.* New York, NY: Ballantine Books.

Mueller, C. M., & Dweck, C. S. (1997). *Implicit theories of intelligence: Malleability beliefs, definitions, and judgments of intelligence.* Unpublished manuscript.

Muraven, M. (1998). *Mechanisms of self-control failure: Motivation and limited resources.* Doctoral dissertation, Case Western Reserve University, Cleveland, OH.

Muraven, M., Baumeister, R. F., & Tice, D. M. (1999). Longitudinal improvement of self-regulation through practice: Building self-control strength through repeated exercise. *Journal of Social Psychology, 139,* 446–457.

Murray, H. A. (2007). *Explorations in personality.* New York, NY: Oxford University Press.

Myers, D. G. (1992). *The pursuit of happiness: Who is happy—and why.* New York: William Morrow.

Myers, D. G. (2000a). *The American paradox: Spiritual hunger in an age of plenty.* New Haven, CT: Yale University Press.

Myers, D. G. (2000b). The funds, friends, and faith of happy people. *American Psychologist, 55,* 56–67.

Myers, D. G. (2001). *Psychology* (6th ed.). New York, NY: Worth.

Myers, D. G. (2002). *Social psychology* (7th ed.). New York, NY: McGraw-Hill.

Myers, D. G. (2004). *Psychology* (7th ed.). New York, NY: Worth.

Nakamura, J., & Csikszentmihalyi, M. (2009). Flow theory and research. In C. R. Snyder & S. J. Lopez (Eds.), *Oxford handbook of positive psychology* (2nd ed., pp. 195–206). New York, NY: Oxford University Press.

National Wellness Institute. (1992). *Making wellness work for you.* Stevens Point, WI: National Wellness Institute.

Neff, K. (2003). Self-compassion: An alternative conceptualization of a healthy attitude toward oneself. *Self and Identity, 2,* 85–101.

Nenkov, G. Y., Morrin, M., Ward, A., Schwartz, B., & Hulland, J. (2008). A short form of the Maximization Scale: Factor structure, reliability and validity studies. *Judgment and Decision Making, 3*(5), 371–388.

Nezlek, J. B., Wesselmann, E. D., Wheeler, L., & Williams, K. D. (2012). Ostracism in everyday life. *Group Dynamics: Theory, Research, and Practice, 16*(2), 91–104. doi:10.1037/a0028029

Niven, D. (2001). *The 100 simple secrets of happy people.* San Francisco, CA: HarperCollins.

Notarius, C., & Markman, H. (1993). *We can work it out: Making sense of marital conflict.* New York, NY: Putnam.

O'Keefe, D. (2002). *Persuasion: Theory and research* (2nd ed.). Newbury Park, CA: Sage.

Oliner, P., & Oliner, S. (1988). *The altruistic personality: Rescuers of Jews in Nazi Europe.* New York, NY: Free Press.

Omarzu, J., Whalen, J., & Harvey, J. H. (2001). How well do you mind your relationship? A preliminary scale to test the minding theory of relating. In J. H. Harvey & A. Wenzel (Eds.), *Close romantic relationships: Maintenance and enhancement* (pp. 345–356). Mahwah, NJ: Erlbaum.

Omoto, A. M., Malsch, A. M., & Barraza, J. A. (2009). Compassionate acts: Motivations for and correlates of volunteerism among older adults. In B. Fehr, S. Sprecher, & L. G. Underwood (Eds.), *The science of compassionate love: Theory, research, and applications* (pp. 257–282). Malden, MA: Wiley-Blackwell.

Oppezzo, M., & Schwartz, D. L. (2014). Give your ideas some legs: The positive effect of walking on creative thinking. *Journal of Experimental Psychology: Learning, Memory, and Cognition 40*(4), 1142–1152. http://dx.doi.org/10.1037/a0036577

Oyserman, D., Elmore, K., & Smith, G. (2012). Self, self-concept, and identity. In M. R. Leary & J. P. Tangney (Eds.), *Handbook of self and identity* (2nd ed.; pp. 69–104). New York, NY: Guilford.

Pallant, J. F. (2000). Development and validation of a scale to measure perceived control of internal states. *Journal of Personality Assessment, 75,* 308–337.

Park, N., Peterson, C., & Seligman, M. E. P. (2004). Strengths of character and well-being. *Journal of Social and Clinical Psychology, 23,* 603–619.

Parke, R. D. (1974). Rules, roles, and resistance to deviation: Recent advances in punishment, discipline, and self-control. In A. Pick (Ed.), *Minnesota symposia of child psychology,* Vol. 8 (pp. 111–143). Minneapolis, MN: University of Minnesota Press.

Paulhus, D. (1983). Sphere-specific measures of perceived control. *Journal of Personality and Social Psychology, 44,* 1253–1265.

Paulus, D. L., Wehr, P., Harms, P. D., & Strasser, D. I. (2002). Use of exemplar surveys to reveal implicit types of intelligence. *Personality and Social Psychology Bulletin, 28,* 1051–1062.

Peale, N. V. (1982). *Positive imaging: The powerful way to change your life.* New York, NY: Fawcett Crest.

Peele, S. (1989). *The diseasing of America.* Boston, MA: Houghton Mifflin.

Pennebaker, J. W. (1985). Traumatic experience and psychosomatic disease: Exploring the roles of behavioral inhibition, obsession, and confiding. *Canadian Psychology, 26,* 82–95.

Pennebaker, J. W. (Ed.). (2002). *Emotion, disclosure, and health.* Washington, DC: American Psychological Association.

Peterson, C. (2006). *A primer in positive psychology.* New York, NY: Oxford University Press.

Peterson, C., & Bossio, L. M. (2001). Optimism and physical well-being. In E. C. Chang (Ed.), *Optimism and pessimism: Implications for theory, research, and practice* (pp. 127–145). Washington, DC: American Psychological Association.

Peterson, C., & Seligman, M. P. (2004). *Character strengths and virtues: A handbook and classification.* Washington, DC: American Psychological Association.

Peterson, C., Seligman, M. E. P., Yurko, K. H., Martin, L. R., & Friedman, H. S. (1998). Catastrophizing and untimely death. *Psychological Science, 9,* 49–52.

Peterson, C., & Steen, T. Optimistic explanatory style. In C. R. Snyder & S. J. Lopez (Eds.), *Handbook of positive psychology* (2nd ed., pp. 313–322). New York, NY: Oxford University Press.

Peterson, K. S. (1992, December). Guiding kids with a curriculum of compassion. *USA Today,* p. 10D.

Pham, L. B., & Taylor, S. E. (1997). *The effects of mental stimulation on exam performance.* Unpublished manuscript.

Piechowski, M. M., & Tyska, C. (1982). Self-actualization profile of Eleanor Roosevelt—A presumed nontranscender. *Genetic Psychology Monographs, 105,* 95–153.

Piliavin, J., & Siegl, E. (2008). Health benefits of volunteering in the Wisconsin Longitudinal Study. *Journal of Health and Social Behavior, 48,* 450–464.

Pinker, S. (2002). *The blank slate: The modern denial of human nature.* New York, NY: Penguin.

Plantinga, N. (1987, October 19). Christian compassion: Obstacles. *The Banner,* p. 17.

Pliner, P., Hart, H., Kohl, J., & Saari, D. (1974). Compliance without pressure: Some further data on the foot-in-the-door technique. *Journal of Experimental Social Psychology, 10,* 17–22.

Poon, K., Chen, Z., & DeWall, C. (2013). Feeling entitled to more: Ostracism increases dishonest behavior. *Personality and Social Psychology Bulletin, 39*(9), 1227–1239. doi:10.1177/0146167213493187

Positive Psychology Center. (2015). Retrieved May 1, 2015, from http://www.positivepsychology.org/

Prime, J., & Salib, E. (2014, May 12). The best leaders are humble leaders. *Harvard Business Review.* Retrieved from http://blogs.hbr.org/2014/05/the-best-leaders-are-humble leaders/?utm_source=Socialflow&utm_medium=Tweet&utm_campaign=Socialflow

Putnam, R. (2000). *Bowling alone.* New York, NY: Simon & Schuster.

Regan, P. C., Kocan, E. R., & Whitlock, T. (1998). Ain't love grand! A prototype analysis of the concept of romantic love. *Journal of Social and Personal Relationships, 15,* 411–420.

Reilly, S., & Simmons, K. (2003, June 9). How satisfied are Americans with life? *USA Today,* p. 1A.

Reis, H. T., & Gable, S. L. (2003). Toward a positive psychology of relationships. In C. L. M. Keyes & J. Haidt (Eds.), *Flourishing: Positive psychology and the life well-lived* (pp. 129–159). Washington, DC: American Psychological Association.

Reynolds, G. (2014, May 6). Want a good idea? Take a walk. *New York Times,* D6.

Rieger, E. (1993). *Correlates of adult hope, including high- and low-hope adults recollections of parents.* Psychology honors thesis, Department of Psychology, University of Kansas, Lawrence, KS.

Rimland, B. (1982). The altruism paradox. *The Southern Psychologist, 2*(1), 8–9.

Roberts, R. (1982). *Spirituality and human emotion.* Grand Rapids, MI: Eerdmans.

Robertson-Kraft, C., & Duckworth, A. L. (2014). True grit: Trait-level perseverance and passion for long-term goals predicts effectiveness and retention among novice teachers. *Teachers College Record, 116*(3), 1–27.

Robitschek, C. (1998). Personal growth initiative: The construct and its measure. *Measurement and Evaluation in Counseling and Development, 30,* 183–198.

Robitschek, C., Ashton, M. W., Spering, C. C., Geiger, N., Byers, D., Schotts, G., & Thoen, M. A. (2012). Development and psychometric evaluation of the Personal Growth Initiative Scale-II. *Journal of Consulting and Clinical Psychology, 59,* 274–287. doi: 10.1037/a0027310

Robitschek, C., & Cook, S. W. (1999). The influence of personal growth initiative and coping styles on career exploration and vocational identity. *Journal of Vocational Behavior, 54,* 127–141.

Roets, A., Schwartz, B., & Guan, Y. (2012). The tyranny of choice: A cross-cultural investigation of maximizing-satisficing effects on well-being. *Judgment and Decision Making, 7*(6), 689–704.

Rogers, C. R. (1951). *Client-centered therapy.* Boston, MA: Houghton Mifflin.

Rogers, C. R. (1956). Review of Reinhold Niebuhr's *The Self and the Dramas of History*. *Chicago Theological Seminary Register, 46*, 13–14.

Rogers, C. R. (1980). *A way of being*. Boston, MA: Houghton Mifflin.

Rosenberg, M. (1989). *Society and the adolescent self-image* (Rev. ed.). Hanover, NH: University Press of New England.

Ross, L. D. (1977). The intuitive psychologist and his shortcomings: Distortions in the attribution process. In L. Berkowitz (Ed.), *Advances in experimental social psychology* (Vol. 10, pp. 173–220). New York, NY: Academic Press.

Rousseau, J. J., & Cole, G. D. H. (2006). *The social contract, a discourse on the origin of inequality, and a discourse on political economy*. Digireads.com.

Rubin, Z., & Peplau, L. A. (1975). Who believes in a just world? *Journal of Social Issues, 31*, 65–89.

Rudd, M., Vohs, K. D., & Aaker, J. (2012). Awe expands people's perception of time, alters decision making, and enhances well-being. *Psychological Science, 23*(10), 1130–1136. doi:10.1177/0956797612438731

Ruthig, J. C., Hanson, B. L., Pedersen, H., Weber, A., & Chipperfield, J. G. (2011). Later life health optimism, pessimism and realism: Psychosocial contributors and health correlates. *Psychology & Health, 26*(7), 835–853. doi:10.1080/08870446.2010. 506574

Ryan, R. M., & Deci, E. L. (2000). Self-determination theory and the facilitation of intrinsic motivation, social development, and well-being. *American Psychologist, 55*, 68–78.

Ryan, R. M., Stiller, J., & Lynch, J. H. (1994). Representations of relationships to teachers, parents, and friends as predictors of academic motivation and self-esteem. *Journal of Early Adolescence, 14*, 226–249.

Ryff, C. D., & Singer, B. (2003). Flourishing under fire: Resilience as a prototype of challenged thriving. In C. L. M. Keyes & J. Haidt (Eds.), *Flourishing: Positive psychology and the life well-lived* (pp. 15–36). Washington, DC: American Psychological Association.

Ryon, H. S., & Gleason, M. J. (2014). The role of locus of control in daily life. *Personality and Social Psychology Bulletin, 40*(1), 121–131. doi:10.1177/0146167213507087

Sabini, J., & Silver, M. (1982). *Moralities of everyday life*. New York, NY: Oxford University Press.

Salovey, P., Mayer, J. D., & Caruso, D. (2002). The positive psychology of emotional intelligence. In C. R. Snyder & S. J. Lopez (Eds.), *Handbook of positive psychology* (pp. 159–171). New York, NY: Oxford University Press.

Salovey, P., Mayer, J. D., Caruso, D., & Yoo, S. H. (2009). The positive psychology of emotional intelligence. In S. J. Lopez & C. R. Snyder (Eds.), *The Oxford handbook of positive psychology* (2nd ed., pp. 237–248). New York, NY: Oxford University Press.

Sapadin, L. A. (1988). Friendship and gender: Perspectives of professional men and women. *Journal of Social and Personal Relationships, 5*, 387–403.

Scheier, M. F., & Carver, C. S. (1985). Optimism, coping, and health: Assessment and implications of generalized outcome expectancies. *Health Psychology, 4*, 219–247.

Scheier, M. F., & Carver, C. S. (2007). Optimism, pessimism, and stress. In G. Fink (Ed.), *Encyclopedia of stress* (Vol. 3, 2nd ed., pp. 26–29). San Diego, CA: Elsevier Academic Press.

Scheier, M. F., Carver, C. S., & Bridges, M. W. (1994). Distinguishing optimism from neuroticism (and trait anxiety, self-mastery, and self-esteem): A reevaluation of the Life Orientation Test. *Journal of Personality and Social Psychology, 67*, 1063–1078.

Scheier, M. F., Carver, C. S., & Bridges, M. W. (2001). Optimism, pessimism, and psychological well-being. In E. C. Chang (Ed.), *Optimism & pessimism: Implications for theory, research, and practice* (pp. 189–216). Washington, DC: American Psychological Association. doi:10.1037/10385-009

Scheier, M. F., Mathews, J. F., Owens, G. J., Magovern, G. R., Lefebvre, R., Abbott, R. C., & Carver, J. S. (1989). Dispositional optimism and recovery from coronary artery bypass surgery: The beneficial effects of optimism on physical and psychological well-being. *Journal of Personality and Social Psychology, 57*, 1024–1040.

Sheldon, K. M., & King, L. (2001). Why positive psychology is necessary. *American Psychologist, 54*(3), 216–217.

Schelling, T. C. (1992). Self-command: A new discipline. In G. F. Loewenstein & J. Elster (Eds.), *Choice over time*. New York, NY: Russell Sage Foundation.

Schimmack, U., & Diener, E. (2003). Predictive validity of explicit and implicit self-esteem for subjective well-being. *Journal of Research in Personality, 37*, 100–106.

Schneider, S. L. (2001). In search of realistic optimism: Meaning, knowledge, and warm fuzziness. *American Psychologist, 56*, 250–263.

Schroeder, D. A., Penner, L. A., Dovidio, J. F., & Piliavin, J. A. (1995). *The psychology of helping and altruism*. New York, NY: McGraw-Hill.

Schutte, N. S., Malouff, J. M., Hall, L. E., Haggerty, D. J., Cooper, J. T., Golden, C. J., & Dornheim, L. (1998). Development and validation of a measure of emotional intelligence. *Personality and Individual Differences, 25*, 167–177.

Schutte, N. S., Malouff, J. M., Simunek, M., McKenley, J., & Hollander, S. (2002). Characteristic emotional intelligence and emotional well-being. *Cognition and Emotion, 16*(6), 769–785. doi:10.1080/02699930143000482

Schutte, N. S., Malouff, J. M., Thorsteinsson, E. B., Bhullar, N., & Rooke, S. E. (2007). A meta-analytic investigation of the relationship between emotional intelligence and health. *Personality and Individual Differences, 42*(6), 921–933. doi:10.1016/j. paid.2006.09.003

Schwartz, B. (2000). Self-determination: The tyranny of freedom. *American Psychologist, 55*, 79–88.

Schwartz, B. (2012). Choice, freedom, and autonomy. In P. R. Shaver, M. Mikulincer (Eds.), *Meaning, mortality, and choice:*

The social psychology of existential concerns (pp. 271–287). Washington, DC: American Psychological Association. doi:10.1037/13748-015

Schwartz, B., Ward, A., Monterosso, J., Lyubomirsky, S., White, K., & Lehman, D. R. (2002). Maximizing versus satisficing: Happiness is a matter of choice. *Journal of Personality and Social Psychology, 83,* 1178–1197.

Schwarz, N. (1990). Feelings as information: Informational and motivational functions of affective states. In E. T. Higgins & R. M. Sorrentino (Eds.), *Handbook of motivation and emotion,* Vol. 2 (pp. 527–561). New York, NY: Guilford Press.

Sears, R. R. (1977). Sources of life satisfaction of the Terman gifted men. *American Psychologist, 32,* 119–128.

Seckel, A. (2002). *More optical illusions.* New York, NY: Carlton Books.

Seligman, M. E. P. (1990). *Learned optimism.* New York, NY: Knopf.

Seligman, M. E. P. (1994). *What you can change and what you can't.* New York, NY: Knopf.

Seligman, M. E. P. (1999). The president's address. *American Psychologist, 54,* 559–562.

Seligman, M. E. P. (2002). *Authentic happiness: Using the new positive psychology to realize your potential for lasting fulfillment.* New York, NY: Free Press.

Seligman, M. E. P., & Schulman, P. (1986). Explanatory style as a predictor of productivity and quitting among life insurance sales agents. *Journal of Personality and Social Psychology, 50,* 832–838.

Seligman, M. E. P., Schulman, P., DeRubeis, R. J., & Hollon, S. D. (1999). The prevention of depression and anxiety. *Prevention and Treatment,* Vol. 2, Article 8. http://journals.apa.org/prevention/volume2/pre0020008a.html

Seligman, M. E. P., Steen, T. A., Park, N., & Peterson, C. (2005). Positive psychology progress: Empirical validation of interventions. *American Psychologist, 60,* 410–421.

Sentyrz, S. M., & Bushman, B. J. (1998). Mirror, mirror on the wall, who's the thinnest one of all? Effects of self-awareness on consumption of full-fat, reduced-fat, and no-fat products. *Journal of Applied Psychology, 83,* 944–949.

Sharabany, R. (1994). Intimate Friendship Scale: Conceptual underpinnings, psychometric properties, and construct validity. *Journal of Social and Personal Relationships, 11,* 449–469.

Shaver, P. R., & Mikulincer, M. (2008). Augmenting the sense of security in romantic, leader-follower, therapeutic, and group relationships: A relational model of psychological change. In J. P. Forgas & J. Fitness (Eds.), *Social relationships: Cognitive, affective, and motivational processes* (pp. 55–74). New York, NY: Psychology Press.

Shaver, P. R., & Mikulincer, M. (2012). Attachment theory. In P. M. Van Lange, A. W. Kruglanski, & E. Higgins (Eds.), *Handbook of theories of social psychology* (Vol. 2, pp. 160–179). Thousand Oaks, CA: Sage Publications.

Shelby, R. A., Crespin, T. R., Wells-Di Gregorio, S. M., Siegel, J. E., Taylor, K. I., & Lamdam, R. M. (2008). Optimism, social support, and adjustment in African American women with breast cancer. *Journal of Behavioral Medicine, 31,* 433–444.

Sheldon, K. M., Elliot, A. J., Kim, Y., & Kasser, T. (2001). What is satisfying about satisfying events? 10 candidate psychological needs. *Journal of Personality and Social Psychology, 80,* 325–339.

Shepell, W. (2000, June). Building and maintaining a healthy relationship. *UM EAP Newsletter,* pp. 1–2.

Shepperd, J. A., Maroto, J. J., & Pbert, L. A. (1996). Dispositional optimism as a predictor of health changes among cardiac patients. *Journal of Research in Personality, 30,* 517–534.

Shubnell, T.F. (2009). *Shubnell's profound thoughts, Book 2.* South Carolina: CreateSpace.

Simon, H. A., & Chase, W. G. (1973). Skill in chess. *American Scientist, 61,* 394–403.

Simpson, J. A., Campbell, B., & Berscheid, E. (1986). The association between romantic love and marriage: Kephart (1967) twice revisited. *Personality and Social Psychology Bulletin, 12,* 363–372.

Slater, L. (2002, February 3). The trouble with self-esteem. *New York Times.* Retrieved from http://www.nytimes.com/2002/02/03/magazine/the-trouble-with-self-esteem.html?pagewanted=3

Slevin, C. (2003, May 9). Hiker describes cutting off arm. *Wisconsin State Journal,* pp. A1, A11.

Smedes, L. B. (1982). *How can it be all right when everything is all wrong?* San Francisco, CA: Harper & Row.

Smedes, L. B. (1987). *The making and keeping of commitments.* Grand Rapids, MI: Calvin College.

Smyth, J. M., Pennebaker, J. W., & Arigo, D. (2012). What are the health effects of disclosure? In A. Baum, T. A. Revenson, J. Singer (Eds.), *Handbook of health psychology* (2nd ed.) (pp. 175–191). New York, NY: Psychology Press.

Snyder, C. R. (1994). *The psychology of hope: You can get there from here.* New York, NY: Free Press.

Snyder, C. R. (1995). Conceptualizing, measuring, and nurturing hope. *Journal of Counseling and Development, 73,* 355–360.

Snyder, C. R., Berg, C., Woodward, J. T., Gum, A., Rand, K. L., Wrobleski, K. K., ... Hackman, A. (2005). Hope against the cold: Individual differences in trait hope and acute pain tolerance on the cold pressor task. *Journal of Personality, 73,* 287–312.

Snyder, C. R., Cheavens, J., & Sympson, S. C. (1997). Hope: An individual motive for social commerce. *Group Dynamics: Theory, Research, and Practice, 1,* 107–118.

Snyder, C. R., & Feldman, D. B. (2000). Hope for the many: An empowering social agenda. In C. R. Snyder (Ed.), *Handbook of hope: Theory, measures, and applications* (pp. 389–412). San Diego, CA: Academic Press.

Snyder, C. R., Harris, C., Anderson, J. R., Holleran, S. A., Irving, L. M., Sigmon, S. T., ... Harney, P. (1991). The will and the ways: Development and validation of an individual-differences measure of hope. *Journal of Personality and Social Psychology, 60,* 570–585.

Snyder, C. R., Hoza, B., Pelham, W. E., Rapoff, M., Ware, L., Danovsky, M., ... Stahl, K. J. (1997). The development and validation of the Children's Hope Scale. *Journal of Pediatric Psychology, 22,* 399–421.

Snyder, C. R., LaPointe, A. B., Crowson, J. J., Jr., & Early, S. (1998). Preferences of high- and low-hope people for self-referential feedback. *Cognition and Emotion, 12,* 807–823.

Sophocles. (1962). *Oedipus at Colonus* (R. Fitzgerald, Trans.). London, England: Faber.

Star of "Camelot," "Potter" films. (2002, October 26). *Grand Rapids Press,* p. D9.

Starr, M. (2003, March 24). Michelle Kwan. *Newsweek,* p. 67.

Staub, E. (1999). Aggression and self-esteem. *APA Monitor, 30,* 4.

Staw, B. M., Bell, N. E., & Clausen, J. A. (1986). The dispositional approach to job attitudes. *Administrative Science Quarterly, 31,* 56–77.

Steele, C. M. (1997). A threat in the air: How stereotypes shape intellectual identity and performance. *American Psychologist, 52,* 613–629.

Steele, C. M. (2010). *Whistling Vivaldi: How stereotypes affect us and what we can do.* New York, NY: W. W. Norton & Co.

Steger, M. F., Frazier, P., Oishi, S., & Kaler, M. (2006). The Meaning in Life Questionnaire: Assessing the presence of and search for meaning in life. *Journal of Counseling Psychology, 53,* 80–93. doi: 10.1037/022-0167.53.1.80

Steger, M. F., & Kashdan, T. B. (2009). Depression and everyday social activity, intimacy, and well-being. *Journal of Counseling Psychology, 56,* 289–300.

Steger, M. F., Mann, J. R., Michels, P., & Cooper, T. C. (2009). Meaning in life, anxiety, depression, and general health among smoking cessation patients. *Journal of Psychosomatic Research, 67,* 353–358.

Steiner, A. (2001, September/October). Got time for friends? *Utne Reader,* pp. 67–71.

Sternberg, R. J. (1985). Implicit theories of intelligence, creativity, and wisdom. *Journal of Personality and Social Psychology, 49,* 607–627.

Sternberg, R. J. (1986a). A triangular theory of love. *Psychological Review, 93*(2), 119–135. doi:10.1037/0033-295X.93.2.119

Sternberg, R. J. (1986b). *Intelligence applied: Understanding and increasing your intellectual skills.* San Diego, CA: Harcourt Brace Jovanovich.

Sternberg, R. J. (1988). Triangulating love. In R. J. Sternberg & M. L. Barnes (Eds.), *The psychology of love* (pp. 119–138). New Haven, CT: Yale University Press.

Sternberg, R. J. (1996). *Successful intelligence: How practical and creative intelligence determine success in life.* New York, NY: Simon & Schuster.

Sternberg, R. J. (2001). Why schools should teach for wisdom: The balance theory of wisdom in educational settings. *Educational Psychologist, 36,* 227–245.

Sternberg, R. J. (2002a, August). *Wisdom, schooling, and society.* Paper presented at the annual convention of the American Psychological Association, Chicago, IL.

Sternberg, R. J. (Ed.). (2002b). *Why smart people can be so stupid.* New Haven, CT: Yale University Press.

Sternberg, R. J. (2003, March). Responsibility: One of the other three Rs. *Monitor on Psychology,* p. 5.

Sternberg, R. J. (2011). The theory of successful intelligence. In R. J. Sternberg & S. Kaufman (Eds.), *The Cambridge handbook of intelligence* (pp. 504–527). New York, NY: Cambridge University Press.

Sternberg, R. J. (2012). The triarchic theory of successful intelligence. In D. P. Flanagan & P. L. Harrison (Eds.), *Contemporary intellectual assessment: Theories, tests, and issues* (3rd ed.) (pp. 156–177). New York, NY: Guilford Press.

Sternberg, R. J., & Horvath, J. A. (Eds.). (1999). *Tacit knowledge in professional practice: Researcher and practitioner perspectives.* Mahwah, NJ: Erlbaum.

Sternberg, R. J., & Whitney, C. (1991). *Love the way you want it: Using your head in matters of the heart.* New York, NY: Bantam Books.

Stevenson, R. L. & Phelps, W. L. (2008). *Essays of Robert Louis Stevenson.* Rockville, MD: Arc Manor.

Stillman, T. F., Lambert, N. M., Fincham, F. D., & Baumeister, R. F. (2011). Meaning as a magnetic force: Evidence that meaning in life promotes interpersonal appeal. *Social Psychological and Personality Science, 2,* 13–20.

Stotland, E. (1969). Exploratory investigations of empathy. In L. Berkowitz (Ed.), *Advances in experimental social psychology* (Vol. 4, pp. 271–314). New York, NY: Academic Press.

Strathman, A., Gleicher, F., Boninger, D. S., & Edwards, C. S. (1994). The consideration of future consequences: Weighing immediate and distant outcomes of behavior. *Journal of Personality and Social Psychology, 66,* 742–752.

Straub, R. O. (2002). *Health psychology.* New York, NY: Worth.

Suh, E., Diener, E., & Fujita, F. (1996). Events and subjective well-being: Only recent events matter. *Journal of Personality and Social Psychology, 70,* 1091–1102.

Suzuki, D. (2000, February 22). A death-bed test for life's priorities. *Sydney Morning Herald.* Retrieved August 22, 2003, from http://old.smh.com.au/news/literarylunches/suzuki.html.

Sympson, S. C. (1999). *Validation of the Domain Specific Hope Scale.* Unpublished doctoral dissertation, University of Kansas, Lawrence, KS.

Tangney, J. P. (2009). Humility. In C. R. Snyder & S. J. Lopez (Eds.), *Oxford handbook of positive psychology* (2nd ed., pp. 483–490). New York, NY: Oxford University Press.

Tangney, J. P., & Baumeister, R. F. (2000). *High self-control predicts good adjustment, less pathology, better grades, and interpersonal success.* Unpublished manuscript, George Mason University, Fairfax, VA.

Thompson, N. J., Coker, J., Krause, J. S., & Henry, E. (2003). Purpose in life as a mediator of adjustment after spinal cord injury. *Rehabilitation Psychology, 48,* 100–108.

Thoreau, H. D., & Emerson, R. W. (2008). Transcendentalism: Essential essays of Emerson & Thoreau. Clayton, DE: Prestwick House.

Tice, D. M., & Baumeister, R. F. (1997). Longitudinal study of procrastination, performance, stress, and health: The costs and benefits of dawdling. *Psychological Science, 8,* 454–458.

Tice, D. M., & Bratslavsky, E. (2000). Giving in to feel good: The place of emotion regulation in the context of general self-control. *Psychological Inquiry, 11,* 149–159.

Titchener, E. B. (1909). *Elementary psychology of the thought processes.* New York, NY: Macmillan.

Tolson, J. (2000, July 3). Into the zone. *U.S. News and World Report,* pp. 38–45.

Travis, L. A., Bliwise, N. G., Binder, J. L., & Horne-Moyer, H. L. (2001). Changes in clients' attachment style over the course of time-limited dynamic psychotherapy. *Psychotherapy: Theory, Research, Practice, Training, 38*(2), 149–159.

Trehan, B. K. & Trehan, I. (2010). *Building great relationships: All about emotional intelligence.* New Delhi, India: Sterling.

Triandis, H. C. (1994). *Culture and social behavior.* New York, NY: McGraw-Hill.

Tsang, J.-A., Rowatt, W. C., & Buechsel, R. K. (2008). Exercising gratitude. In S. J. Lopez (Ed.), *Positive psychology: Exploring the best in people,* Vol. 2: *Capitalizing on emotional experiences* (pp. 37–53). Westport, CT: Praeger.

Tucker, J. S., & Anders, S. L. (1999). Attachment style, interpersonal perception accuracy, and relationship satisfaction in dating couples. *Personality and Social Psychology Bulletin, 25,* 403–412.

Tuckman, B. W. (1991). The development and concurrent validity of the procrastination scale. *Educational and Psychological Measurement, 51,* 473–480.

Twenge, J. M., & Baumeister, R. F. (2002). Self-control: A limited but renewable resource. In Y. Kashima, M. Foddy, & M. J. Platow (Eds.), *Self and identity: Personal, social, and symbolic* (pp. 57–70). Mahwah, NJ: Erlbaum.

Twenge, J. M., & Campbell, W. K. (2003). Isn't it fun to get the respect that we're going to deserve? Narcissism, social rejection, and aggression. *Personality and Social Psychology Bulletin, 29,* 261–272.

Uleman, J. S., & Saribay, S. A. (2012). Initial impressions of others. In K. Deaux & M. Snyder (Eds.), *The Oxford handbook of personality and social psychology* (pp. 337–366). New York, NY: Oxford University Press.

Ullén, F., de Manzano, Ö., Almeida, R., Magnusson, P. E., Pedersen, N. L., Nakamura, J., & ... Madison, G. (2012). Proneness for psychological flow in everyday life: Associations with personality and intelligence. *Personality and Individual Differences, 52,* 167–172. doi:10.1016/j.paid.2011.10.003

Unger, L., & Thumuluri, L. (1997). Trait empathy and continuous helping. *Journal of Social Behavior and Personality, 12,* 785–800.

Urban, H. (2006). Choices that change lives: 15 ways to find more purpose, meaning, and joy. New York, NY: Touchstone.

Uysal, A., & Lu, Q. (2011). Is self-concealment associated with acute and chronic pain? *Health Psychology, 30*(5), 606–614. doi:10.1037/a0024287

Veroff, J., Douvan, E., & Kulka, R. A. (1981). *Mental health in America: Patterns of help-seeking from 1957 to 1976.* New York, NY: Basic Books.

Waters, E. A., Merrick, S., Treboux, D., Crowell, J., & Albersheim, L. (2000). Attachment security in infancy and early adulthood: A twenty-year longitudinal study. *Child Development, 71*(3), 684–689.

Wayment, H. A. (2004). It could have been me: Vicarious victims and disaster-focused distress. *Personality and Social Psychology Bulletin, 30,* 515–528.

Weber, A. (1984). Teaching social psychology. *Contemporary Social Psychology, 10*(3), 9–10.

Weinstein, N. D. (1980). Unrealistic optimism about future life events. *Journal of Personality and Social Psychology, 39,* 806–820.

Weinstein, N. D. (1982). Unrealistic optimism about susceptibility to health problems. *Journal of Behavioral Medicine, 5,* 441–460.

Weinstein, N. D. (2003). Exploring the links between risk perceptions and preventive health behavior. In J. Suls & K. A. Wallston (Eds.), *Social psychological foundations of health and illness* (pp. 22–53). Malden, MA: Blackwell Publishing.

Weinstein, N. D., Slovic, P., & Gibson, G. (2004). Accuracy and optimism in smokers' beliefs about quitting. *Nicotine & Tobacco Research, 6*(Suppl. 3), 375–380.

Weiss, H. M., & Knight, P. A. (1980). The utility of humility: Self-esteem, information search, and problem-solving efficiency. *Organizational Behavior and Human Decision Processes, 25,* 216–223.

Weiten, W. W., Dunn, D. S., & Hammer, E. Y. (2015). *Psychology applied to modern life: Adjustment in the 21st century* (11th ed.). Belmont, CA: Cengage.

Williams, K. D. (2001). *Ostracism: The power of silence.* New York, NY: Guilford.

Williams, K. S. (2007). Ostracism. *Annual Review of Psychology, 58,* 425–452.

Williams, K. D., Govan, C. L., Croker, V., Tynan, D., Cruickshank, M., & Lam, A. (2002). Investigations into differences between social and cyberostracism. *Group Dynamics: Theory, Research, and Practice, 6,* 748–762.

Williams, K. D., & Zadro, L. (2001). Ostracism: On being ignored, excluded, and rejected. In M. R. Leary (Ed.), *Interpersonal rejection.* New York, NY: Oxford University Press.

Wilson, C. (2003, February 5). A mere 10 seconds can stretch a smile for a lifetime. *USA Today,* p. 1D.

Wilson, T. D. (2002). *Strangers to ourselves: Discovering the adaptive unconscious.* Cambridge, MA: Belknap Press/Harvard University Press.

Wilson, T. D. (2011). *Redirect: The surprising new science of psychological change.* Boston, MA: Little, Brown and Co.

Wilson, T. D., & Gilbert, D. T. (2003). Affective forecasting. In M. P. Zanna (Ed.), *Advances in experimental social psychology* (pp. 345–411). San Diego, CA: Elsevier Academic Press.

Wilson, T. D., & Gilbert, D. T. (2005). Affective forecasting: Knowing what to want. *Current Directions in Psychological Science, 14,* 131–134.

Wilson, T. D., Wheatley, T. P., Meyers, J. M., Gilbert, D. T., & Axsom, D. (2000). Focalism: A source of durability bias in affective forecasting. *Journal of Personality and Social Psychology, 78,* 821–836.

Winstead, Z. A. (2009). Friendships, sex differences, and similarities. In H. T. Reis & S. Sprecher (Eds.), *Encyclopedia of human relationships* (Vol. 2, pp. 713–716). Los Angeles, CA: Sage.

Witvliet, C. V. O., Ludwig, T., & Vander Laan, K. (2001). Granting forgiveness or harboring grudges: Implications for emotion, physiology, and health. *Psychological Science, 121,* 117–123.

Witvliet, C. v. O., & McCullough, M. E. (2007). Forgiveness and health: A review and theoretical exploration of emotion pathways. In S. G. Post (Ed.), *Altruism and health: Perspectives from empirical research* (pp. 259–276). New York, NY: Oxford University Press.

Wood, A., Froh, J. J., & Geraghty, A. A. (2010). Gratitude and well-being: A review and theoretical integration. *Clinical Psychology Review, 30,* 890–905.

Wright, P. H. (1998). Toward an expanded orientation to the study of sex differences in friendship. In D. J. Canary & K. Dindia (Eds.), *Sex differences and similarities in communication: Critical essays and empirical investigations of sex and gender in interaction* (pp. 41–63). Mahwah, NJ: Erlbaum.

Wrzesniewski, A. (2012). Callings in work. In K. S. Cameron, G. M. Spreitzer (Eds.), *The Oxford handbook of positive organizational scholarship* (pp. 45–55). New York, NY: Oxford University Press.

Wrzesniewski, A., Dutton, J. E., & Debebe, G. (2003). Interpersonal sensemaking and the meaning of work. In R. M. Kramer, & B. M. Staw (Eds.), *Research in organizational behavior: An annual series of analytical essays and critical reviews,* Vol. 25 (pp. 93–135). Oxford, England: Elsevier Science.

Wrzesniewski, A., McCauley, C., Rozin, P., & Schwartz, B. (1997). Jobs, careers, and callings: People's relations to their work. *Journal of Research in Personality, 31,* 21–33.

Wrzesniewski, A., Rozin, P., & Bennett, G. (2003). Working, playing, and eating: Making the most of most moments. In C. L. M. Keyes & J. Haidt (Eds.), *Flourishing: Positive psychology and the life well-lived* (pp. 185–204). Washington, DC: American Psychological Association.

Wu, P. (1988). *Goal structures of materialists versus nonmaterialists.* Unpublished doctoral dissertation. University of Michigan, Ann Arbor, MI.

Yancey, P. (1989). *I was just wondering.* Nashville, TN: Word.

Yoshinobu, L. R. (1989). *Construct validation of the Hope Scale: Agency and pathways components.* Unpublished master's thesis. University of Kansas, Lawrence, KS.

Young, K. (1998). *Caught in the net.* New York, NY: John Wiley & Sons.

Zubko, A. (2004). *Treasury of spiritual wisdom: A collection of 10,000 inspirational quotations.* New Delhi, India: Motilal Banarsidass.

Index